Taner Can, Berkan Ulu, Koray Melikoğlu (eds.)

ORHAN PAMUK

Critical Essays on
a Novelist between Worlds

Taner Can, Berkan Ulu, Koray Melikoğlu (eds.)

ORHAN PAMUK

Critical Essays on
a Novelist between Worlds

ibidem-Verlag
Stuttgart

Bibliografische Information der Deutschen Nationalbibliothek
Die Deutsche Nationalbibliothek verzeichnet diese Publikation in der Deutschen Nationalbibliografie; detaillierte bibliografische Daten sind im Internet über http://dnb.d-nb.de abrufbar.

Bibliographic information published by the Deutsche Nationalbibliothek
Die Deutsche Nationalbibliothek lists this publication in the Deutsche Nationalbibliografie; detailed bibliographic data are available in the Internet at http://dnb.d-nb.de.

Cover picture: A Portrait of Orhan Pamuk. © copyright 2016 by Sebati Karakurt. Printed with kind permission.

∞

Gedruckt auf alterungsbeständigem, säurefreien Papier
Printed on acid-free paper

ISBN: 978-3-8382-1007-0

© *ibidem*-Verlag
Stuttgart 2017

Alle Rechte vorbehalten

Das Werk einschließlich aller seiner Teile ist urheberrechtlich geschützt. Jede Verwertung außerhalb der engen Grenzen des Urheberrechtsgesetzes ist ohne Zustimmung des Verlages unzulässig und strafbar. Dies gilt insbesondere für Vervielfältigungen, Übersetzungen, Mikroverfilmungen und elektronische Speicherformen sowie die Einspeicherung und Verarbeitung in elektronischen Systemen.

All rights reserved. No part of this publication may be reproduced, stored in or introduced into a retrieval system, or transmitted, in any form, or by any means (electronical, mechanical, photocopying, recording or otherwise) without the prior written permission of the publisher. Any person who does any unauthorized act in relation to this publication may be liable to criminal prosecution and civil claims for damages.

Printed in the EU

Contents

Introduction   1
Taner Can, Berkan Ulu, Koray Melikoğlu

The Arriviste or *görmemişin romanı*:
Pamuk and Tanpınar on New Turkish Literature   9
E. Khayyat

Dependable Content for Political Junctures:
Orhan Pamuk and the Turkish Media   35
Adam McConnel

Voices of Dissent: Belonging and Identity in *Silent House*
and *A Strangeness in My Mind*   59
Hande Gürses

Pamuk, the Storyteller: Elements of *The Thousand*
and One Nights* in *The Black Book   83
Sevinç Türkkan

Provincialism in Orhan Pamuk's *Snow*
and Turkey's Controversial Political History   111
Zafer Doğan

The Hidden Symmetry in Life-Writing:
Pamuk's *Istanbul: Memories and the City*   141
İnci Sarız-Bilge

Provinciality and the City in Pamuk's *Istanbul*   159
Beyza Lorenz

Bridging the Gap between People and Things:
The Politics and Poetics of Collecting in Pamuk's
The Museum of Innocence   185
Hülya Yağcıoğlu

**The Quest for Home and Identity: Modernity and Innocence
in Pamuk's** *The Museum of Innocence* 203
Gönül Eda Özgül

**A Novel Like a Well:
A Girardian Reading of Pamuk's** *The Red-Haired Woman* 231
Elif Türker Gümüş

Contributors 249

Introduction
Taner Can, Berkan Ulu, Koray Melikoğlu

The striking scene in Orhan Pamuk's *Snow* in which soldiers mistaken as part of a stage production fire live bullets into the audience instead of the expected blanks reminds one of an anecdote recounted by Talât Halman in which there is a similarly surreal confusion: A 1962 open-air performance of *Macbeth* in Istanbul enlisted an army battalion stationed nearby as extras to enliven the play's spacious site, an historical fortress. Told to go about their task convincingly, the soldiers charged in Act V with their old battle-cry "Allah! Allah!"

As the audience in *Snow* is confronted with a violence that is more real than they had hoped for, the anecdote's theatregoers are faced with a situation which, if not real in itself, points to a Turkish reality whose Orientalness is stronger than envisaged and ready to pop up in the most unexpected places. This recalcitrance of the Orient to removal is exasperating for Turkish elites who have desperately tried to westernize those whom they feel called upon to lead into modernity.

Halman's anecdote is an amusing exemplification of a phenomenon that serves as a point of departure for the first of the essays collected in this volume: In it Efe Khayyat discusses the sense of belatedness that many regard as hanging over a Turkey struggling to modernize. Just as the old battle-cry perseveres in and clashes with a modern setting, Turkey has not yet fully arrived in the present, and much less in the West. Being aware of that fact without acknowledging it to themselves, the elites and those following them have often compensated with an untamed version of the national pride installed by Atatürk. Atatürk, they feel, has propelled a former empire in decline to the forefront of European nations, a position in which Turkey is entitled to the same respect as in the days of the lost empire. This attitude is mocked on the back cover of a book by Murat Belge which varies official slogans usually employed to praise Turkish exceptionalism:

> Does one, in that world that we want to become part of, in Europe, come across slogans at every turn like "How happy is the one who says I am a Spaniard" or "A Swiss is worth the world"?

> Is it possible in any country to hold a military manoeuvre called "Army-turned Nation"? [...] Those who do such things are the elites in our country who order the people to westernize themselves.[1]

It has been argued that these elites have often been content to ridicule common people clumsily trying to come to terms with a West-orientation ordered from above without much success to show for their own efforts, efforts which are often oriented towards an outmoded model. An indication of this is the frequent Turkish phenomenon that a French pronunciation is attributed to foreign words, no matter what their provenance: The British publishing house is often referred to as "Pengüen," characters popularized by Shakespeare are quoted in their French-mediated form such as "Jül Sezar" or "Brütüs", and the pronunciation of the computer operating system Linux is often equipped with a vowel that is common to French and Turkish, but not suggested by either the term's spelling or origin: Convinced that modernization has to come from the West, some Turks try to deal with the dollar in the language of an empire that, though it outlasted their own, is no longer the dernier cri. And some Turkish adherents of postmodernism seem happy to chime in with such other-orientation as doubts about the possibility of self-identity and self-presence seem to relieve them of the trouble to find a non-derived identity for themselves.

As a corollary of the paralyzing sense of entitlement that seems to persevere from an imperial past, conspiracy theories about dark forces thwarting the country's progress are often used in Turkey to explain any lack of success. It probably does not help that a popular phrase regards the republic as Atatürk's gift to the Turkish people. Waiting for something gift-wrapped, many Turks do not feel called upon to act before Imperialism, the CIA,

---

[1] Translation for this volume of: "[G]irmek istediğimiz o dünyada, Avrupa'da, dağda bayırda, sokakta okulda, 'Ne mutlu İspanyol'um diyene' ya da 'Bir İsveçli dünyaya bedel' gibi sloganlara rastlıyor musunuz? Herhangi bir ülkede 'Ordulaşmış Millet' adında bir askerî tatbikat yapılabilir mi? [...] Bunları yapanlar, bizim ülkemizde halka 'Batılılaşın' emri veren elitlerdir."

Orientalism,[2] the Armenian lobby, the French secret service, Christian missionaries, the EU, more recently: the interest lobby and FETÖ, have not given up their machinations against the country.[3] The view that Orhan Pamuk was awarded the Nobel Prize in 2006 as part of such a conspiracy is quite common in Turkey – and often coexists in a compartmentalized manner with pride in the fact that "we" have received the Nobel Prize. The frustrated sense of entitlement speaking from this non-exhaustive list is discussed in several contributions to this volume as a source of the postimperial melancholy hovering over Pamuk's *Istanbul: Memories and the City*. That the childlike passivity reflected in the enumeration can turn into hostile activism when it feels threatened was experienced by Pamuk when in 2005 his insistence on treating the Turkish public as adults who have to confront their past and present problems led to his being accused of insulting Turkishness (see the essay by Adam McConnel in this volume).

Biographer Falih Rıfkı Atay says about the initiator of Turkey's Westorientation that the "music he loved was Turkish, the music he believed in was Western"[4] and praises the heroism that Atatürk showed in sacrificing his personal tastes for the sake of westernisation. Without belittling the successes of Atatürk's modernization project – for instance, Turkish women received the right to vote decades before their belated Swiss counterparts – it seems legitimate to ask about the price that according to Atay its very instigator had to pay for its successes. Orhan Pamuk's endeavour to explore this price is probably a sign of a greater interest in the complexities of Atatürk's work than Kemalist hardliners can muster. And Pamuk's answer to the question asked in the title of Murat Belge's study cited above, "Where in the world does Turkey stand?" ("Türkiye dünyanın neresinde?") – this answer can be condensed to "not at its centre" or studied in detail in, for instance, *Istanbul: Memories and the City* – opens the way to partici-

---

[2] The Orientalism in this list is particularly noteworthy as a concept developed for imperialized countries that is employed by inhabitants of a formerly imperializing country (see the Pamuk interview in the Works Cited).
[3] Combinations of these and other entities such as "CIA-MOSSAD-MI6-BND-MUHABERAT-FETÖ" are also possible (for an example, see Yılmaz).
[4] "Sevdiği musiki alaturka, inandığı Garp musikisi idi" (410).

pating in this world as a peripheral but actual player rather than as a central but imaginary one.

***

In the first of the contributions to this volume **Efe Khayyat** extends his discussion of a Turkish idiom into a treatise on the literary place of Orhan Pamuk with a view to Ahmet Hamdi Tanpınar, the novelist Pamuk associates with the emergence of modern Turkish writing, and Tanpınar's assessment of the history of modern Turkish literature. Khayyat touches upon numerous works by Pamuk, ranging from *The White Castle* to *The Museum of Innocence*, from *Snow* to his Nobel Lecture. Khayyat adds to the biographical interpretation of this lecture undertaken in the last essay in this volume the aspect of Pamuk's relationship with his audience.

Before the discussion of Orhan Pamuk's oeuvre, begun by Khayyat with an overall look that also includes a treatment of predecessors, is continued with a narrower focus in each of the following essays, historian **Adam McConnel** presents an overview over Pamuk's often troubled relationship with the Turkish media. In McConnel's analysis, no political position has been exempt from making Pamuk as an outstanding representative of the intellectual segment the target of a campaign at one time or another in the attempt to use his works as a springboard for political discussions even when his books had not much bearing on such controversies.

Hande Gürses begins the analysis of individual works with a comparative reading of Pamuk's second novel, *Silent House*, and his recent *A Strangeness in My Mind*. Inspired by Derridean thought, Gürses aims to show that the first-person narration used in both novels leads to different results in the characters' struggle to define their identity. While in *Silent House* each narrator's world appears self-enclosed and shut off against the experiences of other people, *A Strangeness in My Mind* renounces firm boundaries between characters as well as the fixed meanings that the personages in the earlier novel strive after.

Sevinç Türkkan, in her reading of exemplary chapters from *The Black Book*, explores how Pamuk's groundbreaking classic adopts storytelling elements from *The Thousand and One Nights* to shed light on contemporary Turkish society and mount a critique of its authoritarianism. This first literary step within Pamuk's oeuvre towards the East is an instantiation of what

Türkkan regards as the author's theory of writing world literature while avoiding its pitfalls. One of these pitfalls consists in the ignoring of the difference between the centre and the periphery, a theme that the following essay takes up.

While *The Black Book* is rich in political content, that content is treated covertly. **Zafer Doğan** presents a critical evaluation of *Snow*, Pamuk's only openly political work to date. The work discusses the conflict between secularists, leftists and Islamists in Turkey along with the wider issue of the relationship between the centre and provincial backwaters by engaging with theories of thinkers such as the sociologist Şerif Mardin. As an allegory *Snow* describes an identity crisis not just of its personages but of the entire nation. Ultimately Doğan finds Pamuk's treatment of political Islam too favourable for the novel to work as an accurate microcosm of Turkey, despite its aesthetic merits.

İnci Sarız-Bilge traces the way in which the memoir *Istanbul: Memories and the City* connects a view of Pamuk's personal biography with the history of Istanbul. According to Sarız-Bilge what Pamuk refers to as a symmetry between his personal memories and the imperial past of the former capital is in part created by editing out what does not fit in the book's "city creates writer" narrative according to which both are moulded by the same post-imperial melancholy. Sarız-Bilge identifies a similarly constructed symmetry between the author's past and present selves which, driven by the teleological demands of autobiographical self-coherence, views Pamuk's past life as a logical prerequisite for his present writer self.

Beyza Lorenz, who analyses the Istanbul of Pamuk's memoir as a Foucauldian heterotopia in which otherwise incompatible spaces, time periods, and cultures coexist, also provides another contribution to the study of centre and periphery in Pamuk's oeuvre. Lorenz traces the shift of the formerly central Istanbul to the periphery of power and the ensuing melancholy that in İnci Sarız-Bilge's preceding essay was treated under a somewhat different angle. Taking her cue from Walter Benjamin, Lorenz suggests that to cope with that melancholy Pamuk, positioned as both an insider and an outsider, views the city like a collector who attempts to form a new whole out of disparate elements. The permeability characteristic of a heterotopia also extends to generic boundaries which are transgressed in the mixture of text types comprised by *Istanbul*.

Hülya Yağcıoğlu's essay on *The Museum of Innocence* continues the theme of collecting already sounded by Beyza Lorenz for *Istanbul: Memories and the City*. Like Lorenz, Yağcıoğlu dwells on the similarities between collecting and novel writing shown in *The Museum of Innocence*, taking support from Walter Benjamin and Mieke Bal. In Yağcıoğlu's view the protagonist Kemal's museum project, based on his personal life in accordance with Pamuk's theorization in *The Innocence of Objects*, forms an antithesis to Western museums with their emphasis on power and pride.

Gönül Eda Özgül contributes a critical assessment of the view on the East-West divide that she argues is taken by Pamuk's *The Museum of Innocence*. She identifies the renunciation of the past as one of the main difficulties for countries facing the problems of modernization, which in the case of Oriental nations is doubled by their perceived necessity to imitate the West's way of modernizing. The ensuing identity loss leads to the kind of quest for a home that is the theme of *The Museum of Innocence*. Özgül's contention is that the novel, though it is critical of some Turkish attempts to modernize as pointed out in Yağcıoğlu's preceding essay, limits its critique to the "how" of modernization instead of addressing the problems posed by modernization itself. According to Özgül, this limited view ultimately gives in to the perspective of the modernizers and thus enforces an Orientalist view of the East as inferior.

In the last of the essays collected in this volume **Elif Türker Gümüş**, from among the rich mythical, artistic and political canvas presented in Pamuk's latest novel, *The Red-Haired Woman*, focuses on the central subject matter of parent-son conflicts and fatherlessness to discuss a possible biographical background to the text. Drawing on what Pamuk reveals about his own relationship with his father in his Nobel Lecture and other writings, Gümüş views these observations in light of philosopher René Girard's anthropological theory of mimetic desire. According to Girard, desire is derived from a model; with close attention to textual detail, Gümüş argues that for Orhan Pamuk this model or "mediator" is his father, with whom he shares the ambition of being a writer. In her view *The Red-*

Haired Woman is Pamuk's way of coming to terms with the rivalry between himself and his father.

***

"I write because I am angry at all of you, angry at everyone," Orhan Pamuk tells us in his Nobel Lecture. This volume will probably not change his mood to the better. All we can hope for is not to stand in his way when he does what he tells us about in the same lecture: "I write to be happy."

Works Cited

Atay, Falih Rıfkı. *Çankaya: Atatürk'ün doğumundan ölümüne kadar*. İstanbul: Doğan Kardeş, 1969.
Belge, Murat. Back cover. *Türkiye dünyanın neresinde?* İstanbul: Birikim, 1997.
Halman, Talât Sait. *Kahramanlar ve soytarılar: Shakespeare'in dünyası*. İstanbul: Cem, 1991.
Pamuk, Orhan. "My Father's Suitcase: Nobel Lecture." Trans. Maureen Freely. *Nobelprize.org*. 7 Dec. 2006. Accessed 29 May 2017 <http://www.nobelprize.org/nobel_prizes/literature/laureates/2006/pamuk-lecture_en.html>. Trans. of "Babamın bavulu: Nobel konuşması."
___. Interview by Lex ter Braak. *Bidoun* 8 (Fall 2006). Accessed 1 July 2017 <http://bidoun.org/articles/orhan-pamuk>.
Yılmaz, Mehtap. "Osmanlıtokadı budur!" *Yeni Akit* 8 Aug. 2016. Accessed 5 July 2017 <http://www.yeniakit.com.tr/yazarlar/mehtap-yilmaz/osmanli-tokadi-budur-16032.html>.

The Arriviste or *görmemişin romanı*:
Pamuk and Tanpınar on New Turkish Literature

E. Khayyat
Rutgers University

Abstract: Focusing on the Turkish idiom *görmemiş* or *sonradan görme* – 'newcomer,' 'Johnny-come-lately,' 'climber' or 'nouveau riche,' or better still 'arriviste' – as it relates to Turkish modernity and its belatedness, this essay maps out Orhan Pamuk's place in the history of modern Ottoman and Turkish literary culture. It takes its lead from the Turkish poet, novelist, critic and literary historian Ahmet Hamdi Tanpınar's account of this history, elaborating on the thought of the belatedness of non-Western modernity at large, supplementing Tanpınar's vision. It offers a way to overcome the conventional fixation on modernity in accounting for the problematic of belated modernity, and seeks to shift the focus to the implications of belatedness by turning to the newcomers to modernity. This setting enables a rethinking of Orhan Pamuk's extraordinary achievements as a newcomer to the world republic of letters. The essay also scrutinizes the newcomers and arrivistes, new lives and newly discovered pleasures that populate Pamuk's novels, from *The White Castle* to *New Life*, from *My Name is Red* to *Snow* and *The Museum of Innocence*.

I

The Turkish expression *görmemiş* or *sonradan görme* – 'Johnny-come-lately,' 'climber' or 'nouveau riche,' or better still 'arriviste' – contains a kernel of meaning that I believe is most instructive in making better sense of Orhan Pamuk's extraordinary achievements and the place of his thought and writings in modern Turkish cultural history. "Belatedness" of non-Western modernity has been the central issue of Turkish criticism for over a century, and one could certainly consider 'belatedness' as belonging to the pool of possible translations of *görmemişlik* (Gurbilek 2003). *Görmemiş* or *sonradan görme*, literally "the one who has not seen (it) before" or "the one who got to see (it) after the fact," promises to expand the thought of belated modernity in surprising ways, offering a way to overcome the fixation on modernity in accounting for the problematic of non-Western modernity, belated or otherwise, by shifting the focus to the newcomers to modernity, enabling a rethinking of authenticity in that respect. For over a century now the "belatedness" of modernity has implied humiliation in Turkey, for instance, a degree of self-mutilating embarrassment, some discomfort at how the modern Turk, this Johnny-come-lately makes a fool out of himself before the entire world. And as for the rest of the world, Orhan Pamuk suggests, "the great majority of people on this earth live with these same feelings, [...] many suffer from an even deeper sense of insufficiency, lack of security and sense of degradation" ("My Father's Suitcase"). Pamuk, for one, believes that such shift of focus to the newcomers to modernity is necessary, and especially in the humanities, it appears, since

> [w]hat literature needs most to tell and investigate today are humanity's basic fears: the fear of being left outside, and the fear of counting for nothing, and the feelings of worthlessness that come with such fears; the collective humiliations, vulnerabilities, slights, grievances, sensitivities, and imagined insults, and the nationalist boasts and inflations that are their next of kind ... ("My Father's Suitcase")

Modern Turkish thought still has difficulty in coming to terms with the fact that Europeans had Europeanized themselves before the Turks could Europeanize themselves. Many of Pamuk's writings elaborate on this strange paradox. Naturally, all this depends on an immutable faith in a teleology that points to Western European values and modes of living, being and thinking as the ultimate horizon for an entire humanity. It is as if our Oriental embarrassment at our belatedness in arriving at the superior European states of living, being and thinking has to do with how Europeans always appear to be ahead of everyone else in the race to reach those superior states, i.e. in Europeanizing themselves. It is as if each and every stage the modernizing world has to pass through in modernizing itself were previously surpassed by Europe. All this is to say that non-Western modernity is forever a site for newcomers, and obviously Turkish modernity is no exception in that regard. It is as if there is some mysterious trick, some magic strategy that the European has mastered to be always ahead of the game, some secret ingredient alien and unavailable to the Turk, who can at best make as if he were European. The idiom *görmemiş* or *sonradan görme* enables one to give an account of the search for this secret ingredient or this magic strategy in Turkish. Pamuk seems to have figured it out for himself and for his own profession, while his novels certainly have a place in this history of a quest, just as the quest in question itself is one of Pamuk's favorite subjects. Let me explain.

Sonradan görme is obviously a pejorative expression with classist, elitist and at times racist implications. Its cultural baggage cuts through ethnicity and gender, class and sexuality. Here is a popular, modern Turkish idiom that explains who the *görmemiş* might be: "Görmemişin oğlu olmuş, tutmuş çükünü kesmiş" ("The newcomer fathers a son, he ends up cutting off his dong" [clueless as he is, as a newcomer and as a new father, or not knowing what to do with the new son etc.]). The figures of *görmemiş* and *sonradan görme* in Turkish literature and film are typically those who cannot adjust to life in the developing, Europeanizing urban centers, having migrated from rural (for instance Kurdish-majority) areas of the country. They are often presented as wanting in manners and conduct, if not outright vulgar, or as unable to speak the proper, urban Turkish dialect, making a mess out of the opportunities and freedoms they stumble upon. But *sonradan görme* could also be the one who, upon being exposed to European life and thought, cannot decide what to do with the new and superior European ways, but cannot live like before either. These latter could be guest workers of Germany visiting home or those with a training in arts and the humanities in the West or in Western style institutions. They either get caught in perilous paralyses as aspiring writers or intellectuals, or fail to relate to people around them in some other way, but they are often presented as having gone astray, leading those around them astray as well. Newly acquired wealth too is often accompanied by newly discovered European pleasures in this cultural history, the nouveau riche often devouring both the wealth of the nation and those pleasures, without being able to digest either, ending up sick one way or another. The ultimate symptom for this sickness is some perversity that threatens families or family values. All these Johnny-come-latelies typically come out as irreverent, vulgar or immature and childlike. They either make as if they were this or that, which is the best they can do, or they cannot even make as if. What they lack – what secret they need to unearth, what magic trick they need to master – to mature and *be* themselves (be "authentic," Pamuk would say) is never outlined clearly.

As mentioned earlier, one could translate *görmemiş* or *sonradan görme* as 'Johnny-come-lately,' 'newcomer,' 'climber,' 'nouveau riche' or 'arriviste,' and even 'inauthentic.' But its cultural baggage is so heavily marked by the history of modernization and Europeanization that this pool does not suffice. The "belatedness" of Turkish modernity seems to have produced "inauthentic" Europeans, *sonradan görme*s of all hues as modern Turkish subjects, perhaps as postcolonial subjects too. But what perspective enables this vision populated by *sonradan görme*s? For clearly, according to this reasoning, there is something of a *sonradan görme* in every modern Turk, regardless of class, gender or ethnicity.

Newcomers and arrivistes, all kinds of new lives and newly discovered pleasures populate Pamuk's novels, from *The White Castle* to *New Life*, from *My Name is Red* to *Snow* and *A Strangeness in My Mind*. Pamuk also makes it clear that his issues with belatedness and inauthenticity have to do with "the fear that deep inside I was not authentic" ("My Father's Suitcase"). His Johnny-come-latelies are of a different order, then, somewhat more "reflective," as opposed to "naïve" – more inclined to "acknowledge the secret wounds that we carry inside us, the wounds so secret that we ourselves are barely aware of them, and to patiently explore them, know them, illuminate them, to own these pains and wounds, and to make them a conscious part of our spirits and our writing" ("My Father's Suitcase"). It is no coincidence that despite his upper middle class background, Pamuk often enjoys presenting himself as the newcomer, too, as the *sonradan görme* thus broadly conceived – clumsy, somewhat immature and childlike. I will provide some examples. Suffice it for now to note that Pamuk at times owns up to this Johnny-come-lateliness. What makes Pamuk unique as a Johnny-come-lately to the world republic of letters is that he elevates this modern Turkish quest for the magic ingredient, this modern Turkish *görmemişlik* into an art form. He made an ideal out of Johnny-come-lateliness, an ideal to strive towards, perhaps ironically too, not only in Turkey but to the east and west of Istanbul, which makes for an extraordinary literary political statement, as separate from Pamuk's personal opinions on political matters.

The tensions that emanate from an at times awkward struggle to stage *görmemişlik* to one's heart's desire often require him to push back and forth – sometimes in ways that make him appear quite clumsy, quite the newcomer – to make space for his statement, for his literary politics generally, which in turn has everything to do with newcoming and *görmemişlik*. I will provide examples for such responses as well, before engaging the philosophical grounding for this politics, which I believe can be traced back to how Pamuk responds to one of his Turkish predecessors, namely the novelist and humanist Ahmet Hamdi Tanpınar.

II

The troubles his immediately political positions have caused Pamuk and the way in which he dealt with these troubles help us catch a glimpse of how he comes out as a newcomer sometimes, but in a manner that is not entirely convincing either. His comments in an interview for the Swiss news magazine *Das Magazin* ("Der meistgehasste Türke") that one million Armenians and thirty thousand Kurds were murdered in Turkey, and that no one else other than him had the courage to talk about it is a case in point. The comments created an uproar in Turkey while outside Turkey, Pamuk's self-assigned role as an outspoken intellectual buttressed his credibility as Turkey's spokesperson. In Turkey he had to insist that the comments were made in passing, and were not even central to the interview – as if he had no idea these statements would be singled out. And since then he has had to insist that he never desired to be Turkey's spokesperson and/or outspoken about political politics, his interests being primarily aesthetic and literary – that such position was "a burden […] not playful, it's not childlike; it makes me self-conscious, kills the child in me" (qtd. in Walker). As if he were surprised to be approached in this manner outside Turkey. As if he really believed that his comments were just some clumsy digression. Always the Johnny-come-lately! But there is another, more specific context that makes his politics of literature more visible.

Pamuk presents his own father in "My Father's Suitcase," his Nobel speech, in such a way that minimally he comes out as somewhat immature and childlike. He explains how his father, too, had some intellectual aspirations, like Pamuk himself. When his father first tells young Pamuk that he will win the Nobel Prize one day, without really believing it, i.e. to encourage and console Pamuk at once, the son must have felt awkward and embarrassed.[1] The popular idiom I quoted above ("The newcomer fathers a son, he ends up cutting off his dong") often invites the kind of reaction Pamuk incites by telling this story with a certain degree of irony. His father clearly overshoots the destination, intentionally and jokingly too, repeating the joke for years on, not knowing what exactly to do with his beloved, intellectual son, yet willing to encourage him. Obviously young Pamuk would not think that he wrote novels to win awards. His father comes up with those words of encouragement not because he believes in them nor because he sets the prize as a goal for Pamuk. But as a joke, the statement expresses lack of faith as well. That Pamuk carries this baggage all the way to the peak of his international recognition is telling. He concludes his lecture by expressing his wish that his father, who had passed away a few years before, could see him deliver that speech. On the one hand, Pamuk gets back at his late father on the stage. He gets back at his father for encouraging him without believing in him completely – an immaturity that befits an arriviste of Pamuk's caliber! He wins the Nobel Prize, he ends up using the opportunity to get back at his father ("The newcomer fathers a son...")! We have a "naïve" Pamuk here getting back at his father "precisely in the manner of a child" (*Naïve* 17). He carries his father's insecurity to the stage.

On the other hand this account of his father's naïve ways and his own humble origins are but a jibe at that stage to begin with, a mockery of the prize itself. The same address can be interpreted as Pamuk getting back at his audience in acknowledging his father, sharing his lack of faith to a certain extent, or at least understanding it. Because, his father proved to be

---

[1] The English translation of Pamuk's lecture omits the comment concerning "belief." Here is the Turkish original of Pamuk's conclusion to his lecture, available on the same website: "Bu sözü ona inanmaktan ya da bu ödülü bir hedef olarak göstermekten çok, oğlunu desteklemek, yüreklendirmek için ona 'bir gün paşa olacaksın!' diyen bir Türk babası gibi söylemişti."

right! The Nobel committee proves him right and now Pamuk has faith in his father's disbelief, who, in turn, did not have faith in himself or his son, and for a reason! Pamuk's description of the reason why he found his father's writings terrifying helps understand what the reason is. The suitcase itself, once Pamuk opens it, brings the scent of his father's travels to distant lands – to Paris and New York. It is as if the center of his father's world, in his writings too, is not Istanbul but elsewhere. Pamuk fears that his Turkish father may have thought and written in Turkish but as if he were a Frenchman – writing about Istanbul in Turkish as if he were writing in French and about Paris, for instance. He smells insecurity in his father's suitcase and writings, some uncertainty that he says he shared with his father at one point in life. His father seems to him as if he were convinced that neither Istanbul nor the Turkish language are truly worth literature in the modern, European sense. As if in Istanbul one could only pretend to be a novelist – Istanbul being far from the center of the world. As if literature were more of a childish game here, nothing more. Pamuk's father does not seem to have taken the thought of a Turkish literature seriously. Or perhaps he took literature too seriously, being a newcomer, cutting off his own dong! He was no exception either way.

"I write because I am angry at all of you, angry at everyone," Pamuk would proclaim, a little too sincere, a little too disarmed. But "My Father's Suitcase" is a meticulously planned, self-aware and self-conscious, or, according to the way Pamuk understands these terms, an ultimately "sentimental" piece, as opposed to (or in addition to, in Pamuk's account) being naïve. It is as if such play, such immaturity and irreverence comes naturally to Pamuk's way of thinking and being, writing and speaking. But not entirely.

For additionally, it seems to me that all this is to ask a simple question, to his father and to his audience at once. This question is not about centers and peripheries at first sight, but about writing at large. What is being a novelist, if not *making as if* one were a novelist, i.e. walking and talking, thinking and writing as if one were a novelist? What else was he supposed to do to be a novelist, other than making as if he were a novelist in this manner? What else was he supposed to have known or seen? This is his cruel mockery of his father's lack of faith. Of course, Pamuk only made as if he were a novelist, just like his father. This is precisely how one becomes a novelist though, whether in Europe or in the East, which is what his father seems to have missed.

Then again this line of reasoning is at once a cruel mockery of his audience's naïve faith in his anger at his father. For it is also a statement concerning his position as a Turkish Nobel laureate. After all he would always be the *Turkish* novelist despite his recognition – and the spokesperson for a peripheral Turkish culture and politics – and not *just* a novelist. Not *completely* a novelist. He would never be treated as if he were just a novelist, or as a novelist he would always be something of a newcomer. The world does prove to have a center after all, regardless of how one writes, which is how Pamuk acknowledges his father at another register, getting back at his audience in the name of his father. His audience cannot understand what makes a novelist either! For the Nobel committee too, walking and talking, thinking and writing as if one were a novelist is not enough, it appears! The committee too seems to be invested in the naïve faith in some secret ingredient.

The Hoja from Pamuk's *The White Castle* explains this reasoning best. The Turkish Hoja spends years to discover how his Venetian slave, who happens to be his look-alike, manages to tell the most touching tales about his most wretched life. The Hoja and his slave look the same, but they do not see the same, to the master's despair. The Turkish master questions and tortures many a Christian, to dig out from the depths of their souls the secret formula for the slave's way of seeing and saying – the secret formula for experiencing life the way the Venetian slave does, to be able to tell stories like the Christian does. The Hoja eventually masters the Venetian way of storytelling so perfectly and becomes such a great, such a convincing storyteller in the Venetian style that he travels from Istanbul to Venice to live the stolen life of his Christian slave, leaving the Venetian back in Turkey in his place. But this happens only after he understands that the slave's stories owe their strength not to some magic formula or experience, but to the Christian way of making up things, the Christian way of *pretending* and crafting narratives. For we know that he only *pretends* to be his Venetian slave in his new life in Europe.

The White Castle concludes with either the Hoja or the Venetian slave reaching out to us from Turkey, without giving us a clue as to which one of them addresses us, or whether the master and the slave were one and the same person from the outset of the novel – one and the same *Turk*, one and the same *görmemiş*. The Hoja is not only a newcomer to literature in the European sense – to autobiography, to be precise – but he is also quite the *görmemiş* in that he takes his Europeanization to an incomprehensible extreme, ending up turning Christian, cutting off his Turkishness. Perhaps this is the reason why it is the Venetian-slave-turned-Turkish-master half of this most uncanny figure who addresses us to conclude the novel. That half seems to be quite an authentic Turk, and not a newcomer in Turkey or a convert, and quite an authentic European novelist too, despite his pretensions to be a Turk.

III

Now according to Pamuk's somewhat forced reading of Schiller's "Über Naïve und sentimentalische Dichtung," we have a distinction between the writer as a storyteller in the traditional sense, on the one hand, and the modern men and women of letters, on the other. While poetry and storytelling comes almost naturally to the former, the latter is self-aware and self-conscious, "reflective." While the former is more of an artisan in spirit, the latter is an autonomous artist. Pamuk remembers once despising "the naïve, childlike nature of Turkish novelists of the previous generation. They wrote their novels so easily, and never worried about problems of style and technique. And I applied the word 'naïve' (which I increasingly used in a negative sense) not only to them but to writers all over the world who regarded the nineteenth-century Balzacian novel as a natural entity and accepted it without question" (*Naïve* 18). Turkish men and women of letters were once like artisans, perhaps naïvely imitating European novelists, or "unaware" of their circumstances as they produced Venetian-style fictions with ease – in a way similar to Schiller's naïve Goethe. They were no Goethes, though, and their romantic naïveté was somewhat belated, which is why in Pamuk's account the term "naïve" seems to have assumed a particularly "negative sense." They may have sounded just as confident and clueless – as in "unaware" and not "reflective" – as Goethe, but unlike

Goethe's poetry, their writings were marked by some clumsiness, by some insufficiency, i.e. belatedness and *görmemişlik* (stuck as they were to "the nineteenth-century Balzacian novel," minimally, unaware of the conditions surrounding modern arts, perhaps). Thus their naïveté is more of a failure than a feature of their voice to overcome, which is why it would be a mistake to think that Goethe was to Schiller as the "Turkish novelists of the previous generation" were to Pamuk.

But Pamuk thinks that as a sentimental, modern man of letters, he also borrowed from his Turkish predecessors a certain naïveté, and perhaps even reconciled "the naïve novelist and the sentimental novelist" in his own work. On the one hand he follows up on the belated naïveté of the "Turkish novelists of the previous generation," and is indebted to them, on the other hand, where they seem to have failed, he seems to succeed. As I mentioned, Pamuk's debt to one of his predecessors, Ahmet Hamdi Tanpınar, may explain how this came to pass. It could also help better account for the failure I have mentioned in passing, but also the issue of "faith," belatedness, *görmemişlik*, the difference between being and pretending, and Pamuk's "success."

Novelist, poet and critic Ahmet Hamdi Tanpınar was appointed the chair of New Turkish Literature ("Yeni Türk Edebiyatı") at Istanbul University in 1939. The chair was established as part of a project of reorganizing a traditional, somewhat Islamic educational institution, i.e. *İstanbul Darülfünûnu*, into Istanbul University, which in turn was part of the broader project for the institution of a European style humanities curriculum in Turkey (Konuk 2010). It was among the first national, European-style universities in the Muslim world. Many prominent figures who marked Turkish and world literature were involved in this endeavor. Erich Auerbach, for one, having fled Nazi aggression in mid-thirties, chaired the department of Western Languages and Literatures, contributed to the establishment of Romance philology, and penned his canonical *Mimesis* and "Figura" at the same institution, "inventing" the discipline of comparative literature (Apter 2006). Pamuk would study journalism at Istanbul University decades later. Tanpınar's appointment to the chair of New Turkish Literature at Istanbul University marks a crucial moment in the history of Turkish literary and cultural criticism, literary historiography, and modern Turkish fiction.

Above all, it occasioned the first comprehensive history of modern Ottoman and Turkish letters. The incomplete history by Tanpınar, *XIX. asır Türk edebiyatı* [*Nineteenth Century Turkish Literature*] is only the first volume of the planned two-volume work. While his brief account of verbal arts in the "Muslim Orient" prior to the nineteenth century explains why that history could not culminate in a properly literary exchange, and reach novelistic heights, for instance, his lengthy account of nineteenth-century Turkish letters addresses many attempts at creating the space for such exchange for modern Turkish fiction. He describes many of these modern attempts as failures, but regards them all as having paved the way to his own present, when circumstances seem to have changed drastically. According to his very peculiar and somewhat subjective periodization, there is first the failure of the "Muslim Orient" in producing or leading the way to literature in the modern sense, due to its own long established, and at times charming, way of making things with words; then comes the modern Ottoman and Turkish failure to engage in literary activity proper, bound as it was to the ancient ways of the "Muslim Orient"; finally we have Tanpınar's own extraordinary, contemporary struggle and his own reluctant, "melancholy" achievements in producing works of modern literature and literary histories.

Given that Tanpınar, the writer with whom Pamuk feels "the closest bond" (*Istanbul* 110), offers us "the deepest understanding of what it means to live in a rapidly westernizing country among the ruins of Ottoman culture" (209), one could imagine Tanpınar's work as something of a barricade between "the Ottoman past" and Pamuk's present – and Tanpınar as carrying a suitcase to deliver to Pamuk, one that is quite similar to Pamuk's own father's suitcase. This can help us locate the coordinates of Pamuk's writing in the history of Turkish literature. Tanpınar is the ultimate figure that divides the past from Pamuk's present, when there is hardly any link left and when, Tanpınar himself, the barricade "standing tall" (225) and failing to bridge the two sides of the divide, contents himself with giving us a historic image of a world that is no more and a melancholy account of his own present moment in a belated modernity.

Tanpınar's literary history narrates a progression from pre-literary, "Muslim Oriental" verbal arts toward modern Turkish letters. What drives this progression is a conflict between two different ways of relating to and accounting for reality, or relating to words and things. Tanpınar places himself in the middle between two different ways of saying and being, one belonging to the pre-modern, Muslim Orient and the other to his "rapidly," if also belatedly, "westernizing" present. Pamuk deduced "melancholy" as the ultimate legacy of Tanpınar and his companions' impasse in between these two mentalities. Yet Tanpınar also professes literature – a melancholy literature, due to Tanpınar's dedication to "our old poetry," and somewhat "narrow" and restrained too, due to Tanpınar's distance to the European center: but a revolutionary one, in the final analysis, insofar as his literature points to a number of novel paths on Pamuk's side of the barricade. Pamuk's works bear marks of the conflictual history Tanpınar narrates, but at the same time he follows Tanpınar's prescriptions to step out of Tanpınar's melancholy and impasse. Let us follow this trajectory, from what Tanpınar calls the "Muslim Oriental" art, which he also perceived as a dead-end on the way to literary modernity, to the very narrow path that Tanpınar imagines as a way out to literary modernity. I will contextualize Pamuk's writings in these two settings. This will enable us to see how Pamuk can be interpreted as following Tanpınar's prescriptions to step out of Tanpınar's paralysis, surpassing Tanpınar and his predecessors by taking Tanpınar's medicine, i.e. "faith."

IV

"Poetry and Prose" ("Şiir ve inşa," 1868) is the title of one of the first modern literary critical works written in Ottoman Turkish. The author, Ziya Pasha (1825-1880), is thought to have translated the French *littérature* in his title as "Poetry and Prose," in the absence of a word in Ottoman Turkish that corresponds to the French *littérature*. Perhaps this is to say that the Turk was quite the *görmemiş* at this point in time. Prose in the "Muslim Orient" was an almost inexistent genre, Tanpınar would later explain, since Muslim "poetry" surpassed prose in quality and quantity and, due to its prominence, also overburdened prose with its peculiar intransitivity. Let me continue to paraphrase Tanpınar's insights in *XIX. asır Türk edebiyatı* (28-46). The poetry of the "Muslim Orient," moreover, was a way of making things with words that was radically different from Western literature. Tanpınar focusses on the couplet (*beyit*) to prove the difference in question. The essence of "Muslim Oriental art" is the couplet, he argues, the fragmented couplet as opposed to the solid "stanza" of European poetry. The "thematics" that binds stanzas in European poetry is irrelevant in the making of this art. The "narrative" that binds statements into stories or novels, or the "frame," visible or invisible, in Western plastic arts that enables a particular vision and its representation are nowhere to be found in this art form. One could describe similar or corresponding elements for this art, but they would remain secondary to its making. It is the *beyit* that moves and molds. Tanpınar argues that usually the second line of most couplets in Muslim Oriental poetry appears either redundant or superficial, while the two lines together, the couplet as couplet, resemble a jewel.

The saying in the first line of the couplet gives us a motif – a singular object, sentiment or a kernel of thought. The second line says almost nothing, yet expresses a forceful submission to form in following the first line strictly formulaically, thereby making the overall couplet appear empty of discursive content, and transforming the words of the couplet into an embellishment of the motif introduced in the first line. One half of the couplet annuls the content promised in the other, and by rendering the couplet primarily formulaic, pushes the motif presented in the first line to the fore. Individual couplets resemble precious stones bearing the motifs. Couplets do not and cannot join together in a singular and meaningful work, regardless of the length of the poem. Tanpınar translates this into the language of society. Quoting Massignon, he argues that "there is no time in the Muslim Orient, but only moments" (*XIX. asır* 32; my translation). It is as if there were no stories in the "Muslim Orient," not even a story-telling that could enable a historical vision. Poems only inspired impressions and images. These, moreover, were not "realistic" images, but resembled miniatures lacking sense of perspective and proportion. It is as if the trouble with "our old poetry" was that it treated words as things; things resembling precious stones.

This Muslim Oriental, dominantly poetic way of making things with words paralyzed Turkish language and prose, according to Tanpınar. Turkish prose could not have turned literary in the modern sense, could not have enabled the writing of novels, for instance, because it was stuck to the peculiar intransitivity of the Oriental "verbal arts":

> No doubt one of the important reasons for the obsession with the verbal arts overwhelming the old prose was that it was deprived of the *terbiye* [manners, habit of mind, training or discipline] that plastic arts and painting had enabled in other languages, paving the way to the possibility of a clear vision. [...] In a literature [or a "regime" of writing, perhaps], and particularly a prose tradition that had never settled accounts with the line, the image or the sculpture, or simply the volume [also scale or proportion] and the color; in a writing that had never before tested in these the order ["nizam": also system, or regime] of attesting to the real and the accompanying notion of proportion ["nisbet": also relativity, ratio], hence deprived of their *terbiye* of isolation ["tecrit": also abstraction], the contact with the thing and the external world would obviously remain superficial.[2] (*XIX. asır* 46; my translation)

Making things with words, as with lines and colors, conditions vision and relation to the world. Properly literary, "realist" writing, like realist depiction, enables realistic vision. Such vision and relation are possible as a habit of mind, one that is cultivated through exercises in realistic representation, verbal or visual. But the European realist *terbiye* ('manners,' 'habit of mind' or 'discipline') is alien to the Muslim world. Tanpınar himself proves to have developed the habit of mind to forge the kind of "contact with the thing and the external world" that is not "superficial" but here "historical," elsewhere "realist" and literary. His "melancholy" has to do not only with the belatedness of his own mindset, which was too new and

---

[2] "Eski nesri boğan bu söz sanatları iptilâsının mühim bir sebebi de şüphesiz ki başka dillerde plastik sanatlardan ve resimden gelen terbiyeden, onların insana açtığı sarih görüş imkânından mahrum oluşudur. [...] Çizginin, resmin, heykeltraşînin yani rengin ve hacmin tecrübesinden geçmemiş, reel müşahedesinin nizamını ve nisbet fikrini bunlarda dememiş ve bunların tecrit terbiyesini almamış bir edebiyatta; ve bilhassa nesirde, elbetteki eşya ve dış dünya ile temas çok sathî kalacaktı" (*XIX. asır* 46).

perhaps immature, but also with his inability to reconcile his realism with the habits of mind of the Muslim Orient. It is as if, from the perspective of the humanist, he has no option but to describe the old Turkish, Muslim Oriental ways of saying and being as problematic and inaccessible, as an impasse. Yet, he would also repeatedly refer to these ways as "our" old poetry and "our" old prose. "We," newcomers to literary/realist prose, had to lose our old poetry and prose. "Our" words today neither carry the weight of a tradition, nor do they convey our reality maturely.

From Tanpınar's perspective, then, there is the weight of an entire civilizational history, and the immense tension of a civilizational difference and confrontation. The main character of Tanpınar's *The Time Regulation Institute*, Hayri İrdal, a social climber and an arriviste, and certainly a "sonradan görme," carries all this burden as an author. This simple man, cut off from "the past," can hardly understand Ottoman Turkish. He is certainly far from appreciating "our old poetry." His employment in the Institute enables him to mingle with the high society and intellectuals of Europeanizing Istanbul, and initiates him into another way of writing and reading, saying and seeing. His crowning achievement at the institute, whose absurd mission is to popularize the temporal standards of the modern, industrialized world, is to write a best-selling book, a completely fictional (and yet historically probable) biography that almost ends up driving its inventor mad. He writes a story about a Turkish clock smith "who anticipated Graham's calculations two centuries before the fact," but presents it as history (313). People almost believe him, since the story makes, for instance, the expanding network of Turkish railroads more meaningful, and the departure of trains on time sensible. He himself almost believes in his own lies, but not quite. İrdal the newcomer, devoid of a realist *terbiye*, ends up mixing up historical reality and fiction in some mental paralysis. He has nothing real or concrete to achieve, neither in the name of modernity nor in the name of tradition. It is not only that his writing fails to represent reality, he also fails to accomplish anything real and concrete as a writer. The world continues to change, and his words can neither interrupt nor hasten the movement. His words do not carry the weight of a tradition, and his contact with reality, historical and otherwise, is immature, if not superficial. He only *pretends* to be a historian or an intellectual. This is how Tanpınar *inter-*

prets Turkish literary modernity, it appears, himself a major actor in the latter movement.

İrdal's madness could be compared to Galip's perplexity in *The Black Book*. Pamuk is more concerned with the city itself, with what surrounds Galip, than Galip's internal conflicts. When Galip sets on a quest in Istanbul to find his wife, the entire city, real and concrete, transforms itself into a labyrinth of signs, each and every object and event turning overburdened with meaning. The way Pamuk weaves signs together in the novel, and folds the narrative onto itself numerous times, was not meant to simply show how the genius novelist is capable of playing with his readers. Pamuk shows how different ways of relating to words and things can effortlessly transform an entire world beyond one's intentions or understanding – how interpreting the world is already changing it. But the famous scene from *Snow*, when the soldiers on stage fire live rounds at the audience, is helpful here to understand what Pamuk contributes to Tanpınar's position about writing and action:

> As someone from the back rows stood up and made straight for the stage with blood streaming from his head, there came the smell of gunpowder. [...] Even so, the literature teacher Nuriye Hanım, who attended the National Theater every time she visited Ankara and was full of admiration for the beauty of the theatrical effects, rose to her feet for the first time to applaud the actors. (156-57)

The eruption of fiction into reality in these lines must be understood against the background of Tanpınar's commentary on different habits of mind, but in the context of a real and concrete conflict. What is at stake here is the truth of fiction. The stage fires live rounds. Fiction does real things in the real world. Nuriye Hanım, the literature teacher, does not seem to understand what is happening, and appears a little mad, perhaps like İrdal. But the soldiers, the "actors" on *Snow*'s stage with their bullets, and Tanpınar with his history and novels, do real things in the real world, which is what Tanpınar seems to have missed, either underestimating himself or his writing – perhaps due to some melancholy impasse.

Snow, which Pamuk described as his first "political" novel, is not the story of Nuriye Hanım, who is but a comical, minor figure in the narrative. Galip and Pamuk, unlike İrdal and Tanpınar, navigate the city with ease, overburdened with meaning as the city may have become. We will see how Pamuk's literary politics is quite different from Tanpınar's impasse in *The Time Regulation Institute*. Tanpınar himself will prescribe an additional, different sense of politics, a specific politics *of* literature as a way out of his own impasse. Let us continue in the order in which Tanpınar develops his thoughts.

V

Tanpınar describes "Muslim Oriental art" as above all craftsmanship – but craftsmanship of a particular sort: "Our old poetry" was literally making things with words, producing wordy textiles rather than texts perhaps, which relate to reality only superficially. Literary making requires perspective, context, proportion, i.e. a rather more intimate relation to reality. But in his 1960 essay "The Fundamental Differences between the Orient and the Occident" ("Şark ile garp arasında görülen esaslı farklar"), Tanpınar explains how the difference between "Muslim Oriental art" and modern Western *literary* ways comes down to different styles of making, *literally*:

> It is always possible to reduce the most apparent differences between the Occident and the Orient into a few notions, which then would allow critical engagement. As I understand it, first come the behaviors of these two distinct mentalities vis-a-vis the good and the thing. Needless to say, here we take these words in their most general meanings, i.e. we consider the good and the thing, but also the stuff of thinking and imagining, all the material of mental and social life, which is to say, we consider the "object" in the face of the thinking mind and the processing hand. The Orient accepts the thing as is or as it appears in the first differentiation it is assigned at the first encounter. The first traits always suffice. In the first encounter it [the Orient] even arrives at certain perfections, so much so that sometimes after the first encounter, perfection of the same caliber becomes forever unattainable. But in tra-

ditions that take root fast this perfection freezes, it gets rigid. The Occident grabs the thing to turn it around, holds it before the mind, looks for additional traits to assign and other possibilities of perfection to pursue, wrestles to know the thing as thoroughly as possible and as a result of all this endeavor makes the thing into almost something other than itself. It could be argued that the Orient appropriates the good only generally. Sometimes it is as if the Orient simply borrows the good from nature. The Occident owns the good completely by understanding its bodily constitution and testing all of its possibilities.[3] ("Şark ile garp" 132; my translation)

Diamond cutting is the perfect example for Tanpınar. "At least until the conquest of South African mines," he writes, "the Orient was the home of precious metals."[4] While the most precious and the most beautiful jewels are originally Oriental, processing of precious metals has become an Occidental business. It was originally an Oriental business, argues Tanpınar, but "a special care and a way of knowledge that expands all the way to speculation has transformed" this sort of making: "This care is speculative, because it is based on observation and knowledge concerning

---

[3] "Şarkla garp arasında ilk bakışta göze çarpan ayrılıkları birkaç ana fikre indirmek ve onlardan hareket ederek mütalâa etmek daima mümkündür. İtikadımca bunların başında şu iki zihniyetin eşya ve madde karşısındaki davranışları gelir. Söylemeğe hacet yok ki, burada bu kelimeleri en geniş mânâlarında, yani hem madde ve eşya, hem fikir ve hayal, zihnî ve içtimaî hayatın bütün verileri, hülâsa düşünen zekâ ve işleyen el karşısında nesne (Objet) mânâsına alıyoruz. Şark, maddeyi olduğu gibi yahut ilk rastlayışta ona verdiği değişiklikle kabul eder. Telkin ettiği ilk hususiyetlerle yetinir. Bu ilk karşılaşmada bazı mükemmelliklere kadar varır. Hatta erişilmez bir hâl aldığı da olur. Fakat çarçabuk teessüs eden bir gelenekte bu mükemmellik durur, kalıplaşır. Garp ise onu daima elinde evirir çevirir, zihninin karşısında tutar, ondan birtakım başka hususiyetler ve mükemmelleşme imkânları arar, onun hakkında en etraflı bilgiye sahip olmağa çalışır ve bu gayretler sayesinde sonunda bu maddeyi başka bir şey denecek hâle getirir. Denebilir ki, Şark eşyaya ancak umumî şeklinde tasarruf eder. Hattâ bazen onu tabiattan sanki ödünç alır. Garp ise bünye mahiyetini anlamak ve bütün imkânlarını yoklamak suretiyle onu tam benimser."

[4] "Elmas işçiliği bu ayrılığın en iyi misâlidir. Şark, hiç olmazsa Cenubî Afrika madenlerinin keşfine kadar kıymetli taşların vatanı idi."

the capacity of light to be refracted. In the Occident, in poetry, in music and language, in all the fields of fine arts and in all issues concerning thought and society, we always encounter this care and this economy of knowledge."[5] In the Orient, however, "imagination resembles those figures of old fables that stumble upon precious stones. It gathers whatever it can gather on the isolated mountain tops where it flies on the back of a Phoenix" (133). In these few lines, Tanpınar reduces all literary history, an entire history of art, moreover, in the Orient and in the West alike, into a history of manufacture, into a history of *literally* making, even if what is at stake is *literary* making. To answer the question of what art is, one must simply consider "the 'object' in the face of the thinking mind and the processing hand" (132.)

One can interpret Pamuk's carefully crafted, labyrinthine plots, which display a craftsman-like care and precision in light of these insights. The Hoja of *The White Castle*, for instance, as mentioned before, spends years to discover where his Venetian slave's colorful stories come from, to learn how to tell stories himself. But he masters story-telling (so much so that he can *become* the Venetian himself) only after understanding that the slave's stories owe their effectiveness not to the slave's secrets, but to the particular way of crafting narratives. But if there is one single work of art that sets to work with Tanpınar's slogan-like premise in mind ("we consider the 'object' in the face of the thinking mind and the processing hand") it is no doubt Pamuk's *Museum of Innocence* (2010). In it, Kemal introduces us to multiple everyday objects related to his beloved, Füsun, each of them portraying a discrete moment of bliss. In every chapter, together with the narrator, we grab one object after the other, "turn it around, hold it before the mind, [...] make the thing into almost something other than itself" ("Şark ile garp" 132; my translation). But in the meantime, by making the novel itself into a thing, i.e. a ticket to the actual

---

[5] "Elmas işçiliği aslında şarkın malı olan bir işçiliktir. Fakat Şark memleketlerinde olduğu şekilde kalmadı. Hususî bir dikkat, spekülasyona kadar giden bir bilgi onu değiştirdi. Bu dikkat spekülatif'dir, çünkü ışığın kırılıp dağılma kabiliyeti üzerinde müşahedelerin, bilginin neticesidir. Garpde, şiirde, musikide, dilde, güzel san'atların her dalında, fikir ve cemiyet işlerinde daima bu dikkate ve bu bilgili tasarrufa şahit oluruz."

Museum of Innocence of Istanbul (on one of the pages of the book, Pamuk includes a printed ticket to the museum that was conceived in tandem with the novel), the author underlines the dumb reality of the book as an object, selling his books as if they were tickets as well. Moreover, the actual museum displays a collection of objects from the everyday life of Istanbul during the period in which the novel is set. There in the museum, "the same" objects are exhibited as if they were "precious stones," as remnants of a mythic past, of a world that never was or is no more.

Not that there is something specifically "Oriental" about the overall work of art that is "The Museum of Innocence." It simply displays how different ways of relating to words and things, which boil down to real and concrete, conflicting ways of being, can and in fact do exist together in this part of the world. They *do* exist *together*, for better or for worse, at times fraught with tension, sometimes accompanied by indifference. This is to say that Pamuk's own brand of realism simply releases the tensions that emanate from Tanpınar's civilizational conflicts, which seems to have paralyzed Tanpınar. But what enables this?

VI

Ziya Pasha's landmark essay "Poetry and Prose," mentioned earlier, identified a problem relating to the distance between written and vernacular languages, which had disabled the literary address in the absence of properly equipped readers. The pasha proposed educational and curricular shifts and a standardized orthography. These would enable anyone and everyone to take part in a community of letters. Ahmet Midhat Efendi (1844-1912), one of the first novelists of modern Ottoman-Turkish, thought that our failure had to do with the roots or rather rootlessness of literature in Turkish ("İkram-ı aklam," 1897). The problem was that "we don't have classics," which Midhat wanted to recreate for Modern Turkish, rather than simply copy Western classics or embrace them "as ours." Ottoman youth had to read and learn, according to Midhat, but not anything and everything, only what is necessary for the Muslim, which is why we had to create our own classics. Otherwise we would end up producing *sonradan görme*s of all hues – and his novels, like Pamuk's, are populated by *sonradan görme*s' threatening Muslim values. Later Ömer

Seyfeddin (1884-1920) described Midhat's failure by explaining how Midhat's readers, all of them *sonradan görme*s to begin with, traveled all the way to the printing facilities where Midhat had his works published, in order to report to the author that this or that fictional character of his was in fact their neighbor, or to ask him whether or not this or that fictional youth was their neighbor's son or daughter: "[P]eople did not know anything about this genre of writing that is the novel, they took fictional persons to be real persons! And yet, *elhamdülillah*, we do not live in that age that takes the novel to be the real event."[6] ("Sanatı idrak" 2; my translation). Almost a century later, Pamuk would complain about similar circumstances (*Naïve*, ch. 2). Seyfeddin thought that the emerging awareness was just a beginning and acknowledged that there was a long way to go before "we," the newcomers to modern life, started producing works of literature. His diagnosis of the problem poses the question of modern life as the stuff of modern literature:

> Just as on the streets we come across villagers who cannot understand modern life, we can always bump into narrow-minded friends in the intellectual realm [who don't understand modern literature]. No doubt, villagers who bargain for the ticket price before getting on the streetcar or the boat, the old lady who tries to make the streetcar take a turn to drop her off in front of her friend's house, just don't understand the facts of modern life.[7]
> (Seyfeddin 2; my translation)

For Ziya Pasha the building of a new media technology in the form of a common, "simple" tongue and a standardized orthography had priority for the creation of a literary space. This would enable anyone and everyone to

---

[6] "Halk o zaman edebiyatında 'roman' nevinin ne olduğunu bilmediği için hayalî şahısları hakiki adamlar sanırmış! Artık bugün 'elhamdülillah' romanı 'sahih vakıa' zanneden bir devirde değiliz!"

[7] "Nasıl sokakta 'asrî hayat'ı idrak etmeyen köylülere rastgelirsek fikir âleminde de zihninin hacmi gayet dar âşinâlarla karşılaşırız. Tranvayda, tünelde, vapurda biletini pazarlıkla almak isteyen köylü, tranvayı gideceği komşusunun sokağına saptırmak isteyen ihtiyar hanım, şüphesiz asrî hayatın bedihiyyâtını anlayamamıştır."

read and write, to "communicate" in writing and become a new, informed community. For Midhat this could be destructive. One needed to make sure that the emerging literary space and its "public," this new way of *being-in-common*, did not conflict with the traditional, Muslim way of being-in-common, which depended on what one said in the kind of writing that was meant for anyone and everyone. For Seyfeddin, the stuff of modern literature had to come first, i.e. life itself had to be modernized, for literature to make sense. Our lives were not yet ready to be represented by a genre such as the novel, just as we were not ready yet for our "streetcar or the boat." In all these accounts, the question of literature is inextricably linked to an impasse within a particular way of being and *being-in-common*. All of them call for change and prescribe educational measures. "Our" literary failure was our failure to "communicate" and be a "people" in the modern, Western sense, and this was the reason why the literary criticism of this sort was already social critique, and it could not but be political in its call to action. They all theorize "our" newcoming to modernity, expressing fears or acknowledging our Johnny-come-lateliness and *görmemişlik*. They all propose literary exchange, the literary space as potentially a way out of the impasse, deferring "our" late "arrival," "our" becoming ourselves and properly, authentically a people to a moment in the future.

Tanpınar would explain that literary writing is neither a tool to be employed for Ziya Pasha's revolutionary or Midhat's reactionary purposes, nor is it dependent on the modernity of life in common. Beginning with the early nineteenth century, relation to things and words alike change in this part of the world; partially, slowly, even painfully. There is no way around this historic movement, at least not in writing: but people already live, make and share things and words right in the middle of it. Tanpınar juxtaposes what he deems an "idealist" account of "our failure in literature" with a "determinist" one. His idealists argue that the Turkish men of letters do not know their society nor do they show interest in learning about it, but desire to transform it, hence are at best elites cut off from the life in common. Tanpınar accepts that there is a great deal of copying Western examples in modern Turkish letters, yet he also thinks that this issue should be perceived simply as *sonradan görmelik*, and should not be exaggerated, since all art forms travel from culture to culture. All art is imitation to begin with. His determinists argue that Turkish letters fail because "our communal life" is not fit to be represented through a modern aesthetic regime of writing, for a genre such as the novel for instance. Tanpınar agrees with this judgment as well, but proves it to be faulty with the following argument: "Our life is narrow, it is intricate. This said, in the final analysis it is and we are living it, we love and hate, suffer and die. Is this not enough for the novelist?"[8] ("Bizde roman" 37; my translation)

The Time Regulation Institute comes close to putting on paper the narrow and intricate life Tanpınar refers to, although the deep melancholy that emanates from the tragicomedy proves how the fact that "we live, love and die" does not suffice for Tanpınar the novelist. Yet this is exactly what he seems to prescribe for future writers: some sort of indifference, a political indifference or better still, perhaps a politics of indifference. It would be a mistake to associate this indifference with an apolitical position. Tanpınar's fascinating, if still somewhat melancholy, passage below displays its firm political foundations:

> [...] The novelist must believe in the people. It is this faith that produces art. Wherever there is life, there is also the joy that is nothing other than lights and colors overflowing this faith. [...] I believe that when we recognize these issues in their actuality, we will find ourselves elsewhere, in a place where we don't anymore take life to be something we bear, something like fate. A place where we take hold of life, looking around us with the self-confidence of the great makers. Yet to find this spirit of making we need first to find the pleasure of life. We need to taste the happiness of life in the exact same way the great nature appears to be happy simply to be. This is only possible by believing in the people of this society. It is futile to look at this society under alien lenses, or to recreate it as if it was a product of the intellect, as if

---

[8] "Hayatımız dardır; karışıktır, iyi ama, bu hayat nihayet vardır ve yaşıyoruz, seviyoruz, nefret ediyor, ıztırap çekiyor, ölüyoruz. Bir romancı için bu kadarı yetmez mi?"

it did not have a reality of its own.[9] ("Hayat karşısında romancı" 44-45; my translation)

Faith in the people, then, in the life in common, requires coming to terms with the realities of the life in common, even when this life is narrow and intricate. Neither nostalgia for bygone glory nor ideals about origins nor fixation on the greener grass will do. What marks the spirit of great makers, of which Pamuk certainly has his share, is "the joy that is nothing other than lights and colors overflowing this faith." (44) What makes Pamuk a "Turkish" novelist, then, is not what makes Ziya Pasha, Midhat, Seyfeddin or Tanpınar Turkish men of letters. Pamuk stands out of this crowd, perhaps in the direction Tanpınar points to, as a great, naïve, and sentimental novelist of world literature, with Istanbul at the narrow center of his world. He stands out as a great maker, an artisan who gives us a glimpse of the "lights and colors" of the city, crafting stories out of memories, hopes and despairs, angers and joys of its past and present occupants.

He is a great "arriviste" to the world republic of letters – not simply authentic, nor just inauthentic, pretending to be novelist sometimes, pretending to be an artisan at times. On the one hand, his faithful conclusion seems to be that we the Turks have no other option than to pretend to be Europeans with this ceaseless ambition of ours to Europeanize ourselves, no other option to come out as pretenders. Then

---

[9] "Romancı insana inanmalıdır. Çünkü hayatı bu iman yapar. Nerede hayat varsa, orada bu imanın renk ve ışık tufanı olan neş'e vardır. [...] insanı realiteye, realiteyi altındaki kökleşmiş mes'eleye irca etmeden bu memleketin edebiyatının yapılacağına ben de kani değilim. Hatta bu mes'eleleri hakikî yüzü ve diliyle tanıdığımız zaman, kendimizi çok başka bulacağımıza, hayatı sadece tahammül edilmesi lâzım gelen bir şey, bir kader gibi kabul edeceğimiz yerde, ona hâkim olacağımıza, etrafımıza büyük yapıcıların nefis güvenleriyle bakacağımıza inanıyorum. Fakat bu yapıcı ruhu bulabilmek için yaşamanın tadını bulmamız lâzımdır. Büyük tabiat var olmaktan ne kadar mes'ut görünüyorsa, biz de yaşamanın saadetini öyle tatmalıyız. Bu da, bu cemiyetin insanına güvenmekle olur. Onu yabancı adeselerin tuttuğu ışıklar altında görmekle, yahut hiç realitesine bakmadan sadece zihnin bir mahsûlü gibi yaratmakla, hiçbir şey elde edilemez."

again, what does it mean to be (oneself, European, a novelist, modern or even "human" etc.), Pamuk seems to ask, if not to pretend to be (oneself, European, a novelist, modern or even "human" etc.)?

Works Cited

Ahmet Mithat Efendi. "İkram-ı aklam." Tercüman-ı hakikat 5 Sept. 1897.

Auerbach, Erich. *Mimesis.* 1953. Trans. Willard R. Trask. Princeton: Princeton UP. 1974.

___. Figura." Trans. Ralph Manheim and Catherine Garvin. *"Scenes from the Drama of European Literature.* Minneapolis: University of Minnesota Press, 1985.

Apter, Emily. *The Translation Zone: A New Comparative Literature.* Princeton: Princeton UP, 2006.

Gurbilek, Nurdan. "Dandies and Originals: Authenticity, Belatedness, and the Turkish Novel." *South Atlantic Quarterly* 102.2/3 (2003): 599-628.

Konuk, Kader. *East-West Mimesis: Auerbach in Turkey.* Stanford: Stanford UP, 2010.

Massignon, Louis. "Islam milletlerinin sanat yaratışlarındaki usuller." *Din ve sanat.* İstanbul 1937. 15-41.

Pamuk, Orhan. *The Black Book.* Trans. Maureen Freely. 1990. New York: Vintage, 2006. Trans. of *Kara kitap.*

___. *Istanbul: Memories and the City.* Trans. Maureen Freely. New York: Knopf, 2006. Trans. of *İstanbul: Hatıralar ve şehir.*

___. "Der meistgehasste Türke." Interview by Peer Teuwsen. *Tages-Anzeiger. Das Magazin* 5 Feb. 2005. Accessed 14 May 2017 <https://web.archive.org/web/20090116123035/http://sc.tagesanzeiger.ch:80/dyn/news/kultur/560264.html>.

___. *My Name Is Red.* Trans. Erdağ M. Göknar. New York: Knopf, 2001. Trans. of *Benim adım kırmızı.*

___. *The Museum of Innocence.* Trans. Maureen Freeley. New York: Knopf, 2010. Trans. of *Masumiyet müzesi.*

___. "My Father's Suitcase: The Nobel Lecture." Trans. Maureen Freely. Accessed 3 Jan. 2017 <https://www.nobelprize.org/nobel_prizes/

literature/laureates/2006/pamuk-lecture_en.html>. Trans. of "Babamın bavulu: Nobel konuşması."

___. *The Naïve and the Sentimental Novelist*. The Charles Eliot Norton Lectures 2009. Trans. Nazım Dikbaş. Cambridge, MA and London: Harvard UP, 2010. Trans. of *Saf ve düşünceli romancı*.

___. *The New Life*. Trans. Güneli Gün. New York: Vintage, 1998. Trans. of *Yeni hayat*.

___. *Snow*. Trans. Maureen Freely. London: Faber, 2004. Trans. of *Kar*.

___. *The White Castle*. Trans. Maureen Freely. London: Faber and Faber, 2001. Trans. of *Beyaz kale*.

Seyfeddin, Ömer. "Sanatı idrak." *Vakit Gazetesi* 45. 5 Kanun-ı evvel 1334 [1918].

Tanpınar, Ahmet Hamdi. *XIX. asır Türk edebiyatı*. 1949. Istanbul: Yapı Kredi, 2006.

___. "Bizde roman." *Edebiyat üzerine makaleler*. By Tanpınar. Istanbul: MEB, 1969. 33-37.

___. "Hayat karşısında romancı." *Edebiyat üzerine makaleler*. By Tanpınar. Istanbul: MEB, 1969. 42-45.

___. "Şark ile garp arasında görülen esaslı farklar." *Edebiyat üzerine makaleler*. By Tanpınar. İstanbul: MEB, 1969. 132-35.

___. *The Time Regulation Institute*. 1954. Trans. Ender Gürol. Madison: Turko-Tatar Press, 2002.

Walker, Shaun. "Orhan Pamuk: Turkey's Enemy Within Finds Peace." *Independent* 19 Aug. 2012. Accessed 3 Jan. 2017 <http://www.independent.co.uk/news/world/europe/orhan-pamuk-turkeys-enemy-within-finds-peace-8061626.html>.

Ziya Paşa. "Şiir ve inşa." *Hürriyet* 11. 7 Sept. 1868.

Dependable Content for Political Junctures: Orhan Pamuk and the Turkish Media

Adam McConnel
Sabancı University

Abstract: Turkish press controversies regarding Orhan Pamuk are not a recent development. Since the 1980s, when Pamuk's novels began to receive domestic and international attention, Pamuk has been subjected to domestic press debates that reflect far more on the contemporary discussions in Turkish society than on the themes or meanings of Pamuk's books. This chapter examines the reasons for these intense but superficial attacks directed at Pamuk. The role designated for the intelligentsia by Turkish state institutional traditions and the political atmosphere in Turkish society are identified as the primary factors fueling these polemics. Because the disputes centered on Pamuk are sourced in the socio-political topics of the moment, and can also draw upon comments that Pamuk has provided to the press, all political standpoints in the Turkish political sphere have participated in the anti-Pamuk rhetoric at one point or another. As long as Turkish intellectuals are seen foremost as socio-political role models, the controversies surrounding Pamuk, his novels, and his opinions are likely to continue.

> I asked him about his enemies. He recounted, and recounted, and recounted.
> – Orhan Pamuk, *The Black Book*, epigraph for ch. 8, "The Three Musketeers"

Unlike many other countries, domestic press polemics about figures from Turkey's arts and culture community are a frequent occurrence. These controversies are connected to the role given to intellectuals by Kemalist state ideology, which sees intellectuals as public guides for the masses concerning academic and cultural subjects.

The result of this situation is that, if any certain intellectual is perceived as rocking the boat, or in some way not fulfilling the role provided to them by the Turkish state, they become the subject of public scrutiny, controversy arises, arguments ensue, and the entire process is carried out through the press. Furthermore, many different ideological stances are represented in Turkish media, so different perspectives may find something to criticize at different times.

Orhan Pamuk is certainly Turkey's most internationally-recognized novelist. But as a member of the intelligentsia, He is also subject to the traditional expectations that Turkish society holds towards its intellectuals. As the examples below will illustrate, Pamuk has long been the subject of controversies because of his novels' content and success, and because of his public statements. Those disputes have waxed and waned according to the Turkish political topics of the moment, but all sides of the political spectrum have taken their turns at targeting Pamuk.

When Pamuk's most recent novel, *Kırmızı saçlı kadın* (*The Red-Haired Woman*), appeared in early 2016, noted Turkish TV journalist and amateur historian Murat Bardakçı quickly published an article heatedly criticizing one aspect of the book. Published on the *Habertürk* news website and titled "Orhan Pamuk, What the Hell is This?!" ("*Çüş Orhan Pamuk, Çüş!*"),[1] Bardakçı's column voiced an aggressive, insulting attack against both the novel's content and the advertising campaign that accompanied the book's appearance.

Bardakçı first excerpts a section from page 114 in which the narrator discusses the frequency of Oedipal-themed crimes in Turkish newspapers and society. After the excerpt, Bardakçı proceeds to an angry condemnation of the novel's "perverted" content, claiming that such incidents cannot appear in Turkish newspapers because reporting them is banned, that even in European countries similar bans exist, and that in 40 years as a journalist he had never seen a single newspaper report of a son raping his mother, killing his father, and then being murdered in prison. Bardakçı is offended by the novel's implication that such crimes are common in Turkish society.

Bardakçı then ends his brief commentary by leveling accusations at Pamuk that are similar to those repeated endlessly over the past 25 years: the plot's salacious nature is intended to boost sales, and the same plot and

---

[1] Bardakçı accused Pamuk of plagiarizing parts of *The White Castle* and *My Name is Red*. More specifically, Bardakçı ("Reşad Ekrem") claimed that *My Name is Red* was copied from Norman Mailer's *Ancient Evenings*. Translations are mine unless otherwise stated.

strong sales will get the novella translated and published abroad. Finally, because the book will then be bought by scores of foreigners, the world will end up getting the idea that Turkey is populated by a vile mass acting out their Oedipal complexes. In the last sentences, Bardakçı enumerates some additional emphatic verbal reactions that he wanted to include in the title, and summarizes the novel's basic plot as "shameful." From the right-of-center, Bardakçı gives the reader moralizing and cheap populism as his literary critique.

Only two weeks later, one of Turkey's many progressive-leftist websites, *5Harfliler*,[2] published a broadside against the same Pamuk novel. This piece by "Özüm Hanım,"[3] titled "A Red-Haired Green Light for Feminism from Your Uncle Orhan (feat. Come On, You'll Be Alright)" (*"Orhan Eniştenizden feminizme kırmızı saçlı yeşil ışık [feat. Hadi Yine İyisiniz]"*), provides all of the juvenile smirk promised by the title.

The author begins the article by describing how she overcame her initial reaction to the novel's title and forced herself to read it. The second paragraph purports to summarize the text in a list of keywords (town, well, father, son, master, apprentice, murder, Oedipus, Rostam, 12 September [1980], love, urban renewal, construction, individualism, life as a writer, East, West),[4] following which the author relates how Pamuk includes every detail of the Oedipus and Shahnameh stories through his narrator, pedantically making sure that the reader understands the subject. After a derogatory caricature inserted into the article, "Özüm Hanım" continues on to complain that Pamuk does not leave literary interpretation to the reader, and that Pamuk's novels, post-Nobel Prize, have lost their intellectual quality.

Three final short paragraphs turn to the author's main worry: why did Pamuk call this novel his most "feminist" book? What is the writer's

---

[2] The name translates to "five-lettered ones," a reference to the spelling of the Turkish word for woman, *kadın*. The website describes itself as focused on women and women's issues and features a variety of writers.

[3] A *nom de plume* which means something similar to "my nature is that of a lady."

[4] "Kasaba, kuyu, baba, oğul, usta, çırak, cinayet, Oidipus, Rüstem, 12 Eylül, aşk, kentsel dönüşüm, inşaat, bireylik, yazarlık, doğu, batı."

conclusion? Simply the fact that the title's "red-haired woman" speaks with her own voice in the text makes this Pamuk's most feminist novel.

"Özüm Hanım's" critique, coming from the other side of the political aisle from Bardakçı's and from the self-declared opposite of mainstream Turkish media, is equally as sneering and arrogant. Taking a stance from the leftist intelligentsia and utilizing a thoroughly adolescent tone, the author provides references to literature, psychology, and sociology that should impress university sophomores, and then tops off the analysis by claiming that Pamuk has become spoiled and intellectually lazy since winning the Nobel Prize. For the reader's amusement, the author even includes a brief list of lessons to take away from Pamuk's novella:

1) Don't win the Nobel Prize.
2) Don't out-do your older brother.[5]
3) If you produce a novel every four years on average, don't publish a novel you wrote in one year. Instead, work on it for another three-and-a-half years.
4) Identify carefully what makes you look clever, then use it well. Don't trust anything else.
5) As a writer, don't bite off more than you can chew.
6) Forget about feminism."[6]

A foreign Orhan Pamuk reader who came upon such articles might be taken aback by the distinctly uncivil language with which they were written. Subsequently, the reader may also think that Bardakçı or "Özüm Hanım" was especially irritated by this particular book, or that the current political situation in Turkey provided a basis for such inflammatory writing. That foreign reader would be mistaken, though, because such

---

[5] This is a reference to Pamuk's older brother, Şevket Pamuk, an economist, economic historian, and Boğaziçi University professor.
[6] 1. Nobel almayın 2. Abinizi yenmeyin. 3. Bir romanı ortalama dört buçuk yılda yazıyorsanız, bir yılda yazdığınız romanı piyasaya sürmeyin. Üç buçuk yıl daha üzerinde çalışın. 4. Sizi zeki gösteren şeyi iyi tahlil edin. Ona sıkı tutunun. Ondan başka hiç bir şeye güvenmeyin. 5. Kalıbınızın yazarı olun. 6. Feminizmi karıştırmayın.

articles are actually completely normal and have many precedents. Pamuk has been subjected to similar verbal assaults for more than 25 years. Those unaware of this situation may be surprised or even misled by some of the rhetoric about Pamuk that appears in the Turkish press.

Pamuk's most recent major novel, *A Strangeness in My Mind* (*Kafamda bir tuhaflık*) was short-listed for the 2016 Man Booker Prize, yet another honor to add to his extensive resume. But in the past when Pamuk was awarded international recognition, such as the Nobel Prize, the domestic Turkish media response was often uncomprehending. The ideas[7] that Turkish citizens, parroting the Turkish press, repeat about Pamuk's international accolades can be summarized under the following themes: "Pamuk's popular abroad, but no one reads him in Turkey"; "he has good translations"; "they're rewarding his political stances." Such responses appear to be a mixture of envy and political prejudice, but they are fueled by Turkish press commentary.

On the other hand, gullible foreigners may also be deceived by information published in the Turkish press. For example, in late 2014, both the *Guardian* and the *New York Times* fell victim to the complexities of Turkey's political polemics concerning Pamuk. An article (Yüksel) in the right-wing Turkish tabloid *Takvim* claiming that Pamuk was part of an anti-Turkish "international literature lobby"[8] somehow made its way to the *Guardian*, which then published an alarmed reaction to it (Flood). The *Guardian* article, in turn, apparently served as the source for the *New York Times* editors' assertions, in a slapdash staff editorial ("Turkey's Descent"), that Orhan Pamuk and Elif Şafak were under attack for being the *avant-garde* of an "international literature lobby" focused on slandering the Turkish governing party AKP (Adalet ve Kalkınma Partisi), the Justice and Development Party.

Neither the *Guardian* nor the *New York Times* bothered to explore whether the *Takvim* article should be taken seriously. However, the claims in the *Takvim* article were immediately denied by the person supposedly

---

[7] Examples will be discussed below.
[8] Takvim's article anticipates both Bardakçı and "Özüm Hanım" by complaining that Pamuk had once again given negative comments to foreigners about Turkey in order to make money for himself.

quoted in the article, Professor Şengül Hablemitoğlu, who stated that the article's author fabricated the interview used as the source for the information about Pamuk.[9] This would not be surprising at all because similar fictions appear in the Turkish media on a daily basis. Since the early 1990s, Pamuk has been attacked by different sectors of the Turkish press and political classes for supposedly tarnishing Turkey's image abroad by expressing criticisms. And Pamuk has provided public comments over the years that can be cherry-picked by anyone who wants to put together a newspaper article for provocative purposes.[10]

In fact, the week before the *NYT* published the editorial mentioned above, Pamuk was forced to cancel an appearance at Boğaziçi University in Istanbul because of opposition from a leftist student group (Nazım Hikmet Merkezi). Turkey's Kemalist left has long disliked Pamuk because he has expressed views that violated their various ideological precepts, including discussing the situation of minorities in Turkey such as the Armenians. The students that succeeded in preventing Pamuk from appearing claimed that he was not worthy of speaking at the inauguration of a facility bearing the name of Nazım Hikmet, Turkey's globally-renowned Marxist poet. The students described Hikmet as "enlightened, peaceful, and anti-imperialist,"[11] implying that Pamuk did not represent the same ideals.

Domestically, the Boğaziçi University scandal got more attention than the *Takvim* article because few Turkish citizens take *Takvim* seriously. And, predictably, no more similar accusations have appeared concerning an "international literature lobby" in the nearly two years since the *Takvim* article appeared.

The situation's essence is that criticism of Pamuk from across Turkey's political spectrum, even criticism that can be considered slander or incitement, is nothing unusual; wild claims directed at him by politically-

---

[9] https://twitter.com/s_hablemitoglu/status/542394317944274945?ref_src=twsrc%5Etfw>; <https://twitter.com/s_hablemitoglu/status/542395121187053568?ref_src=twsrc%5Etfw>; <https://twitter.com/s_hablemitoglu/status/542395710436433920?ref_src= twsrc% 5 Etfw>. All accessed 12 Oct. 2016.

[10] Examples will be provided below.

[11] "Aydınlamacı, barışsever ve anti-emperyalist."

motivated Turkish newspapers are definitely not new. But comprehending how this situation developed is closely linked to grasping the role that intellectuals have been expected to play in the Turkish Republic's politics and society. Only then will the abuse that Pamuk has been subjected to during his writing career become more understandable, even if the rhetorical assaults are hardly intellectual, sometimes threatening, and never acceptable.

The Intellectual's Role in the Turkish Republic

Pamuk has been the most prominent member of Turkey's intelligentsia for several decades, and that is the primary motivating factor behind the intense domestic political polemics about him. Turkey's modern intellectual class emerged only around 150 years ago, during the Tanzimat Era (1839-1870s), when the Ottoman/Turkish modern state and society began to take shape.[12] That intelligentsia developed in close contact with the strengthening state bureaucracy, and in the shadow of ideas flowing in from Europe. As a result the Ottoman intelligentsia, from an early point, saw their role as modernizers leading social change.[13]

Eventually a situation emerged similar to that taking shape in other global societies coming into contact with the rapidly industrializing states of Europe.[14] By the end of the 19th century, Ottoman elites were dominated

---

[12] A summary can be found in Findley 76-132. "Tanzimat" means literally "reforms" or "reordering," but the term applied specifically to Ottoman institutions. During that period bureaucrats were the primary political decision-makers and military officers also emerged as a social class. The Tanzimat's ultimate result was the promulgation of an Ottoman constitution in 1876.

[13] Findley 104-05.

[14] See, for example, Hobsbawm, *Age of Capital* 116-34 and *Age of Empire* 30-33, 76-81, 283-85. Hobsbawm describes how elites in societies that had been colonized, or were independent but struggling to stave off Western encroachment, turned to the Western societies as their model for modernization/industrialization. This meant that modernization would be carried out top-down using the socio-political power that those elites possessed, and that the effort was specifically aimed at breaking down traditional ways of life and belief systems in order to substitute models adapted either partially or wholesale from Western European societies. Especially Britain and France served as examples, but Germany also became important later in the 19th century.

by the state bureaucracy, intelligentsia, and educated military officers, and had largely embraced radical, Western ideas dramatically opposed to what was acceptable to the mass of Ottoman citizens (Hanioğlu, *Young Turks* 7-32). Those elites saw themselves as guiding the Ottoman citizenry to enlightenment and civilization in the name of preserving and strengthening the Ottoman state (200-12). During the Tanzimat, state bureaucrats had the ability to enact top-down reforms on society, but Sultan Abdülhamit II (1876-1909) reasserted the primary role of the monarch during his reign. For that reason, elite opposition to Abdülhamit's policies took the shape of secret societies.

The most important opposition organization was the Committee of Union and Progress (*İttihad ve Terakki Cemiyeti*), which got its name from concepts associated with Comtean Positivism (Hanioğlu, *Young Turks* 202-05). This covert network was more popularly known as the Young Turks, from the French *Les Jeunes Turcs*, an echo of the many nationalist movements that blossomed in 19th-century Europe. Princeton professor Şükrü Hanioğlu has defined the ideological currents that formed the outlook of the Committee of Union and Progress (CUP), which step-by-step asserted its control over the Ottoman state from 1908-1913 (see *Young Turks* and *Preparation*). Mustafa Kemal (Atatürk), who embraced most of the contemporary CUP ideology, would then find himself in a position to impose his interpretation of those beliefs on Turkish society after the Turkish War for Independence (Hanioğlu, *Atatürk* passim).

The Turkish Republic was founded in 1923, in the aftermath of eleven years of nearly constant war. The territory remaining to the newly-born republic was greatly reduced from the Ottoman Empire's previous extent. Anatolia made up the vast bulk of the state's possessions, but it had been devastated by the war, famine, disease, massacres, and forced population expulsions and transfers. The intellectual classes of the late Ottoman Empire were also decimated by the war.

From the first years of the young republic, intellectuals continued in the socio-political role they had filled in the late Ottoman period, but now in a different project, creating the culture and society for the Turkish nation-state, and modernizing its citizens. This meant furthering the cultural and ideological construction of Turkish society within the guidelines provided by state elites, most specifically Mustafa Kemal. Moreover, most of the radical socio-cultural reforms enacted by Mustafa Kemal can be traced to CUP precedents.[15] Turkey's intellectuals, in other words, were expected to transmit what was essentially CUP ideology, in the form of Kemalist (or Atatürkist) prescriptions, to Turkish citizens through the education system, the Village Institutes (until their closure),[16] and the press. This also meant that Turkey's intellectuals were meant to assume an overtly political role and function in Turkish society, but a role and function that was closely monitored by Turkish state institutions, which remained under the influence of Kemalist bureaucrats and, ultimately, the Turkish military (see Kahraman, vol. 2, 437-39).

Strangely, for a party program intended to be a guiding philosophy for Turkish society, Kemalism was never defined or systematized as a totalizing ideological system. Cemil Koçak ("Kemalist Nationalism") uses the phrase "murky waters" to describe Kemalism's content because Kemalism was never precisely delineated or elaborated in detail during Mustafa Kemal's life or afterwards. Mustafa Kemal was a politician who said whatever was necessary, and took whatever action deemed necessary according to political expediency. This has meant that different aspects of Kemalism gained emphasis according to political junctures in the decades since Atatürk's death. No matter what the political atmosphere or events, a quote from Atatürk can be dug up to justify nearly any sort of stance or action.

---

[15] See: Hanioğlu, *Atatürk* 129-225 *passim*, and Kahraman, vol. 1 147-60. The attitudes of the early Turkish Republic's intellectuals are also well-expressed by Fatma Darvinoğlu's internal monologues in Pamuk's second novel, *The Silent House*. *Öteki renkler*, a collection of essays, articles, and interviews by Pamuk contains an article in which Pamuk explains that some of the inspiration for Fatma's monologues came from his own grandparents' letters ("Dünyayı Ateşler"; qtd. in *Öteki renkler* 142). That particular item was not included in the English translation, *Other Colors*.

[16] The Village Institutes were designed as a way of projecting educational goals and standards desired by state elites to the village level in a society that lacked teachers and resources. Citizens were selected from villages for training in literacy, agricultural techniques, and vocational skills, and then sent back to their original villages as teachers. This effort continued from 1936 until the mid-1950s.

The combination of a prominent role for intellectuals in the nation-state construction project, a vague state ideology, recurrent bouts of political instability, and massive, dramatic social change has always posed dangers to Turkish intellectuals. Starting immediately after the Republic's foundation, the dominant political narrative within Turkish society made intellectuals who did not sense which way the wind was blowing, or who stubbornly extolled ideals not in favor with state elites, subject to imprisonment, loss of employment, or exile. Intellectuals who did not follow the interpretation preferred by state and military elites of any current political controversy received intense public reprobation through the press for "deviation." Early Republican intelligentsia figures such as Halide Edip Adıvar, Nazım Hikmet, and Ahmet Emin Yalman, for example, encountered various types of difficulties vis-a-vis the Turkish state.

The conclusion of WW II and the slow expansion of democracy made little difference to the situation that Turkish intellectuals faced. The developing Cold War atmosphere caused leftist academicians Behice Boran, Pertev Naili Boratav, and Niyazi Berkes to be expelled from their university posts in 1948; leftist novelist Sabahattin Ali was murdered the same year. When military coups began to mar Turkish politics, intellectuals were also targets. Especially the 1971 and 1980 coups resulted in the arrests, jailings, and even torture of large numbers of Turkish intellectuals.

Likewise, the Turkish press has often been subject to censorship, to physical attacks, and even assassinations. In the Turkish Republic's early decades, newspapers were often closed for periods of time as punishment for violating the limits on what could be published. In late 1945, the facilities and machinery of the newspaper *Tan*[17] were ransacked by a right-wing mob. The late 1970s to the 1990s was an era during which a number of prominent Turkish journalists, such as Abdi İpekçi and Uğur Mumcu, were assassinated. In early 2007, Turkish-Armenian journalist Hrant Dink was assassinated by a nationalist triggerman, a crime which still has not been entirely illuminated. Though the situation has improved over the past

---

[17] *Tan* was targeted because of its prominent leftist writers, especially Zekeriya and Sabiha Sertel.

ten years since he was put on trial for violating the infamous clause 301 of the Turkish Penal Code,[18] Orhan Pamuk has faced similar public pressures during his entire career as a novelist.

To summarize, modern Turkish intellectuals have always been expected to perform an overtly political role in Turkish society. In order to "enlighten" the Turkish masses, intellectuals were expected to support Kemalist ideals and to transmit those ideals to the citizens. This role, however, became dangerous in certain political circumstances. If any specific intellectual did not say the right things according to the particular political juncture, that person could be singled out by the Turkish state, and by publications friendly to elements in the Turkish state, for retribution.

Orhan Pamuk's Relationship with the Media

Pamuk's novels garnered awards from the beginning, and with that attention controversy arose concerning the reasons for the attention given to Pamuk's writing. But because the determination of whether a public intellectual is fulfilling their role correctly is an inherently political judgment, the causes and subjects of politically-inspired press controversies also have changed according to Turkey's political atmosphere. Correspondingly, domestic media polemics concerning Orhan Pamuk have not remained constant as his writing career has developed over the past thirty-five years.

The main forum where those debates played out was the Turkish media. In the 1980s and 1990s, Pamuk was largely subject to speculation about why his novels were so popular abroad, and about his writing style. In the first years of the new millennium, He then became a center of controversy concerning the 1915 Armenian deportations and massacres issue. In recent years, Pamuk was targeted by the hard-line pro-AKP press.

Pamuk's first major work was *Cevdet Bey ve oğulları* [*Cevdet Bey and His Sons*; untranslated], which was published in 1982. That novel won Pamuk the *Milliyet* Publications Novel Competition more than two years

---

[18] This clause made "insulting Turkishness" ("Türklüğü aşağılamak") a crime punishable by six months to three years imprisonment until the phrase was changed to "insulting the Turkish nation" ("Türk milletini aşağılamak") in 2008.

before the book actually appeared. Even though the novel had won a prize, Pamuk still struggled to get it published ("Orhan Pamuk: Her şeyin"; qtd in *Öteki renkler* 138).[19] After it finally came out in 1982, *Cevdet Bey ve oğulları* received the 1983 Orhan Kemal Novel Award. Those were the first prizes on the road eventually leading to the Nobel Prize for Literature in 2006. That also meant Pamuk's first attention from the Turkish press. As early as 1983, Pamuk provided interviews to Istanbul newspapers interested in his writing (see his interview by Ertop about *Cevdet Bey and His Sons*).

The 1980s were also the years following the 12 September 1980 coup. At that point domestic issues in Turkey already intruded on Pamuk's writing, even though the politics of his novels are notoriously opaque. In the English-language edition of *Other Colors*, Pamuk included a 2005 interview from the *Paris Review*. In that interview, which was not included in the 2011 Turkish-language edition of *Öteki renkler*, Pamuk explained that the first book he began writing after *Cevdet Bey and His Sons* was a neutral but political novel that featured violence against politicians. The moment the coup occurred he realized that the book, of which he had already written 250 pages, could not be published any time soon. Instead, he began work on the text which would become *Sessiz ev* (*The Silent House*), also a political work but with a different, allegorical approach (Pamuk, "Art of Fiction").

By the early 1990s Pamuk had become a major literary figure and the first two of his novels translated to English – *The White Castle* and *The Black Book* – were met with wide acclaim abroad. Then *The New Life* and *My Name is Red* added to Pamuk's fame and sales figures. This sparked a domestic discussion about why Pamuk's novels sold so well and were admired internationally.

Several clichéd themes were developed and then reiterated endlessly in the Turkish press during the 1990s about the popularity of Pamuk's novels outside of Turkey.[20] The first was that Pamuk purposefully wrote for a for-

---

[19] That item about *Cevdet Bey and His Sons* was not included in the English language edition of *Öteki renkler*.

[20] The general attitude that had emerged in the Turkish press towards Pamuk in the 1990s is acerbically summarized by a caricature included in *Öteki renkler* on p. 417.

eign audience so that he would have strong foreign sales; that his writing also purposefully was not meant to appeal to Turkish readers was suggested by that theme. A second theme was the accusation that the advertising and publicity devoted to the new appearance of each Pamuk novel was responsible for their popularity. In other words, the content of the books was not what created strong sales, but rather capitalist propaganda was to blame.[21]

Part of the reason was the popularity of *The Black Book* despite its difficult content. *The Black Book* was the most successful novel by a Turkish writer determined to write with the techniques developed during the 20th century by other international authors. It was also dramatically different than almost the entirety of Turkish literature that had preceded it. For that reason in the 1990s an intense debate, which has resulted in a number of academic studies,[22] developed around *The Black Book* and Pamuk's writing more generally. Much of that debate took place in the Turkish media.

However, some of the reactions to Pamuk, especially in the 1990s, stemmed from intellectual jealousy amongst the Turkish elites. Kemalism instructs its believers to admire Western civilization, and Pamuk has received the highest awards that can be conferred upon a writer or intellectual by the West. That is, he has succeeded in gaining the admiration of "the West," something which most Kemalists, despite all of the anti-imperialist rhetoric, also desperately want to enjoy.

Two articles that appeared at the end of the 1990s can be examined to understand the then-current domestic discussion on Pamuk. Doğan

---

In the caricature, Pamuk is confronted by a thuggish figure, brandishing a club with a nail driven through it, who questions Pamuk rhetorically, "Dude, why do you sell so many [books]? You must be a traitor to the nation!" ("Niye çok satıyorsun ulan? Vatan haini misin, yoksa!"). The caricature was published in *Dünya* by Ferruh Doğan on 2 March 1999.

[21] For a reference to these themes, see: Pamuk, *"Art of Fiction."*

[22] See, for example: Hadzibegovic, ed.; Esen, ed., *Kara Kitap*; Kılıç, ed.; Esen and Kılıç, eds.

Hızlan,[23] one of the doyens of Turkish literary criticism, published a response for *Hürriyet* to Pamuk's inclusion in the *Observer*'s 21 important writers for the 21st century ("Millenium yazarı"). Hızlan begins his comment by grudgingly acknowledging the worth of Pamuk's novels and then, with no hesitation, claims that the reason Pamuk is known abroad, and thus was accorded a place on the *Observer*'s list, is simply because his works have been translated into a number of foreign languages. While protesting that Pamuk does deserve a place on such a list, Hızlan claims that other Turkish writers could also have been included, but because they have not been translated to foreign languages, they are overlooked.

Hızlan then goes one step further and asserts that Pamuk was singled out by Western publishing houses and received positive attention from literary reviewers, asserting that "Western publishers chose him specially."[24] That is, according to Hızlan, the sole reasons for Pamuk's reputation abroad are that he has been translated and gotten good press. Only at the end of his column does Hızlan quickly admit that, because Pamuk's novels also sold well, there must be something more to his popularity than just good promotion. But he does not care to explore what the reasons might be since he does not discuss the content, quality, or technical aspects of Pamuk's writing.

Another column appearing in the same time frame was by Ayşe Arman, a popular culture journalist for *Hürriyet* who usually writes on topics relevant to Istanbul's high society, titled "Keep on Condemning!" ("Kınamaya devam ediniz!"). Arman's text was written in response to an anonymous, rude email she had received after publishing a two-part interview with Orhan Pamuk.[25] In the interview, she inquired about several unusual topics, including a pointed gender question about a passage in *My Name is Red*, along with the more typical interview fare asked of successful novelists.

---

[23] In late 2006, Sabancı University hosted a symposium to commemorate Pamuk's Nobel Prize for Literature that the author also attended. Hızlan was one of the keynote speakers and provided vague, but positive comments.

[24] "Batılı yayıncılar da onu özellikle seçtiler."

[25] The two parts of the interview, which is quite entertaining, were published under the titles "Ayşe'nin gözlüğü" and "Ayşe'nin günlüğü," respectively.

The email Arman received begins by claiming that the writer always defended Arman against those who derided her journalistic credentials and, after a banal comment referring to the erosion of literature in contemporary societies, states that the mail was sent in order to condemn Arman's interview with Pamuk. The writer terms the interview terrible ("çok kötü") and questions whether Arman actually read *My Name is Red*. Then the writer opines that the questions seem as if Arman was forced to do the interview and did not actually have questions that she wanted to ask; for that reason the writer feels embarrassed for having defended her journalistic credibility. The message ends by saying that the questions that Arman did ask are the sort that a teenager would ask, and then gives a couple of examples with insulting reactions tacked on in parentheses.

The person sending that email to Arman did not even include their name, but the message's tone is typical of media controversies in Turkey: harsh and insulting. Arman rightfully reacts to the message with anger and pens a long list of reasons why she chose to interview Pamuk. She states forcefully that a main reason was that she had indeed read *My Name is Red* and loved the novel. Other reasons that she provides are simply that she wanted to meet Pamuk, that Pamuk was Turkey's foremost writer, and that she found some of the things that Pamuk had written to be fascinating. Sprinkled between the lines of Arman's response are allusions to the ongoing debates in Turkish society about "high" and "low" culture, and about who has the right to read and comment on both.

The articles and interviews by Hızlan and Arman in the paragraphs above were typical of the controversies swirling around Pamuk in the Turkish press in the 1990s. That is, the controversies were more about Turkish cultural life and Turkey's position in relation to the Western societies. In the new millennium, political issues began to overshadow the more mundane and envy-driven arguments about Pamuk's writing. Possibly, this was unintentionally heralded by Pamuk's publication of *Snow* in 2002, which he admitted was a "political" novel (see R. Çakır). Set in Kars, a mostly Kurdish city in Turkey's Eastern Anatolian Kurdish provinces, even the novel's name evokes the manner in which certain so-socio-political issues in Turkish history have been suppressed.²⁶

The 1915 deportations and massacres of Ottoman Armenians (as well as a number of other incidents of state violence that accompanied the late Ottoman and early Turkish Republican eras) by the Committee of Union and Progress Ottoman leadership was an issue long suppressed by official Turkish state ideology. Starting in the late 1990s and the early years of the 21st century, a number of Turkish intellectuals began to forcefully insert the 1915 issue into the public space. The most prominent were Halil Berktay and Taner Akçam.²⁷ This initial push to bring the 1915 issue to the attention of the Turkish public culminated in September 2005 when an unprecedented conference on the 1915 issue was held at Istanbul's Bilgi University (see, for example, "Ermeni konferansı").

Earlier in 2005, Orhan Pamuk gave an interview to the Swiss newspaper *Tages-Anzeiger* in which he said that thirty thousand Kurds and one million Armenians had been killed on Turkish territory, and that no one was brave enough to talk about it other than him ("Der meistgehasste Türke" [The Most-Hated Turk]; see also the Pamuk interview "Kimse"). Pamuk's statements caused a furor that resulted in charges being filed against him under section 301 of the Turkish Penal Code, for insulting Turkishness. After an international outcry, the case was eventually struck down by the courts.²⁸

---

[26] Falling snow and scenes of snow-covered landscapes are often used to represent the forgotten, or the act of attempting to forget something unpleasant. The name of the city Kars contains the Turkish word for snow (*kar*), which implies an ironic historical message about the minority (Armenians) who used to populate the city and were physically eliminated from there by Ottoman state elites, who then tried to cover up the entire event; it is a reference as well to the minority (Kurds) who currently populate the city and whose existence was also suppressed by the Turkish state for many decades. Finally, the city itself receives heavy annual snowfall, so it makes for an appropriate setting to metaphorically discuss such issues.

[27] For examples of Berktay's interviews in the Turkish press, see the Works Cited. Akçam began publishing studies on the Armenian issue in Turkish starting in 1999.

[28] For a detailed account of the controversy around Pamuk in 2005-2006, see: McGaha 1-16.

After that point, controversies about Pamuk took on an overtly political aspect. From 2005, continuing through his trial and then for several years afterwards, Pamuk was aggressively criticized by different sectors of the media for his stance on the Armenian and Kurdish issues. Interviews that he gave to the press almost invariably rubbed some sector of Turkish society the wrong way, and the media outlets catering to those sectors used Pamuk's quotes against him. That was also an era of heightening political tension in Turkish society because of the clash between Turkey's traditional Kemalist state elites and the AKP, led by Prime Minister Recep Tayyip Erdoğan. The assassination of Hrant Dink in 2007 (and other acts of violence), the Ergenekon case, the Republic Rallies before the 2007 general elections, and the closure case brought against the AKP by the Turkish Constitutional Court in 2008 were all features of that political juncture.

Between 2011 and 2013 other concerns began to invade the Turkish media, mostly connected to the growing reaction to the policies of the governing Justice and Development Party.[29] Starting even before the May-July 2013 Gezi Park protests, Pamuk gave press comments that, though not strongly critical of the government, were nonetheless not entirely sympathetic. Subsequently, criticism of Pamuk began to emerge from a sector of the Turkish press, the pro-AKP publications, that had previously been largely friendly to him.[30]

---

[29] A word can be said here about the alliance that some leftists formed with the AKP in the years since 2007. The touchstone event for this period was the September 2010 constitutional referendum, for which a segment of the left-leaning intelligentsia gave their provisional support through the slogan "It's not Sufficient, but Yes!" ("Yetmez ama evet!"). Orhan Pamuk is generally understood as left-leaning politically and he expressed support for the AKP's policies in that same time frame. As the years passed, many of those left intellectuals switched to the anti-AKP opposition, but at different points and for different reasons; some remain friendly to the AKP's policies. Because of the topic's complexity and still-contentious nature, it is not possible to provide a detailed discussion here, but this is an important Turkish political debate of the last ten years.

[30] For examples from that time period, see: "Orhan Pamuk'tan AKP yorumu"; Ünlü; E. Çakır; Altuğ. *Cumhuriyet* newspaper is the flagship publication of the Kemalist old guard; *Hürriyet* is the main paper of the Doğan Holding Company, which is widely understood as friendly to the CHP and the Turkish military; *Sabah* was sold

Since 2013 at least, political criticism of Pamuk has appeared in every sector of the Turkish press according to the stance that any particular publication maintains, whether pro-government or anti-government, and all of the varying shades in between. That is why the articles I examined at the beginning of this essay should not be seen as something unusual. Because of Pamuk's prominent stature, and because he has not shied away from telling interviewers his personal opinion on many different subjects, including sensitive political issues, Pamuk is not seen as an ally by any Turkish political perspective. Even ludicrous conspiracy theories such as the one floated by *Takvim* (discussed above) get published and are taken seriously abroad by publications with an entirely different aim.

That is the overall pattern: Pamuk says something in an interview that someone or group does not like, so they criticize him, usually with malicious, emotional language. Then other groups with different intentions use either Pamuk's words or the attacks written about him for their own ends. Until political debates in Turkey can be carried out with a calmer and more respectful tone, Pamuk's past statements will continue to circulate and be utilized by those with malevolent intentions. Pamuk's status as Turkey's foremost internationally-known intellectual, and the status that intellectuals are accorded in Turkish society, provide the fuel for the arguments and assaults.

In the past year, between Elif Şafak's *Guardian* interview with Pamuk, and the 16 April 2017 constitutional referendum, the domestic press rhetoric concerning Pamuk has been more subdued. But that, in itself, does not mean that attitudes toward Pamuk have changed. In the wake of the 15 July 2016 failed coup attempt, Pamuk gave an interview to the BBC (interview to the BBC) in which he criticized both the apparent disinterest of the West and the consequent purges from state institutions of those accused of membership in Fethullah Gülen's organization. Possibly because he chastised multiple sides connected to the issue, that interview

---

by the Turkish state to a private company ten years ago after its previous owners fell into financial difficulties, and consequently became a steadfastly pro-AKP news source.

sparked relatively little reaction in Turkey.[31] Two months before the referendum, a brief controversy occurred when *Hürriyet* apparently refused to publish an interview with Pamuk in which he explained why he intended to vote "no" in the referendum ("Hürriyet, Orhan Pamuk'un").[32]

So I want to end this discussion on a more positive note. Even though the conversation about Orhan Pamuk in the Turkish press has often been disgraceful, there are some voices which have analyzed Pamuk's novels and other publications thoughtfully and with appreciation. In the wake of the articles that I began this essay with, Oral Çalışlar published a short, admiring essay on *The Red-Haired Woman* that provided a welcome contrast to the invective of Murat Bardakçı and Özüm Hanım. In that article, titled "The Red-Haired Woman, or Mahmut Usta's Revenge," Çalışlar recounts the novel's conclusion and then closes with laudatory remarks on Pamuk's latest novel as well as his literary career. He states simple regard for the two great literary creations, the *Shahnameh* and *Oedipus Rex*, that the novel draws upon, and then describes the novel as different from Pamuk's other novels. But then again, he avers, all of Pamuk's novels are different from one another, and each is a rich literary text that contains its own surprises. Çalışlar concludes by urging, "We owe Orhan Pamuk gratitude because he has enriched our literature and made it internationally appreciated. Despite all of the thuggishness he has encountered he has remained tied to this land and has succeeded in remaining so."[33]

If only those taking the time to compose articles or essays on Pamuk displayed the same esteem for and comprehension of Pamuk's importance in the literary world.

---

[31] For an example, see: "Obama'nın Sisi toleransı." This *Hürriyet* article simply reports Pamuk's comments.

[32] A transcript of Pamuk's *Hürriyet* interview has never surfaced, so it is not possible to know exactly what Pamuk said or whether the interview actually exists.

[33] "Orhan Pamuk'a teşekkür borçluyuz. Edebiyatımızı zenginleştirdiği için, daha küresel bir değer haline getirdiği için. Bunca hoyratlıkla karşılaşmasına rağmen, bu topraklara bağlı kaldığı, kalmayı başardığı için."

Works Cited

Books and Book Chapters

Aral, Fahri, ed. *Orhan Pamuk edebiyatı sempozyum tutanakları* [*Proceedings of the Orhan Pamuk Literature Symposium*]. Sabancı University, 19-20 Dec. 2006. İstanbul: Agora, 2007.

Esen, Nüket, ed. *Kara Kitap üzerine yazılar* [*Articles on* The Black Book]. İstanbul: İletişim, 1996.

___, and Engin Kılıç, eds. *Orhan Pamuk'un edebi dünyası* [*Orhan Pamuk's Literary World*]. İstanbul: İletişim, 2008.

Findley, Carter. *Turkey, Islam, Nationalism, and Modernity*. New Haven: Yale UP, 2010.

Hadzibegovic, Darmin, ed. *Kara Kitap'ın sırları* [*The Black Book's Secrets*]. İstanbul: Yapı Kredi, 2013.

Hanioğlu, Şükrü. *Atatürk: An Intellectual Biography*. Princeton: Princeton UP, 2011.

___. *Preparation for a Revolution: The Young Turks, 1902-1908*. New York: Oxford UP, 2001.

___. *The Young Turks in Opposition*. New York: Oxford UP, 1995.

Hobsbawm, Eric. *The Age of Capital: 1848-1875*. New York: Vintage, 1996.

___. *The Age of Empire: 1875-1914*. New York: Vintage, 1989.

Kahraman, Hasan Bülent. *Türk siyasetinin yapısal analizi I: Kavramlar, kuramlar, kurumlar* [*Structural Analysis of Turkish Politics I: Notions, Theories, Institutions*]. İstanbul: Agora, 2008.

___. *Türk siyasetinin yapısal analizi II: 1920-1960*. İstanbul: Agora, 2010.

Kılıç, Engin, ed. *Orhan Pamuk'u anlamak* [*Understanding Orhan Pamuk*]. İstanbul: İletişim, 2006.

Koçak, Cemil. "Kemalist Nationalism's Murky Waters." *Turkey between Nationalism and Globalization*. Ed. Riva Kastoryano. London: Routledge, 2013. 63-70.

McGaha, Michael. *Autobiographies of Orhan Pamuk: The Writer in His Novels*. Salt Lake City: University of Utah Press, 2008.

Pamuk, Orhan. ["Art of Fiction"] "The Paris Review Interview." Interview by Ángel Gurría-Quintana. *Other Colors: Essays and a Story.* By Pamuk. New York: Knopf, 2007. 355-78.

___. *The Black Book.* Trans. Güneli Gün. London: Faber and Faber, 1996.

___. *Other Colors: Essays and a Story.* New York: Alfred A. Knopf, 2007. Partial trans. of *Öteki renkler: Seçme yazılar ve bir hikâye.* 1999.

___. *Öteki renkler: Seçme yazılar ve bir hikâye.* 1999. İstanbul: İletişim, 2011.

Articles from Newspapers or Internet Sources

Altuğ, Evrim. "Orhan Pamuk: Ayıplıyorum." *Cumhuriyet* 28 Nov. 2015. Accessed 1 Nov. 2016 <http://www.cumhuriyet.com.tr/haber/kultur -sanat/434799/Orhan_Pamuk__Ayipliyorum.html>.

Arman, Ayşe. "Ayşe'nin gözlüğü." *Hürriyet* 18 Dec. 1998. Accessed 1 Nov. 2016 <http://www.hurriyet.com.tr/aysenin-gozlugu-3905376 5>.

___. "Ayşe'nin günlüğü." *Hürriyet* 19 Dec. 1998. Accessed 1 Nov. 2016 <http://www.hurriyet.com.tr/aysenin-gunlugu-39053942>.

___. "Kınamaya devam ediniz!" ["Keep on Condemning!"]. *Hürriyet* 22 Dec. 1998. Accessed 1 Nov. 2016 <http://www.hurriyet.com.tr/kinamaya-devam-ediniz-39054358>.

Bardakçı, Murat. "Çüş Orhan Pamuk, cüş!" *Habertürk* 17 Feb. 2016. Accessed 12 Oct. 2016 <http://www.haberturk.com/yazarlar/murat-bardakci/1196692-cus-orhan-pamuk-cus>.

___. "Reşad Ekrem 'cemal aşığı'idi ama intihalci değildi!" *Hürriyet* 25 May 2002. Accessed 1 Nov. 2016 <http://www.hurriyet.com.tr/ resad-ekrem-cemal-sigi-idi-ama-intihalci-degildi-74394>.

Berktay, Halil. "A Special Organization Killed Armenians." Interview by Neşe Düzel. Trans. Marc David Baer. *Radikal* 30 June 2000. Accessed 15 May 2017 <http://www.atour.com/~aahgn/news/20010 105d.html>.

Çakır, Esma. "Orhan Pamuk: AKP 8 yıl önce daha saygın bir yerdeydi." *Hürriyet* 11 Sept. 2015. Accessed 1 Nov. 2016 <http://www.hurriyet .com.tr/orhan-pamuk-akp-8-yil-once-daha-saygin-bir-yerdeydi-300 43371>.

Çakır, Ruşen. "Orhan Pamuk 'Kar'ı anlattı." *NTV* 27 Jan. [2002]. Accessed 1 Nov. 2016 <http://arsiv.ntv.com.tr/news/131480.asp>.

Çalışlar, Oral. "'Kırmızı saçlı kadın' ya da Mahmut Ustanın intikamı." *Serbestiyet* 7 Apr. 2016. Accessed 1 Nov. 2016 <http://serbestiyet.com/yazarlar/oral-calislar/kirmizi-sacli-kadin-ya-da-mahmut-ustanin-intikami-677566>.

"Ermeni konferansı Bilgi Üniversitesi'nde başladı." *Hürriyet*. 24 Sep. 2005. Accessed 1 Nov. 2016 <http://www.hurriyet.com .tr/ermeni-konferansi-bilgi-universitesinde-basladi-352577>.

Flood, Alison. "Turkish Novelists Orhan Pamuk and Elif Shafak Accused of Being Western Stooges by Pro-government Press." *Guardian* 12 Dec. 2014. Accessed 12 Oct. 2016 <https://www.theguardian.com /books /2014/dec/12/pamuk-shafak-turkish-press-campaign>.

"Halil Berktay." *European Stability Initiative*. August 2009. Accessed 1 Nov. 2016 <http://www.esiweb.org/index.php?lang=en&id=322&debate_ID =2&slide_ID=3>.

Hızlan, Doğan. "Millenium yazarı Orhan Pamuk." *Hürriyet* 23 June 1999. Accessed 1 Nov. 2016 <http://www.hurriyet.com.tr/dogan-hizlan-millennium-yazari-orhan-pamuk-39087325>.

"Hürriyet, Orhan Pamuk'un 'başkanlığa hayır' dediği röportajı yayımlamadı!" *Cumhuriyet* 14. Feb. 2017. Accessed 12 June 2017 <http://www.cumhuriyet.com.tr/haber/turkiye/675924/Hurriyet__Orhan_Pamuk_un__baskanliga_hayir__dedigi_roportaji_yayimlamadi_.html#>.

"Nazım Hikmet Merkezi Orhan Pamuk'suz açıldı!" ["Nazım Hikmet Center Opened Without Orhan Pamuk!"] *Radikal* 16 Dec. 2014. Accessed 15 May 2017 <http://www.radikal.com.tr/kultur/nazim-hikmet-merkezi-orhan-pamuksuz-acildi-1252597/>.

"Obama'nın Sisi toleransı Türkiye'deki darbe girişiminin önünü açtı." *Hürriyet* 16 Oct. 2016. Accessed 12 June 2017 <http://www.hurriyet.com.tr/obamanin-sisi-toleransi-turkiyedeki-darbe-girisiminin-onunu-acti-40249959>.

"Orhan Pamuk'tan AKP yorumu." *T24*. 29 Apr. 2012. Accessed 1 Nov. 2016 <http://t24.com.tr/haber/orhan-pamuktan-akp-yorumu,202760>.

Özüm Hanım. "Orhan Eniştenizden feminizme kırmızı saçlı yeşil ışık (feat. Hadi Yine İyisiniz)." *5Harfliler.* 3 March 2016. Accessed 12 Oct. 2016 <http://www.5harfliler.com/orhan-enistenizden-feminizm e/>.

Pamuk, Orhan. "Dünyayı ateşler içine atmak isterdim." Interview by Nuray Kızıltan. *Güneş Gençlik* 28 Sept. 1990. 130-33.

___. Interview by Konur Ertop. *Metrukat kalemiyesi. Milliyet sanat* 15 June 1983. Accessed 1 Nov. 2016 <http://metrukatkalemiyesi.blog spot.com.tr/2015/08/orhan-pamuk-soylesisi-milliyet-sanat.html>.

___. Interview to the BBC. *bbc.com.* 14 Oct. 2016. Accessed 12 June 2017. <http: //www.bbc.com/news/av/world-europe-37645191/wr iter-pamuk-chides-erdogan-and-west-over-failed-turkey-coup>.

___. "Kimse söylemiyor, bari ben söyleyeyim." Interview by İsmail Erel. *Hürriyet* 9 Feb. 2005. Accessed 1 Nov. 2016 <http://www.hurriyet. com.tr/kimse-soylemiyor-bari-ben-soyleyeyim -295331>.

___. "Der meistgehasste Türke" ["The Most-Hated Turk"]. Interview by Peer Teuwsen. *Tages-Anzeiger. Das Magazin* 5 Feb. 2005. Accessed 14 May 2017 <https://web.archive.org/web/2009011612 3035/http:// sc.tagesanzeiger.ch/dyn/news/kultur/560264.html>.

___. "Orhan Pamuk: Her şeyin, günlük hayat denilen sıkıcı şeyin kahredici bayağılığına battığını göstermek istediğimi belki söyleyebilirim şimdi." Interview by Konur Ertop. *Milliyet Sanat* 15 June 1983. 128.

Shafak [Şafak], Elif. "Orhan Pamuk and Elif Shafak: Istanbul, City of Dreams and Nightmares." *Guardian* 27 Jan. 2016. Accessed 15 May 2017 <https://www.theguardian.com/artanddesign/2016/jan/27/orha n-pamuk-museum-of-innocence-istanbul-turkey-somerset-house-london-elif-safak-interview>.

"Turkey's Descent into Paranoia." Staff Editorial. *New York Times* 19 Dec. 2014. Accessed 12 Oct. 2016 <https://www.nytimes.com/ 2014/12/20/ opinion/turkeys-descent-into-paranoia.html?_r=1>.

Uruş, Alper. "1 milyon Ermeni'yi ve 30 bin Kürt'ü kestik mi?" *Vatan* 9 Feb. 2005. Accessed 15 May 2017 <http://www.gazetevatan.com/1-milyon-ermeni-yi-ve-30-bin-kurt-u-kestik-mi--46650-gundem/>.

Ünlü, Ferhat. "Türk romanının Özal'ı: Orhan Pamuk." *Sabah* 2 Sept. 2012. Accessed 1 Nov. 2016 <http://www.sabah.com.tr/ pazar/2012/09/02/ turk-romaninin-ozali-orhan-pamuk>.

Yüksel, Mevlüt. "Pamuk projesi." *Takvim* 9 Dec. 2014. Accessed 12 Oct. 2016 <http://www.takvim.com.tr/guncel/2014/12/09/pamuk-projesi>.

Voices of Dissent: Belonging and Identity in *Silent House* and *A Strangeness in My Mind*

Hande Gürses
University of Massachusetts Amherst

Abstract: Contrary to the conventional artistic principle, Pamuk's books do not show but "are" the very thing that they are addressing. The struggle of defining one's identity underlying his oeuvre finds a different form of embodiment in each of Pamuk's novels. This paper focuses on two novels that use a polyphonic narrative style to discuss the implications of voice in the expression and experience of identity. *Silent House* and *A Strangeness in My Mind* are novels where the reader can hear the voice of each character through their individual first-person narration. *Silent House*, Pamuk's second novel, recently translated into English is marked by a sense of impending doom during the days leading to the 1980 military coup. The claustrophobic environment of *Silent House* is contrasted with the sense of scattering that marks *A Strangeness in My Mind*, which spans the period of 1954-2012, through a profusion of characters. In both novels the characters speak in the first person, conveying their individual perspectives on the events. This narrative style provides highly individualized voices to the characters as well as a diverse and fragmented structure to the novel and requires a more active reading from the part of the reader. This essay will discuss how this narrative strategy operates in the two selected novels. It will analyze how the narrative technique affects the contextual issues that the two novels deal with. By looking at two novels from different periods in Pamuk's career this paper will bring to light the various directions that his oeuvre has taken.

Orhan Pamuk's second novel *Silent House*, published in Turkish in 1983 (*Sessiz ev*), only became available in English translation in 2012. As a result of this temporal gap, *Silent House* offers two distinct experiences for Turkish and English readers. For English readers, it functions as a retrospective gaze into the early works of the Nobel laureate while for Turkish readers it represents the second novel of a young author, introducing various stylistic and contextual novelties during a period of transition in the aftermath of the military coup of September 12, 1980. *Silent House* tells the story of the Darvinoğlu[1] family through the eyes of its members from different generations. The novel spans the period of one week in July 1980, when the grandchildren visit their grandmother in Cennethisar, a small town near Istanbul. The grandmother Fatma, her grandchildren Faruk and Metin, Recep, the servant and the illegitimate son of doctor Selâhattin and his nephew Hasan, are the five narrators of the individual chapters. The multiplicity of voices is the main stylistic innovation of the novel within Pamuk's oeuvre, allowing the reader access to different perspectives and different generations[2] while preventing the dominance of one voice over the others. This narrative technique subsequently recurs in *My Name is Red* (2001; trans. of *Benim Adım kırmızı*, 1998) where the reader is invited to find clues regarding the murder through the individual voices of the narrators.

In *A Strangeness in My Mind* (2015; trans. of *Kafamda bir tuhaflık*, 2014) Pamuk introduces a modified version of this narrative technique. The story of Mevlut Karataş, a boza[3] and yogurt seller, is told by various members of his family, his friends as well as an occasional overseeing narrator. The implications of this particular narrative technique alongside other narrative elements including place, time, plot and character are the main focus of this essay. Its comparative perspective will bring together *Silent House* and *A Strangeness in My Mind* to discuss how the specific narrative elements and stylistic preferences operate in relation to the contextual elements of these novels. The temporal gap between the two novels will enable an overview of Pamuk's transformation as an author and will also highlight the transitions that the Turkish political and cultural scene has under-

---

[1] The name Darvinoğlu means "sons of Darvin." The name Darvin, unusual to the Turkish ear, is a near-homonymic of (Charles) Darwin. It is implied that following the Surname Law of 1934 Selâhattin decided on this name for his family as a homage to the Western rationalist tradition.

[2] Pamuk's first novel *Cevdet Bey ve oğulları* (1982; *Cevdet Bey and His Sons*, untranslated) is a family saga of over 600 pages. The narrative strategy that Pamuk uses in *Silent House* allows him to bring together three generations as he did in *Cevdet Bey and His Sons* in a more concise manner.

[3] Boza, as explained in the novel, is "a traditional Asian beverage made of fermented wheat, with a thick consistency, a pleasant aroma, a dark yellowish color, and a low alcohol content" (*Strangeness* 19).

gone in the scope of three decades. The primary theoretical framework of this chapter is provided by the writings of Jacques Derrida and his critique of the problematic equation of meaning with presence.

For the Western philosophical tradition meaning is only possible as presence. It is transmitted through the presence of the interlocutors via the spoken word. The immediacy of speech guarantees an ultimate transmission of meaning without any disruptions/misrepresentations or delays. Writing, within this framework, is considered to be a secondary tool, a "supplement" that is merely a replacement for the immediacy of speech. Disregarding the dynamic nature of time and the impossibility of a fixed present, this view resorts to writing only as a device that records the originary meaning captured in speech.

Consequently the Western metaphysical tradition establishes speech and writing as binary oppositions and places them in a hierarchical scale where speech is accorded superiority due to its immediacy whereas writing is viewed as inferior because of its supplementary nature. Derrida challenges this binary positioning by highlighting the impossibility of an originary and present meaning in the first place. He argues that since all language is composed of arbitrary signs that operate on a system of difference, all representations as language will have to be mediated through these signs. It is this structure of language as difference that makes an inherent meaning as presence an impossibility. Every sign, whether visual, textual or auditory, "represents the present in its absence" (Derrida, "Différance" 9), thus enabling the production of meaning only through differentiation. And this differentiation is what Derrida calls *différance.*

The impossibility to re-present presence results in temporal and spatial displacement in all forms of representation, and this includes both speech and writing, thus undermining the immediacy and superiority of speech. Derrida suggests that language, whether it is spoken or written, is a form of signification and could never represent meaning as presence since language as such is made possible through differentiation. Language is always and already a play of *différance*; it is never the reference to an originary presence but only produces meaning through difference and deferral.

Speech vs. writing is just one in a long list of concept pairs: self/other, man/woman, presence/absence, sun/moon, fact/fiction, each and every one of these pairs contains a party that is considered to be superior and hence shapes the way we perceive all identities. These binaries are also present in Pamuk's oeuvre and this chapter will explore the narrative strategies that he uses in an effort to undermine such binary positions.

Space

While both *Silent House* and *A Strangeness in My Mind* have distinct spatial settings, their main focus remains on Istanbul, the city that has shaped and defined Pamuk's writings. The particular angle through which Istanbul is depicted in the two novels is an embodiment of the changing social and political identities within Turkey. Istanbul, in other words, is not solely an element of ornamental background but rather an agent that shapes and affects the lives of the characters in the two novels.

Silent House is set in Cennethisar,[4] a fictional town that Pamuk locates in the Gebze area, on the outskirts of Istanbul. After spending the first four years of their marriage in Istanbul, Fatma and Selâhattin Darvinoğlu move to Cennethisar; a move that is more enforced than voluntary.

> One summer evening, Selâhattin came straight to me instead of going to his library and he said, "We're not going to live in Istanbul anymore, Fatma!" I didn't ask, "Why, Selahâttin?" but he told me anyway, jumping around like a gangly kid. We're not going to live in Istanbul anymore, Fatma, because Talat Pasha called me today and this is what he said: Dr. Selâhattin, you will no longer live in Istanbul, and you will have nothing to do with politics! (*Silent House* 23)

As the reference to Talat Pasha implies, Dr. Selâhattin's exile from the imperial capital is the result of his falling out with the Committee of Union and Progress.[5] After considering various options that include Paris, Da-

---

[4] Cennethisar can be translated as "fortress of heaven" or "heavenly fortress."
[5] The Committee of Union and Progress (CUP) was founded in 1889 with the aim of reforming the Ottoman Empire and of bringing it back to its glorious days. The CUP remained in power until 1918. Enver, Talat and Cemal were the three leaders of the party.

mascus and Izmir, Selâhattin finally decides on Cennethisar as the destination of his exile.

Selâhattin is initially optimistic as he views the exile to be temporary. He hopes to go back to what he calls "Istanbul of the Future" (28) once the Unionists fall out of power. His sense of optimism, however, gradually fades and is eventually replaced by self-deception since the long anticipated fall of the Unionists comes with the fall of the Ottoman Empire at the end of World War I. As his dreams of going back to Istanbul collapse along with the empire, Selâhattin seeks solace in what he deems to be his masterpiece, an "encyclopedia of everything" (28). For Selâhattin, who is an avid admirer of European rationalism, Istanbul represents hope, a place where he could put into practice his modernizing project. Selâhattin's interactions with the local villagers of Cennethisar and his encyclopedia mimic the general attitude of the modernization project. Reşat Kasaba identifies the characteristics of the project as follows:

> The first of these was a total admiration for science, not as something one engages in critically but as an omnipotent tool that can be borrowed and used for a variety of purposes, including inducing social change. To the reformers, the Ottoman-Turkish scene was a blank slate onto which they were determined to inscribe a firm signature of science and reason. According to them, this and only this could create the right conditions for the kind of social change they deemed necessary for the country. (26)

Selâhattin follows this pattern in his interactions with the villagers and aims to familiarize the ignorant inhabitants of Cennethisar with rationalism. His interactions with the locals only serve to generate more conflict as they are marked by his sense of superiority and arrogance. Selâhattin's approach appears as a mirror image of the broader politics of the Ottoman Empire identified by Çağlar Keyder as "modernization-from-above" ("Whither" 39).

Selâhattin's denigrating discourse not only results in him losing his patients but also creates a self-inflicted exile in Cennethisar as the boundaries separating him from the rest of the village become consolidated. These boundaries still prevail during Fatma's old age as they not only ensure the security but also keep the family's purity intact by preventing all contact with the outside world: "'Did you make sure the doors are closed?' she said. 'Yes, Madam,' I said, but then I went back in and this time slammed them so she could be assured" (72).

The firmly closed doors create a claustrophobic setting, which is also mirrored in the narrative structure of the novel with the individual chapters accorded to each narrator. In the Turkish original the chapters have numbers that separate one from the other but no distinguishing information can be found regarding the identity of each narrator.[6] The reader, with each chapter, is invited to delve right into the individual world of that specific narrator without an introductory title that would connect it to the overall plotline of the narrative. This sense of disconnection created by form is reinforced with the internal monologues of the narrators. The tension between the internal and the external manifests itself as interrupted speech.

> I get out, we walk among the gravestones with one of them on each arm, moving slowly, God, forgive me, these gravestones just give me the creeps,
> "Are you okay, Grandmother?"
> slowly in the heat, with nobody, this burnt smell of the dried weeds, me, too, one day, I'd be
> "Where was it?"
> among them, the graves – But don't think of that now, Fatma,
> (72)

The clash between the external world and Fatma's internal monologue produces two distinct lines of dissonant narratives. These two lines of narrative only interact by interruption and not complementation. Immersed in their thoughts, the narrators of *Silent House* do not address an outside listener but retreat further into their internal worlds, enhancing the overall claustrophobic effect.

---

[6] The English translation, on the other hand, has chapter titles such as "Recep Goes to the Movies" or "Metin Spins Out of Control," helping the reader identify the narrator of each chapter.

An additional element that contributes to this sense of seclusion is created by the different focus of each narrator. While Fatma is primarily busy reminiscing, Faruk is trying to make peace with his uncertain future. While Metin's focus is in finding ways to enchant the beautiful Ceylan, Recep is preoccupied with coming to terms with his late father. Each narrator is absorbed in his/her narrative and is deaf to the story of others. The narrators' disinterest for each other's stories contributes to the claustrophobic atmosphere, making each narrator a prisoner of his/her own secluded narrative.

The seclusion is also replicated in the domestic spaces of the narrative. Fatma rarely leaves her room and spends most of her time in bed. Recep, on the other hand, is "downstairs," both socially, as he is the servant of the family, and physically as he runs the kitchen of the house. On one of the rare occasions that they cohabitate the same space, the characters unite around the dinner table in the kitchen. This occasion is marked by silence, reflecting how despite their spatial affinity the inhabitants of the *Silent House* still remain enslaved by their own individual narratives. Recep, who is not allowed to sit at the same table with the rest of the family, observes the silence:

> They fell quiet, and I was waiting two or three feet away, behind the table. No sound but that of the knives and forks under the pale light the sleepy moths kept circling: at that hour, the garden fell quiet too, a few crickets, some rustling trees [...]. In the winter they, too, would be gone, and the silent darkness of the trees on the other side of the walls would make my hair stand on end so I'd want to scream, but I can't, or I'd even like to talk to Madam, but she won't, so I'm quiet and I look at her wondering how a person can live like that without talking [...]. (78)

The silence of this scene stands in sharp contrast with the cacophony of each narrator's internal monologue. The communal space of the kitchen, while physically bringing the narrators together, does not enable dialogue among them. The only voice that can be heard is the internal voice of Recep, who is the narrator of the section.

Another space that brings the family members together is the cemetery where Selâhattin, his son Doğan and his wife Gül are buried. While life fails to take the narrators out of their secluded spaces, death in the form of a cemetery manages to bring them together in the open; it is only in the cemetery that their individual boundaries are removed:

> Just as they were leaving, Grandmother wanted to say one more prayer, and this time only Nilgün lifted her hands to pray with her; Faruk had pulled out a handkerchief the size of a sheet and was mopping his sweat, Uncle Recep was holding Grandmother's for her, and Metin had stuck his hands in the back pockets of his blue jeans, not even pretending to pray anymore. (88)

The scene is depicted from the point of view of Hasan who is watching the family from a distance. His position as an outsider is foregrounded by the voyeuristic qualities of his narration. Unlike Recep, who despite his illegitimate position can nevertheless cohabitate the same space as the other members of the Darvınoğlu family, Hasan is an outsider who is denied access to the terrain of the family. The distance from which he observes the family echoes the distance that exists between him and the other members of the family. The space of the cemetery thus brings to the foreground dynamics that were hidden within the domestic domain and challenges the purity and seclusion that Fatma the Grandmother so desperately wants to preserve. By bringing the narrators together, the space of the cemetery provides an insight into the tensions and affinities that exist among the narrators.

While in *Silent House* spaces are very much constricted and separated from one another by clear boundaries, *A Strangeness in My Mind* offers an entirely distinct spatial experience. Both personal and communal uses of space in the novel aim towards an obliteration of boundaries and eventually create a much more permeable and amorphous experience of space. The portrayal of Istanbul is the first and most evident distinction in terms of representation of space between the two novels. The city that appeared as a remainder of past failures and lost hopes in *Silent House* becomes a city of dreams and opportunities in *A Strangeness in My Mind*. It appears almost without boundaries and allows the newcomers a chance to build a new life by creating a new neighborhood in the peripheries, thus integrating themselves into the structure and identity of the big city.

The two brothers, Hasan Aktaş and Mustafa Karataş,[7] the protagonist Mevlut's uncle and father respectively, come to Istanbul in 1963 leaving the village of Cennetpınar[8] in the district of the central Anatolian Konya. Mevlut enters Istanbul through the Haydarpaşa train station, which offers an impressive view of the old city, including the Topkapı Palace, the heart of the Ottoman Empire. Since they cannot afford living in the established central neighborhoods, Mevlut and his father follow the common trend and settle in Kültepe, a fictional shantytown that mimics the newly emerging slums on the outskirts of the city. These illegal *gecekondus*[9] were the primary new settlements of Istanbul during the 1950s as the immigration from villages across Anatolia increased. Çağlar Keyder defines the new Istanbul as follows:

> The picture that emerged when immigrants started settling in the city was an urban planner's nightmare: the jigsaw pattern of established private property, abandoned non-Muslim holdings, waqf land without claimants, former agricultural holdings, and above all various kinds of publicly owned land, translated to a similarly unpredictable intertwining of zones and gecekondu settlements, resulting in a surprising juxtaposition of villas and expensive blocs of flats with shacks, even in the wealthiest neighborhoods of the city. ("Housing Market" 146)

With the emergence of the slums, the boundaries of the city dissolve as the social boundaries remain rigid. Mevlut's sister-in-law Samiha, who works as a maid in a house in the wealthy Şişli district, has an experience that is uncannily similar to Recep's in *Silent House*:

---

[7] The novel informs the reader that the two brothers have chosen two distinct surnames. Aktaş means "white stone," Karataş "black stone." The latter is also the surname of Recep from *Silent House*.

[8] Like Cennethisar, this is a fictional town name meaning "heavenly spring."

[9] The word literally means "built overnight."

> But Madam (that's what I used to call her – I never used her name) would not sit at the table with me, and I wasn't allowed to eat when she did. She wanted me near enough to hear her when she said, "Where's the salt?" or "Clear this away now," so I would stand in the doorway to the dining room watching her eat, but she wouldn't talk to me. (*Strangeness* 364)

Recep in the same manner addresses Fatma as Madam, he is not allowed to sit at the kitchen table with the rest of the family, lingering around waiting for her orders instead. The presence of both Samiha and Recep in these domestic spaces appear to be peripheral. The owners of the domestic spaces undermine Samiha and Recep's presence by exercising control over their voices and bodies.

While the politics of the domestic space in the two novels show similarities, the representation of urban space differs, primarily reflecting the dynamics of their respective temporal setting. Unlike the stationary Istanbul of *Silent House* that is mostly observed from a distance and hence subject to various forms of idealization and projection, Mevlut's interaction with the city in *A Strangeness in My Mind* offers an outlook that invites fluidity and results in a constantly changing, inexhaustible narrative. As a street vendor, Mevlut is always on the move, strolling the city's different quarters, interacting with the city in innumerable ways. Echoing Baudelaire's *flâneur*, Mevlut is at home on the streets of Istanbul.

> During these walks, he discovered that the shadows of the trees in some neighborhoods moved even when there was no breeze at all, stray dogs got braver and cockier where streetlamps were broken or switched off, and the flyers for circumcision ceremonies and cram schools pasted on utility poles and in doorways were all written in rhyming couplets. Hearing the things the city told him at night and reading the language of the streets filled Mevlut with pride. (*Strangeness* 304)

What makes Mevlut's strolls distinct from those of the *flâneur* is the bilateral movement. The city for Mevlut is not a passive entity that is waiting to be observed but rather a dynamic agent that interacts with him. The city is not a text waiting to be deciphered but rather an interlocutor with which Mevlut engages in a conversation. This conversation is also echoed in the narrative structure of the novel. Unlike the isolated and distant characters of *Silent House* that were confined to their individual chapters, the voices of the narrators in *A Strangeness in My Mind* mix and interact with each other constantly. The constricted spaces allocated to individual narrators in *Silent House* are replaced with a communal space cohabitated by multiple narrators.

This polyphonic structure is evident in parts III, IV and V of the novel. These lengthy sections are each composed of numerous smaller sections with two headings.[10] These smaller sections are narrated by multiple characters and each time a different narrator starts to talk, his or her name appears in bold, notifying the reader of the shift while also highlighting the distinct personal narratives. The narrators thus cohabitate both the physical space of the book as they appear on the same page and also the literary space as they respond to what the other narrator say, at times in contestation and at others in agreement. In addition to these personal narratives there is also a heterodiegetic narrator who primarily follows Mevlut, whose individual voice is never heard. The narrator's parts are indicated with the image of a man carrying boza shown from behind, a symbol for Mevlut. This visual sign, while marking the anonymity of the narration, also adds a visual dimension to the role of the narrator as someone who follows Mevlut closely. The section below displays the cohabitation of the different levels of narration and their interaction:

> The local dogs barked only at those who came from outside the village, anyone who was a threat or a foreigner. But sometimes a dog would bark at someone local, like Mevlut's cousin Süleyman, who was his best friend. [...]

---

[10] The relevance of these headings will be discussed in more detail in the following sections.

Süleyman. Actually, the village dogs never barked at me. We've moved to Istanbul now, and I'm sad that Mevlut had to stay behind in the village, I miss him ... But the dogs in the village treated me the same way they treated Mevlut. I just thought I should make that clear.

[...] From atop Mevlut and Kâmil's hill you could see, when it was windy an the sky was clear, and especially in the mornings, the little houses of Gümüşdere and the sweet little white mosque with its slender minaret.

Abdurrahman Efendi. I will take the liberty to quickly interrupt here, as I actually live in the abovementioned village of Gümüşdere. (46)

The claustrophobic and secluded individual chapters of *Silent House* are replaced in *A Strangeness in My Mind* with a polyphonic texture that promotes interaction between the different narrators. The narrators share a communal space where they freely voice their individual stories while also communicating with one another. This narrative technique is both dynamic and egalitarian as it allows all the characters of the novel to become narrators, without a sense of hierarchy. Depending on the development of the plot, characters who are involved in a particular scene become narrators, providing their individual perspectives to the events. In other words, the plotline emerges as each narrator shares his or her part of the story.

The absence of a prevalent figure of authority becomes even more evident when the narrators challenge the accuracy of the information provided by the anonymous heterodiegetic narrator. While on the one hand contributing to the overall sense of equality by undermining the alleged authority and objectivity of this narrator, this strategy also enables Pamuk to explore the dynamic, communal and non-linear nature of stories. While the protagonist Mevlut's voice is never heard directly, his story is created by the multitude of fragments that each narrator provides. "The death of the narrator" as a figure of authority therefore is not only an undermining of the grand narratives but rather emerges as a gesture that highlights the collective and dynamic nature of creation.

The inclusion of the reader into the creation process is another strategy that Pamuk explores in his attempt to highlight the collective and polyphonic aspect of the narrative. Rather than being assigned the role of a passive listener, the reader is invited to be an active collaborator. The sense of complicity is created with the use of the first person plural, which brings the narrator and the reader into the same creative space: "In order to understand Mevlut's decision, his devotion to Rayiha, and his fear of dogs, we must look back at his childhood" (45).

Another noteworthy instance of the involvement of the reader as an active agent takes place when Vediha, Mevlut's sister-in-law, makes a long list of the various occasions that made her feel unhappy and disrespected and asks the reader whether it is right. Vediha's list goes on for almost three pages and repeats the question "is it right?" with each point.

> Is it right for Korkut to tell Samiha what she can and can't do and order her around like his wife, just because she's living with us now? [...] Is it proper for them to keep those disgusting magazines in their room? Is it right for their father to come home so late every other evening? [...] Is it fine for them to ask for fries every day even though their faces are covered in pimples? (587)

In addition to the humor, the repetition creates a sense of familiarity and makes the reader complicit in Vediha's complaints. The reader can no longer remain as a passive listener but is impelled to take sides, to give a verdict and thus take part in the unfolding of the narrative. From being totally absent in *Silent House*, the reader advances into the role of an indispensable agent in the creative process in *A Strangeness in My Mind*.

The communal use of narrative space is also mirrored in the use of domestic space in both novels. While *Silent House* is marked by doors, windows and different floors that isolate each narrator, the domestic spaces in *A Strangeness in My Mind* are always communal, without any boundaries. During the early years of their marriage, Mevlut and his family live crammed into one room.

> At night, Mevlut and Rayiha slept in the same bed as their two daughters, Fatma and Fevziye. [...] The girls had their own little bed next to the window, but they were scared of being alone, and even in the same room they would start crying if they were put there. (389)

Although poverty also plays a role in this arrangement, even when the family is wealthier a similar structure is created years later. Mevlut and his cousins all move onto different floors of the same apartment building and continue sharing a communal space, under different circumstances. The space thus appears as permeable and collective in *A Strangeness in My Mind* whereas *Silent House* clings to firm boundaries that separate and isolate.

Time

There are two temporal axes in *Silent House*. The first one is the present that brings together all the characters in the scope of a week in July 1980. The second axis spans a period of 100 years and is created by the narrators' reminiscences and future dreams. The linear flow of events on the diegetic level that constitutes the present is interrupted by the flashbacks of each narrator taking the reader as far back as the early 1900s. The coexistence of these two temporal axes further reinforces the claustrophobic setting of the narrative created through the use of space. By bringing together three generations in the scope of a seven-day period, the narrative creates a sense of condensed time that doesn't allow expansion. The prevailing sense of impending doom is thus further highlighted with the constricted time span of the diegetic level of the narrative. It is only through their memories and imaginations that the narrators can escape the constrictions of their present. The depiction of the present follows a linear chronological structure as the events start the day before the grandchildren arrive in Cennethisar and conclude at the end of the seventh day with Nilgün's sudden and violent death. This linear temporality helps to highlight the climax as the tension gradually augments, and reaches its height towards the very end of the novel. This linear structure is perpetually disrupted by the internal monologues of each narrator that take the reader to different periods of time. The past, present and future are all represented and given voice by different narrators. The grandmother Fatma can attest to the history of the family as the oldest surviving member. In her internal monologues Fatma is obsessing about the past, trying to reconcile the unhappiness of her marriage with her conservative values. She is almost like a voice from the underworld, only talking to deceased members of the family and otherwise silent in her daily interactions.

The generation that follows is muted, as both Fatma's son Doğan and his wife Gül are dead. The dates on Doğan's tombstone inform the reader that Doğan Darvinoğlu, the district administrator, was born in 1915 and died in 1967. The absence of a narrator from this period is significant not only for the personal history of the Darvinoğlu family but also for the history of the Turkish Republic. The absence of a witness from this period of upheaval and violence that marks the end of the Ottoman Empire and the foundation of the Turkish Republic has two major implications. Firstly it attests to the unspeakable nature of the events and secondly, by eliminating testimony, it obliterates all possibility of literature. For Derrida testimony is another domain where the definition of presence becomes problematic. He deems testimony not as an attestation of an ultimate singular presence but rather as intricately tied to the possibility of fiction: "there is no testimony that does not structurally imply in itself the possibility of fiction, simulacra, dissimulation, lie, and perjury" (*Demeure* 29). The absence of a testimony from a specific period in *Silent House* thus obliterates the possibility of fiction, of stories from that era. The only voice from that period is the voice of Recep, Selâhattin's illegitimate son. Born in 1925, Recep is the symbol of the break with the Ottoman Empire and the hopeful new beginnings of the Turkish Republic. Although Recep's conception reflects Selâhattin's defiance of the traditional values of society, he is promptly crippled by Fatma's beatings. Recep's prospects are thus "dwarfed"[11] alongside the ideals of modernization.

Faruk, Metin and their illegitimate cousin Hasan represent the younger generation. While Faruk as the eldest is filled with worry and disillusion for the future, Metin and Hasan provide a more hopeful prospect. Despite

---

[11] Ahmet Kuyaş identifies Recep with humanism and his brother Ismail with goodwill.

the discrepancy in their directions, these two narrators are the only ones in the novel who speak of a future. Hasan, who is part of the fascist fraction, believes that he is worthy of better things and imagines a day when he will become famous and that "The television and newspapers will talk about me one day [...]" (183).

Metin, on the other hand, aspires to a life in America: "next year at this time I would be in New York [...] I imagined the freedom along the city's avenues, the blacks who would play jazz for me on the street corners [...]" (102). The fact that all the narrators reflect on the temporality to which they belong mimics the spatial segregation created. There is almost no interaction between the different narrators who belong to different temporalities and each remains secluded within his/her respective past, present or future.

While *Silent House* offers a temporality that clearly distinguishes between past, present and future, *A Strangeness in My Mind* challenges such separations as temporalities merge with one another without a sense of linear direction. The novel spans a period of four decades, from 1968 to 2012. Mevlut, the protagonist, is born in 1957 but the part of his life before his arrival in Istanbul is not covered in the novel, since, as the subtitle explains, this is the story of Istanbul as much as it is the story of Mevlut: "Being the Adventures and Dreams of Mevlut Karataş, a Seller of Boza, and of His Friends, and Also a Portrait of Life in Istanbul Between 1969 and 2012 from Many Different Points of View."

Although 1968 is the chronological beginning, the novel starts *in media res* in 1982, when Mevlut and Rayiha elope. This is also echoed in Mevlut's odyssey-like journey that the narrative traces out. This initial part of the novel is narrated entirely by the heterodiegetic narrator without any intervention from the other narrators.

> In fact, let me take this opportunity to point out that there are no exaggerations anywhere in this book, which is based entirely on a true story; I will narrate some strange events that have come and gone and limit my part to ordering them in such a fashion as to allow my reader to follow and understand them more easily. So I

will start in the middle from the day in June 1982 when Mevlut eloped with a girl from the village of Gümüşdere [...]. (4)

The unconventional role of the narrator evident in relation to space is once again highlighted in the temporality of the narrative. The narrator, who is the sole narrator in the first and last two parts of the narrative, is not an overseer who creates stories behind the scenes. The narrator's role is primarily similar to the mythological figure Chronos, as the one who mends time. The creative process therefore emerges not as a solitary act that depends on a singular source of authority but rather as a collaborative act where the narrator is only one of the many contributors. The narrator is not one who creates, but rather one who organizes.

Part II of the novel fast-forwards in time to March 30, 1994 and describes the evening that Mevlut is robbed while selling boza on the streets of Istanbul. This section is not particularly crucial in terms of plot development but rather provides an insight into the life Mevlut will have in Istanbul. The freedom with which the narrative moves between different time periods creates a sense of fluidity that is also present in the spatial explorations. The non-linear movement liberates the narrative from the restrictions of time, and generates a particular rhythm that in many ways echoes the chaotic, unpredictable structure of Istanbul, growing in various unpredictable directions. Very much in parallel to the story of Mevlut, Istanbul, too, over the span of forty years grows and matures in unpredictable and multiple directions.

It is only with part III that the narrative gains a linear temporality. Part III depicts the period between September 1968 and June 1982, part IV the period between June 1982 and March 1994 and part V the period between March 1994 and September 2002. The last two parts mirror the first two, in the sense that they depict one day rather than longer periods of time; part VI depicts April 15, 2009 and the final part VII October 25, 2012. This unusual structure and timeline allows the chapters not only to move between the past and the present but also provides the reader with various experiences of temporality that range from snapshots of instances to longer durations of times. This fluidity and fragmentation eventually creates an organic connection to life and memory. Unlike *Silent House*, which relies on a structured and linear temporality for the plot development, *A Strangeness in My Mind*, mirrors the workings of memory in its unpredictability and disorder. The narrative is not structured around a singular decisive event but appears as a texture composed of multiple different fragments that perpetually unfold.

Reminiscent of Roland Barthes' distinction between "work" and "text," *Silent House* remains devoted to the quest of a singular meaning epitomized by Nilgün's death, whereas *A Strangeness in My Mind* comfortably navigates the plurality and inexhaustibility of meaning. In other words, temporality in *Silent House* operates as yet another element that firmly foregrounds identity as a unique and originary presence, while in *A Strangeness in My Mind* it becomes the expression of its fluidity and ephemerality.

The dissimilarity in the temporal experience offered by the two narratives is evident in their exploration of the possibility of event. The plot of *Silent House* with its linear temporality revolves around a main climactic event: Nilgün's violent and sudden death, at the end of chapter 30. The various tensions between the personal and the political, the modern and the traditional, self and other, all continuously build up until the moment of Nilgün's death. This event, on a symbolic level indicates the death of communism at the hands of fascism; on the diegetic level it marks the end of the novel, not the resolution but at least the conclusion of the tensions within the narrative. Within the linear temporality of the narrative, Nilgün's death appears as the singular and non-repeatable event that marks the present, separating it from the past and the future.

The fragmented and fluid structure of *A Strangeness in My Mind*, on the other hand, makes it impossible to identify such a singular and decisive event. Pamuk strategically begins the novel with what might be considered the major event, the elopement of Mevlut and Rayiha. By taking this event out of its chronological and diegetic temporal setting and placing it at the beginning of the novel Pamuk undermines the definition of a singular and non-repeatable event. Another strategy are the titles of the individual chapters that essentially reveal the principal event taking place in that specific chapter. Each of the 57 chapters has a title and a subtitle, which is either a reference to an important scene or a phrase from that section. Titles like

"Samiha Runs Away: Blood Will be Shed Over This" or "After Rayiha: People Can't Get Cross with You If You're Crying" give away the main elements that contribute to the plot development, so much so that it is almost possible to get an idea of the action by just reading the titles of each chapter.

These titles are not spoilers that aim to ruin the reading experience but rather operate as significant elements contributing to an alternative definition of event. Within the framework of *A Strangeness in My Mind* there are no singular, non-repeatable events but rather a perpetual dissemination that enables the interaction of the past, present and future. The temporality, in parallel to the meaning, is not the product of a unique presence. It is a perpetual movement created by different *traces* that enable dissemination of meanings alongside temporalities.

To further subvert the singularity of the event, Mevlut and Rayiha's elopement described in the first chapter of the novel reappears in chapter 19 of part III, this time depicted from Süleyman's point of view. The repetition of the same event in two sections creates a temporal and spatial displacement by taking the reader back in time while also obliterating the possibility of a singular event. In the absence of an ultimate climax, the reader is left with micro-narratives that highlight distinct aspects of the same day, undermining both the originary presence and meaning.

Additionally, for readers who are keen on a linear temporal setting Pamuk places a chronology at the end of the narrative. This rather ironic appendix blurs boundaries and includes both the historical and fictional events that appear in the narrative. The coexistence of these two realms illustrates that the sense of belonging to time and space does not come from the events but rather from their appearance in the personal narratives. The order in which these events appear and the space allocated to their depiction is what gives them their meaning as well as a sense of belonging.

Characters

The prevalent context that connects the characters in both novels is the family. The family structures, however, show distinct characteristics that are also reflected in the narrative structure. *Silent House* primarily focuses on the father-son dynamic within a nuclear family, whereas *A Strangeness in My Mind* emphasizes siblings in a more extensive family structure.

Selâhattin Darvinoğlu fails to bring to life his encyclopedia but fathers three sons; Doğan, his rightful heir, and Recep and Ismail, the illegitimate sons he has with the maid of the house. Selâhattin never acknowledges Recep and Ismail as his own children, casting them to an ambiguous role on the periphery of the family. Recep as the servant of the family is mostly "downstairs" in the kitchen preparing food for Fatma and her grandchildren. While Doğan and Faruk, who represent the legitimate lineage of Selâhattin, are only preoccupied with utopian ideas that bring more harm than benefit to their families, Recep is in touch with the coarsest reality of human existence: sustenance. Ironically, it is not the legitimate rational and educated lineage but the illegitimate dwarf son who feeds the family.

While *Silent House* portrays a rather compact family structure, *A Strangeness in Mind* presents a more complex and crowded setting, which is reflected in the number of its narrators. The family structures in the later novel are less homogeneous since a family consists of a larger circle that includes in-laws and neighbors as well as fellow countrymen.

A protagonist in the conventional sense is lacking in *Silent House*, since there is no one character that stands out from the others. The five narrators, although they have different numbers of chapters allocated to them, seem to be standing at an equal distance from the reader and from one another. No one of the narrators generates more love or antipathy than the other. They are merely immersed in their internal monologues and do not seem to be aware of the existence of a reader.

A Strangeness in My Mind, on the other hand, offers an entirely different interaction with its characters. The protagonist is Mevlut Karataş and the narrative claims to be his life story. Mevlut's story is created by the various stories told by numerous characters. The abundance of characters gives a sense of a perpetual fluidity and movement as the reader is navigating between these different voices. As the structure of the narrative illustrates, the characters are not separated from one another with individual chapters. They appear on the same page with an indication of their name in bold when they start to talk. This flow between the narrators enables interaction and exchange, mirroring the sense of perpetual displacement that dominates the narrative. The family structures are also reflected in this loose texture as cousins, in-laws, siblings are all in contact, and part of the family. In *A Strangeness in My Mind* no character is left out in the periphery, as there are no strict boundaries to create peripheries. Each character takes his or her turn and plays the role within the story without necessarily being placed within a hierarchy.

The multiplicity and complexity of the ties between the characters at times gets too overwhelming and as a precaution Pamuk places a family chart at the beginning of the novel, showing the names of and connections between the characters. An additional feature is the character index at the end that is almost four pages long. This index not only fulfils an informative function, it also redefines the role assigned to the reader. Unlike in *Silent House*, the reader cannot be a mere observer in *A Strangeness in My Mind*. The index of characters offers readers the freedom to create their individual narratives by concentrating on the story of an individual character. Although Mevlut appears to be the protagonist of the novel, the reader is free to choose any character in the index and read his/her story, thus re-ordering the narrative and maintaining the possibility to re-invent it with yet another protagonist. There are no hierarchies in the novel that prioritize one story over the other. It is up to the readers to decide whose story they wish to listen to. The narrative thus not only obliterates a linear temporal and spatial setting but also incites perpetual displacement in terms of its characters.

Concluding Remarks

Both *Silent House* and *A Strangeness in My Mind* are polyphonic narratives with characters who also act as narrators. While the narrative technique remains the same, the effect it produces is drastically different. In *Silent House* the firm boundaries of each narrator create a claustrophobic environment with no interaction with the outside. The various tensions that prevail in the narrative, including self/other, inside/outside, modern/traditional, past/present, left/right, are reinforced by the boundaries between each narrator's chapters. The narrative strategy, in other words, allows each identity to be firmly defined in opposition to its other, without providing a space where they can come into contact. The narrators of *Silent*

House create their individual grand narratives, aiming to find an ultimate and fixed meaning. Rather than interacting with one another and being exposed to different points of view, they aim to find an originary meaning within their own stories. They are more interested in keeping the territory of their "self" safe than in having an exchange with the "other."

The concluding passage of the novel highlights another opposition, that between the real and the fictional:

> You can't start out again in life, that's a carriage ride you only take once, but with a book in your hand, no matter how confusing and perplexing it might be, once you've finished it, you can always go back to the beginning; if you like, you can read it through again, in order to figure out what you couldn't understand before, in order to understand life, isn't that so, Fatma? (*Silent House* 402)

The main difference between the real experience and the fictional one is described as the possibility of repetition. While the real experience is a singular event, the fictional one offers the chance of repetition. This difference between the "real" and the "fictional" not only introduces another layer to the already prevalent binaries but also operates on the illusion of an inherent and ultimate meaning waiting to be discovered. While stories appear to be the best way to unravel this meaning, the illusion of a fixed and ultimate meaning is what dooms this endeavor to failure

A Strangeness in My Mind, on the other hand, is not looking for a hidden meaning; instead, it offers a space of continuous displacement where meaning is constantly being re-invented. The different narrators with their individual voices perpetually displace the possibility of a stable position for the reader while the characters are displaced within the big city. Identity is not firmly defined within time and space but is always already displaced; it is this movement that generates meaning as *différance* in *A Strangeness in My Mind*. The boundaries of *Silent House* no longer exist, instead there is fluidity between identities; similar to the ease with which Mevlut moves through the city, the reader can move between times, spaces and voices. The voice of each narrator exists alongside others; there is no distinction between the internal and external. There is no ultimate meaning waiting to be unraveled but only stories that are told. The stories told by different narrators who interact with each other perpetually displace the idea of an ultimate meaning as presence. The eradication of the boundaries becomes evident as Mevlut becomes one with the city:

> So this is how Mevlut came to understand the truth that a part of him had known all along: walking around the city at night made him feel as if he were wandering around inside his own head. That was why whenever he spoke to the walls, advertisements, shadows, and strange and mysterious shapes he couldn't see in the night, he always felt as if he were talking to himself. (*Strangeness* 728)

Despite being the protagonist Mevlut is the only character in the novel who doesn't speak in the first person. His silence is explained in the dissolution of the boundaries between his self and the other. The novel claims to be the story of his life, and Mevlut knows that there is no story that belongs to oneself only. The self can only be known through the stories of others.

Works Cited

Barthes, Roland. "From Work to Text." *Image, Music, Texts*. New York: Noonday, 1988.

Derrida, Jacques. "A Certain Impossible Possibility of Saying the Event." Trans. Gila Walker. *Critical Inquiry* 33.2 (Winter, 2007): 441-61.

___. *Demeure: Fiction and Testimony*. Trans. Elizabeth Rottenberg. Stanford: Stanford UP, 2000.

___. "Différance." *Margins of Philosophy*. By Derrida. Trans. Alan Bass. Chicago: University of Chicago Press, 1982. 1-28.

Kasaba, Reşat. "Kemalist Certainties and Modern Ambiguities." *Rethinking Modernity and National Identity in Turkey*. Ed. Sibel Bozdoğan and Reşat Kasaba. Seattle: University of Washington Press, 1997. 15-37.

Keyder, Çağlar. "The Housing Market from Informal to Global." *Istanbul: Between the Global and the Local*. Ed. by Keyder. Boulder: Rowman & Littlefield, 1999: 143-61.

___. "Whither the Project of Modernity? Turkey in the 1990s." *Rethinking Modernity and National Identity in Turkey*. Ed. Sibel Bozdoğan and Reşat Kasaba. Seattle: University of Washington Press, 1997: 37-52.

Kuyaş, Ahmet. "Tarihçi gözüyle *Sessiz ev*." *Orhan Pamuk'u anlamak*. Ed. Engin Kılıç. İstanbul: İletişim, 2000: 71-74.

Pamuk, Orhan. *My Name Is Red*. Trans. Erdağ Göknar. NY: Alfred A. Knopf, 2001. Trans. of *Benim adım kırmızı*, 1998.

___. *Silent House*. Trans. Robert Finn. London: Faber & Faber, 2012. Trans. of *Sessiz ev*.

___. *A Strangeness in My Mind*. Trans. Ekin Oklap. London: Faber & Faber, 2015. Trans. of *Kafamda bir tuhaflık*.

Pamuk, the Storyteller:
Elements of *The Thousand and One Nights* in *The Black Book*

Sevinç Türkkan
University of Rochester

Abstract: This article focuses on those elements of Orhan Pamuk's *The Black Book* (*Kara kitap*) that adopt and adapt the storytelling technique and other elements from *The Thousand and One Nights* (more popularly known as *The Arabian Nights*) to comment on Turkish society's socio-political predicaments in the 1980s. Two chapters in the novel, "Love Tales on a Snowy Night" and "A Very Long Chess Game," are exemplary of how *The Black Book* performs cultural mobility and political critique by way of adopting material from the *Nights*. By probing the acts of rewriting, translating, and literary appropriation, *The Black Book* enters the domain of *Weltliteratur*. Yet, Pamuk's novel is also a pointed critique that acquires a special force in the context of authoritarian regimes in Turkey, which the novel condenses in the overarching motif of the *Doppelgänger* and its logical extension, the master-slave relationship. Pamuk's home, therefore, is the world of storytelling and cultural critique as much as Istanbul.

> "*The Book of One Thousand and One Nights* is a treasure chest of secret logic, in-jokes, richness, strangeness, impudence and vulgarity. More profoundly than any other book, it shows us what life is made of."
> - Orhan Pamuk

What are the "secret logic, in-jokes, richness" and in particular, the "strangeness" of the *Nights* that Pamuk finds so mysterious and inspiring? How can a book of tales about "impudence and vulgarity" be a blueprint for life? What aspects of Pamuk's work can help us answer these questions? Above all, what does this tell us about the impact of one text on another, of one literature on another, and of cross-cultural interaction and continuity of tradition in world literature?

By now, Pamuk has secured himself a solid place in "world literature" and has often been associated with the category "cosmopolitan" rather than anything essentially "Turkish." Goethe coined the term *Weltliteratur* in 1827 when he admitted that he preferred to "look about [himself] in foreign nations. [...] National literature is now a rather unmeaning term; the epoch of world literature is at hand, and everyone must strive to hasten its approach" (Eckermann; qtd. in Damrosch 1). Similarly, but this time in relation to global economy, in 1847 Marx and Engels used the term "world literature" to hail a new epoch: "National one-sidedness and narrow-mindedness become more and more impossible, and from the numerous national and local literatures there arises a world literature" (Eckermann; qtd. in Damrosch 2). Distinct from Goethe's cross-cultural context, Marx and Engels' approach is grounded in the close affinities between national and global industries. The bourgeoisie's exploitation of the world market destroyed the old-established national industries and granted cosmopolitan guise to all national production and consumerism. Consequently, in the realm of arts and cultures, national literatures have been superseded by world literature. Pamuk is certainly its prime example as a writer who has surpassed national one-sidedness and who has successfully negotiated literary influences both western and eastern.

Pamuk's fourth novel *The Black Book* [1] has become a cult book since its publication in 1990, so much so that in Turkey, readers have come to categorize modern Turkish literature as "before *The Black Book*" and "after *The Black Book*." With 46 editions in Turkish it is among the best-sellers in the country. In 2015, following the book's twenty-fifth anniversary, Pamuk's current publisher Yapı Kredi issued a special edition of the novel and in 2013 published the supplemental volume Kara kitap*'ın sırları* (*The Secrets of* The Black Book) featuring the writer's reflections on the process of creation side by side with pictures from his handwritten spiral notebooks and of his drawings (Hadzibegovic and Pamuk). The reception of the novel in academic circles has equally been positive. It has been subject to academic articles, and to chapters in edited volumes and books.[2] For instance, Seyhan read the novel as a *Bildungsroman* (150), Parla intriguingly called it a "meta-novel" (104), Adak read it as an "encyclopedic novel," Mattar called it a "*Künstlerroman*" (50), Brendemoen analyzed its narrative as an

---

[1] Available in English in Maureen Freely's translation (2006); the previous English translation (1994) by Güneli Gün is out of print now.
[2] In English see McGaha (2008), Anadolu-Okur (2009), Afridi and Buyze (2012), Göknar (2013); in Turkish see Kılıç (1999), Esen (1996).

experiment in innovation of the Turkish language and syntax (129), Kim saw it as a quest in the tradition of mystical Islam (23), Goytisolo named it "an aesthetic of multivoicedness" (297) and Moran read it as a metafictional meditation on identity (98). I was intrigued by its translations and transformations in English and German and in two previous and one forthcoming publications, I analyzed the book as the source text of three stylistically divergent translations which, I argued, taken together, can open insights into the original in a way the original by itself would not have been able to accomplish. I further suggested that Pamuk's image as a world writer has been significantly shaped by his multiple translators in English and German (Türkkan 2011, 2012 and forthcoming).

What makes this novel distinct from Pamuk's previously penned three novels is the writer's sincere interest in and turning to the literary archives of the Sufi, Persian, and Ottoman traditions he inherited. The previous three novels[3] consciously distance themselves from that tradition. Formally and thematically, *Cevdet Bey* echoes Mann's masterpiece *Buddenbrooks*. *The Silent House*'s multiple first person narrative style was inspired by Faulkner and by the earlier Japanese Akutagawa. *The White Castle*, on the other hand, is in close reminiscence with the *Doppelgänger* narratives of Poe, Conrad, E.T.A. Hoffmann, Dostoyevsky, Cervantes, and Stevenson, to name a few. That is, initially Pamuk's literary and artistic inspirations were heavily marked by western literary models. For *The Black Book*, Pamuk turned his eye in-ward and east-ward.

Pamuk's exercise in "turning east-ward" needs to be understood in a proper context. The essay collection, *Öteki renkler* includes a piece on world literature ("Dünya edebiyatı") in which, Pamuk comments, in a somewhat dark voice, on the exclusive nature and "fraternal order" the term entails ("Kitap okuyanların yüksek kardeşliği!" 218). This short piece was not included in the English edition of the collection (*Other Colors*) and left in the dark many Anglophone readers of Pamuk's novels regarding his perception of himself as a self-conscious and incomplete writer. In "Dünya edebiyatı," Pamuk criticizes the notion of world literature and the childlike assumption that all literatures of the world can come together,

---

[3] *Cevdet Bey and His Sons* (*Cevdet Bey ve oğulları*, 1982; untranslated), *The Silent House* (*Sessiz ev*, 1983), *The White Castle* (*Beyaz kale*, 1985).

crossing the barriers of unequal power distribution, and shed off their attachments to the "authoritative and restrictive demands of national traditions."[4] In his struggle to master the art of the novel, to combine the stories of Istanbul and the Ottoman tradition he inherited at home with modernist and postmodernist literary techniques he encountered in the novels of "world writers," Pamuk came to recognize the "subtle remembering" and "cunning forgetting" the order of world literature entails.[5] World literature has not been a dialogue or even cross-cultural exchange but the imposition of literary forms and styles of powerful nations upon the less powerful ones. In contrast to the rhetoric of effortless influence, seamless borrowings, admiration and reception, Pamuk makes a strong case for the "difficulty of literary forms traveling across borders" in spite of assumptions of equal access through globalization. Pamuk writes:

> While some research the identity of the murderer, the meaning of life, the structure of the world and of language, the depths of the human soul, certain others can only have their voices heard if they tell stories about poverty, misery, violence, and backwardness. As my books get translated into foreign languages, I am most often confronted with this accusatory question in Turkey: "Do you write for readers in Turkey or for readers around the world?" Behind this question lurks an extremely suspicious reaction to the literary division of labor in the world. Not to mention the frightening nationalism that can only be overcome through more exchange and libraries, through a culture of writers who read each other's work and through a rich tradition of translation. (All translations mine unless otherwise indicated.)[6]

---

[4] "Bu düşünce ilk anda bizi hem ulusal geleneklerin buyurucu ve sınırlayıcı taleplerinden kurtarıyor hem de çocuksu bir saflıkla bütün ülkelerin edebiyatlarının kardeş olduğunu hayal ettiriyor!" ("Dünya edebiyatı" 218-19).

[5] "[Z]arafetle yapılmış bir hatırlama olduğu kadar incelikle yapılan bir unutma" (219).

[6] "Bazıları katilin kim olduğunu, hayatın anlamını, dünyanın ve dilin yapısını, insan ruhunun derinliklerini araştırırken başka bazıları seslerini ancak yoksulluk, eziklik, şiddet ve gerilik üzerine hikayeler anlatarak duyurabildiler. Kitaplarım yabancı dillere çevrildikçe Türkiye'de en çok karşılaştığım suçlayıcı soru: "Türk okuru için mi, dünya okuru için mi yazıyorsunuz?" Bu sorunun arkasında dünyadaki edebi

Pamuk sees through "world literature"'s nationalistic aspirations and its binary logic with a center that imposes its tastes upon a periphery and a periphery that is compelled to mimic that center. A way out of this impasse, according to Pamuk, is the model of William Faulkner and Thomas Bernhard who write as if they were in the periphery although they are in the center and that of Dostoyevsky and Borges who write as if they were in the center while residing at the periphery. In this sense, *The Black Book* presents a theory of Pamukian world literature and of becoming the other as Galip searches for and eventually becomes Rüya/Celal. Similarly, Pamuk's career trajectory mimics this ideal as his interest in the "marginal/forgotten/erased" Ottoman, Persian, and Arabic literary traditions has increased, the more he has become central at home and beyond.

The Black Book *and* The Thousand and One Nights

The Black Book has a simple plot inserted into an intricate structure. The protagonist Galip's search for his runaway wife Rüya physically in the backstreets of Istanbul and mentally through his cousin Celal's newspaper columns constitutes the allegorical path of the narrative. The search for a beloved is superimposed on the search for "the other," and ultimately on the search for oneself. In the beginning, Rüya constitutes everything for Galip: she is his cousin, first love, wife, and confidante all at the same time. Galip's search for her is narrated in odd-numbered chapters of the novel, at least in the first part of the novel. The narrative point of view becomes blurred, difficult to dissect, and the tone darker in the second part as Galip and Celal's voices blend into one. The odd-numbered chapters consist of fictional newspaper columns written by Celal. They can be read independently from the rest of the novel and display Pamuk's mastery in reproducing minutely the style and tone of Turkish newspaper commentators notorious for pretending to be jacks-of-all-trade. Reading through the novel across these chapters in the first part is relatively effortless. The reader's desire to distinguish between Galip's search and Galip's reading of Celal's

---

işbölümüne aşırı aşırı kuşkucu bir tepki var. Ve ancak etkiler, kütüphaneler, birbirlerini okuyan yazarlar ve zengin bir çeviri geleceğiyle yenilebilecek korkutucu bir milliyetçilik" (*KK* 219).

columns is denied in the second part, where the two voices merge to deliver Galip's ultimate transformation into a writer. All this transpires during seven cold days in Istanbul while a mysterious green pen keeps writing, underlining, and crossing out sections of the narrative. Pamuk interweaves numerous stories into the book, from executioners' haunting tales to apocalyptic narratives of the Bosphorus' receding waters, from generals' nocturnal journeys in disguise to the mysteries of letters inscribed on faces, from stories about crown princes to haunting airshafts, from the memorable citizens of Istanbul to its strange and, at times, absurd inhabitants. Istanbul-themed endless stories and histories supply the secular setting for Galip's spiritual path and make the novel a literary history of Istanbul's past and present.

The Black Book builds on material Pamuk compiled in 1986 when he was at Columbia University and had access to Butler Library's expansive collection of Turkish, Ottoman, and Persian literary traditions. Being away from Turkey allowed Pamuk to gain an alternative perspective to works which he previously associated with conservative Islam (Hadzibegovic and Pamuk 66). In brilliant publications Sooyon Kim and Didem Havlıoğlu, for instance, have discussed Pamuk's allusions to Mevlânâ Celâleddin Rumi's *Masnavi-i Ma'navi* (1273, *Mesnevi*, [1881]), Şeyh Galip's *Hüsn ü Aşk* (1783, *Beauty and Love* [2005]), and Farid ud-Din Attar's *Mantiq ut-Tair* (1177, *Conference of the Birds* [1954]). Indeed, these works inspired *The Black Book*'s allegorical aspects as a search for a beloved, an ideal, and ultimately a search for oneself. However, not much has been written about the structural, thematic, and stylistic elements it borrows from *The Thousand and One Nights*.

In his insightful discussion of the novel, Berna Moran argues that Pamuk wrote a modern novel in the context of "Eastern literary tradition" (94). In particular, the *Night*'s structure influenced *The Black Book*'s in that, as in the *Nights*, the novel consists of the frame story of Galip and Rüya, which circumscribes numerous other stories, Celal's newspaper columns, and autobiographical references. Even though I do not subscribe to the notion of hemispheric divisions in literary tradition (in this case, it is not clear whether Pamuk read translations of the European *Nights* or of the Arabic

Nights[7]), I agree with Moran's point that there is a close structural affinity between the *Nights* and Pamuk's novel. Moran's discussion however, does not go beyond this point, nor does it give any analyses of the stories within stories in the novel, which is what I attempt to do here.

The Arabian Nights *in Turkey*

The stories of the *Nights* were familiar to the Turkish culture even before they reached prominence in Europe since the territory of the Ottoman Empire (1299-1922) included the regions where the stories circulated: a significant portion of the Arab peninsula, the fertile crescents of the Tigris and Euphrates rivers (Mesopotamia and Syria) bordering Persia and the Gulf, and Egypt. The centuries-old exchange among the Turkish, Persian, and Arab cultures populating these territories inevitably fostered the mutual influences between the *Nights* and the Turkish oral tradition.

Many of the stories, characters, and motifs of the *Nights* were already present in the archives of the Turkish oral tradition even before the first Turkish translation (as *Binbir Gece Masalları* [Stories of the Thousand and One Nights]) appeared in 15th century (Birkalan 221). The Turkish influence on the *Arabian Nights* is already visible in the collection's title in Turkish: *Bin bir gece masalları*. "Bin bir" means "a thousand and one" but in this context, it is not meant to designate a specific number. Instead, the alliteration reinforces the meaning of numerous and endless stories in the collection. It is the Turkish title "Bin bir gece" that gave the *Arabian Nights* the numeric designation that appeared in the title later on, in Arabic (*Alf Layla wa Laylah*), in Persian (*Hazar Afsana*), and in the European languages (*Les mille et une nuit* in Antoine Galland, *Stories from the Thousand and One Nights* in Edward Lane, *Tausend und eine Nacht* in Gustav Weil, *Erzählungen aus den Tausendundein Nächten* in Enno Littmann). By now, it is a well-known fact that the French Galland acquired a copy of the *Nights* (most probably a Turkish translation of an Arabic text) when he was appointed an assistant to the ambassador in Istanbul and initiated the

---

[7] In "Love, Death and Storytelling" Pamuk mentions that he read Raif Karadağ's translation, *1001 Gece Masalları*. Interestingly, Karadağ presents himself as the writer ("yazan") on the cover of his four-volume translation and does not reference any original source.

Nights frenzy in Europe. The acclaimed folklorists Eberhard and Boratav for instance, include the stories of "Aladdin and the Magic Lamp" and "Ali Baba and the Forty Thieves" in their work on the typologies of Turkish folktales (1953). Birkalan notes that the cycle of stories featuring the Caliph Harun al-Rashid, in fact, represents "the Arab imagination of how a Turkish sultan in the fifteenth century might have lived" (223). Ironically, it is exactly this character that Pamuk borrows from the *Nights* to articulate a harsh critique of oppressive and dictatorial regimes in Turkey. I will discuss this point in more detail below.

Most Turkish translations of the *Nights* are ambiguous when it comes to specifying the language of the original or the translator, and at times they lack both (Birkalan 222). More importantly, and as Birkalan argues, the project of making the *Nights* available in Turkish was more a political than an aesthetic one. Scholars have long remarked that the project of modernization and westernization in the Turkish context was also a project of translation as confirmed by the language reform of the early Republican period (Gürçağlar). The ideology of modernization of the late Ottoman Empire and early modern Turkish Republic imagined the Turk as a rational and advanced subject in pursuit of European modernity. This projection necessarily defined the Arab and its culture as "the other" or as oriented towards the East and therefore backward. This ideology also informs the readers' and publishers' ambivalent relationship to the *Nights* in Turkey. While early Turkish translations of the *Nights* were from Arabic texts, modern Turkish translations were based on European versions, ironically disregarding the proximity of Turkish to Arabic. As Pamuk points out "because we live in a culture that has severed its links with its own cultural heritage and forgotten what it owes to India and Iran, surrendering instead to the jolts of western literature, [the *Nights*] came back to us via Europe" ("Love, Death and Storytelling" 34).

Pamuk's Love Stories

One of the best instances of storytelling in *The Black Book* – unimpeded by Pamuk's endless hermeneutic circles – is the chapter "Love Tales on a Snowy Night" ("Karlı Gecenin Aşk Hikâyeleri"). After his visit to a brothel and during one of his urban rounds, Galip comes across İskender and a group of journalists who intend to do "the-thousand-and-one-nights tour of Istanbul" ("bir binbir gece Istanbul'u yaptırmak"; *Kara kitap*[8] 160). Similar to Boccaccio's ten Florentine narrators in *The Decameron*, Pamuk's seven characters gather in a bar to spend the cold snowy evening narrating stories. These stories have a strange and uncanny resemblance to the various layers that constitute *The Black Book,* and that aspect makes the novel a variation on the *Nights*. *The Black Book* is not a diachronically progressive linear narrative. Rather, like *The Thousand and One Nights,* it is a collection of stories, types, motifs, and events that bear resemblance to one another and constantly refer back to the frame tale of Galip's search for Rüya.

The metafictional aspect of this chapter is evident in the references to beautiful women who abandon their husbands, to writers who cannot write, to true stories that are taken to be fictional and to fictional stories assumed to be true, to the uncanny resemblances between people and events, to people who effortlessly become somebody else, and to the sublime aspects of literature versus the debased nature of reality – all themes subject to the novel's hermeneutic investigations. There are autobiographical references to the historical figure Pamuk, and to two of his novels – the previously published *The White Castle* (*Beyaz kale* 1985) and the subsequent *The New Life* (*Yeni hayat* 1994). The chapter itself is a frame tale – a tale framing Pamuk's desire to tell stories and our desire to listen to them. But before that, the chapter is one of the many stories framed by the most external search in the novel, that of Galip's for Rüya. The "love" content of the stories directly comments on Galip's trauma, on his misconception of Rüya as representing ideal beauty, and on his "love" for her – his devotion to and his futile search for her. The love stories of this chapter are poignant, tragicomic, and evocative of one another. None of them are climactic – *á la* Shahrazad's stories. Each time a story-teller brings a story to an agreeable make-believe end, the listeners fall respectfully silent – *á la* Shahrazad And, all of the stories involve a triangle of characters – *á la Arabian Nights*.

---

[8] *KK* from here on.

In *The Arabian Nights*, the betrayed and disillusioned king Shahrayar vows to marry for one night only and kills his wife the next morning, "in order to save himself from the wickedness and cunning of women" (Haddawy and Mahdi 14). Shahrazad asks her father to marry her to Shahrayar so that she may either succeed in saving the people or perish and die like the rest. In a gesture of female bonding, she invites her sister Dinarzad to join her and to divert the king's attention from killing Shahrazad by requesting a story in the morning. This diversion translates into a narrative refrain which recurs in the narrative as many times as there are mornings:

> But morning overtook Shahrazad, and she lapsed into silence, leaving King Shahrayar burning with curiosity to hear the rest of the story. Then Dinarzad said to her sister Shahrazad, "What a strange and lovely story!" Shahrazad replied, "What is this compared with what I shall tell you tomorrow night if the king spares me and lets me live? It will be something even stranger and more wonderful than this. When it was night and Shahrazad was in bed with the king, Dinarzad said to her sister Shahrazad, "Please, if you are not sleepy, tell us one of your lovely little tales to while away the night." (23)

The king asks to hear the ending of the story Shahrazad strategically left unfinished the previous night. This refrain – just like many of the stories, characters, tropes, motifs, and stock sayings in the *Nights* – repeats over and over for a thousand and one times. Similarly, *The Black Book*'s spiraling effect is partly due to the events that repeat, recur, and return. The *Nights*' triangle of the King (Shahrayar), the Queen, and the Slave (Shahrazad) is replaced in the novel by the triangle of the Husband (Galip), the Wife (Rüya), and the Beau (Celal). On an unconscious level, Galip embarks on a journey not to find his runaway wife *per se* but to come across experiences and stories that confirm his own experience, the way Shahrayar and Shahzaman do in the frame tale after they witness their wives' betrayal. As Beaumont remarks, in the *Nights* a story comes to an end provisionally only to invite another story that is more amazing than the one we just read. Yet, the story that is introduced in this way contains elements from or is a variation on the preceding one. That is, what qualifies it as "even stranger and more wonderful" are the "uncanny recurrences of events found in the preceding story" (Beaumont, *Slave* 150). It is the repetition that makes it "stranger and more wonderful." For instance, at the end of the English journalist's story in which "a beautiful woman" abandons "her dolt of a husband," we are told that Galip laughs at its "tragic ending" and finds the silence that follows it "meaningless" (*BB* 162). I am not suggesting that Galip ridicules the English journalist's story here. Rather, I contend, he laughs at its uncanny recurrence because its recurrence is what makes it stranger and even more amazing than his own personal situation. That is, the English journalist's story happens to be just another variation on the theme of love and abandonment which Pamuk's *magnum opus* explores in great detail.

The Black Book opens with Galip and Rüya in bed, Rüya asleep and heedless to Galip whose eyes carefully trace every curve and expression on her face; his mind restlessly wonders over the content of her dreams. He is suspicious, jealous, self-conscious, impotent, infatuated, and narcissistic – simply, the neurotic male subject or another Shahrayar. Both Galip and Sharayar are deeply and fundamentally afraid of women's sexuality, power, and betrayal, and each book is a potent expression of the dramas and traumas of male anxiety, of the fear of being abandoned and condemned to eternal solitude. Above all, both books tell the story of human anxiety in the face of death – "the destroyer of delights" (Haddawy 518). But before that, we need to analyze Pamuk's anxiety of not being able to write, of not being able to finish *The Black Book*, of eternally being misunderstood, and condemned to death.

We know well that the stories Shahrazad tells Shahrayar are commentaries and variations on the frame story. Shahrazad spins a dream narrative of condensation and displacement in which Shahrayar's drama repeats in different settings and situations, and through different characters. Her tales comment on various forms of trauma, (in)justice, love(sickness), and take us down the forked path of the vicissitudes of desire as demonstrated in the story of the Hunchback, for instance (Beaumont, *Slave* 105). All these themes are variations on the frame tale. *The Arabian Nights* is about *The Arabian Nights*. Similarly, *The Black Book* is about itself and about the process of writing it. Pamuk constantly gestures towards the relationship between his novel and other texts which inspired him, underlines similarities, and creates writer figures like himself who deny that their stories are about themselves – the perennial denial as affirmation. For instance, the second story in the chapter on "Love Tales" is narrated by a tall man who introduces himself as a writer (Pamuk?) and who intends to tell a story about a writer. The storyteller/writer is quick to dissipate his audience's suspicion that the writer who is the subject of his story is not himself (a tongue-in-cheek remark that "this is *not* Pamuk"!). Galip remembers having heard the name of this writer somewhere before. The metafictional aspects of this story are evident, again. This story is not just another variation on a man abandoned by his wife, it is also a redemption of the anxieties of writing and creating. It is about the black hole that is the writer's block, and the fear and anticipation of a negative critical reception, even of being misunderstood. This writer compares the feeling of being abandoned to the feeling of "writing a novel that was refusing to go according to plan: It was as if there were a secret locked inside his dream that refused to reveal itself, that kept luring him into cul-de-sacs to confirm his incompetence, compound his confusion," in Freely's translation (*BB* 163).

In *Other Colors*, Pamuk writes about the pleasures and fears of the dizzying mental fatigue that descended on him when he came close to the end of writing *The Black Book*. He admits that he lost control over its mysterious core which at times was closed even to him – similar to the writer/storyteller in "Love Tales." Pamuk writes,

> As I sat in that distant place, working on this book that refused to end, a strange and miserable fear began to taint the joy of my writing, and my solitude, a fear that slowly came to resemble that suffered by the hero, Galip. [...] as the writing progressed and the book grew broader, the pleasure of writing it grew deeper, but I was unable to take pleasure in that fact because of the obsessive goal that eluded me. [...] I felt all alone, like Galip – perhaps I felt like this so I could carry the emotion into the book – but he was subsumed by melancholy, while my isolation was in anger. Because they wouldn't understand this book that was becoming

steadily stranger, because it was hard to understand, because they would point to the book's more obscure parts to prove it a failure, and also, perhaps, because I was never going to finish it; I'd written the wrong book. [...] there were times when I feared that the book was going nowhere, that all these pages I had written would lead neither me nor the reader anywhere but a state of confusion. (253-54)

The writer-storyteller in "Love Tales" remembers the novel he wrote before his wife left him, "later his readers called it 'historical'" and because this writer wanted to overcome the feeling of abandonment and become his previous self again, he found himself writing a book about look-alikes and doubles over and over again (*BB* 164). Later on, bored of witnessing a world full of copies and doubles, this writer decides to invent another, a surreal world and for this reason, decides to roam the backstreets and alleys of Istanbul, to explore its underground passages, cafes, and dives at night. He comes to realize that the world he dreamed of and the world he witnessed on the streets are alike. Therefore, he concludes, the world is a book. Like the *Night*'s refrain which never lets us lose ourselves in the narrative world of Shahrazade's stories and reminds us of the predicament under which she narrates, *The Black Book* constantly affirms itself and its status as a lens through which we perceive Galip. It is no surprise that the writer's story ends with a comment on the silence that follows it: the audience fell silent not because the story was about love but because it was about storytelling and loneliness (164).

Similarly, the bar girl's story is modeled after the story of "Aziz and Aziza" from the *Nights* (Lyons 489-593) even as the bar girl/storyteller insists that the story is "true" and demands complete suspension of disbelief (165). The *Nights*' "Aziz and Aziza" tells the story of two cousins who are about to get married. On the wedding day, Aziz leaves to pay a visit to a friend whom he forgot to invite to the wedding. On his way back, he falls in love with a mysterious woman. He arrives late to the wedding which gets postponed. Aziz admits that he has fallen in love. Aziza pines for love and selflessly helps Aziz to decipher some mysterious messages the woman sends him. It is only with the help of Aziza that Aziz can understand

and communicate with the woman. Aziza dies of love while Aziz narcissistically pursues his new love affair until he himself falls prey to lovesickness. Pamuk borrows the structure of falling in love and the wound created by this trauma from the *Nights* and complicates it by situating it in a local context. Pamuk's mysterious woman is the "bastard child of the Queen of England and the Shah of Iran" ("İran Şahı'yla İngiliz Kraliçesi'nin piçiymiş"; *KK* 165). Her visit to Turkey is part of her plan to avenge herself by locating a map divided into two halves, one in the hands of the National Security Bureau and the other with the secret police. By the time the pieces of the story are sealed together, Pamuk's "Aziza" realizes that her cousin/fiancé betrayed her, and she betrays him. Pamuk's "Aziz" realizes that he has been trapped by the mysterious woman and returns to "Aziza" but it is too late. The various triangles that structure the inner and outer circles of *The Black Book* are mirrored in this story; before it even comes to an end, a new story – *á la Arabian Nights* – begins: Seeing that some of her listeners have doubts about the authenticity of her story, the bar girl invites the photographer, who had pictured some of its events and happens to be at the bar, to confirm the events and to tell a love story of his own.

In *The Black Book* there are stories within stories akin to those in the *Nights*. There are also other formal aspects such as thematic resonances in the form of meta-commentary similar to the thematic resonances between stories in the *Nights*. One such example is the thematic relation between the stories of the chapter on "Love Tales" and the novel's two overlapping layers: Galip's search for Rüya and Galip's search for Celal. The waiter, for instance, tells a story about performance and acting, about the ease with which one can become somebody else and the failure of people around him to recognize the "electrifying, confusing, dreamlike substitution" which occurs when he is asked to appear in a movie. When he sees the finished film, the waiter comes to realize that "his back, shoulder, and neck weren't his own" ("sırtı, omuzları ve ensesi kendisinin değilmiş" *KK* 170). In an unmistakable gesture of meta-commentary, the waiter's story remarks on the second layer that constitutes *The Black Book*'s concentric circles – on the relationship between Galip and Celal, and on Galip's eventual conversion. By the end of the novel, Galip assumes Celal's self and, in the waiter's words, "embark[s] on a brand-new life" ("yepyeni bir hayata başlayabileceğine"; *KK* 170). While the *Nights* leaves it to the reader to uncover the significance of various resonances and Shahrazad's purpose in creating them for Shahrayar, in *The Black Book* the tongue-in-cheek comments characteristic of Pamuk do the job for us.

The sixth tale comes from a retired army officer whose story is the exact replica of Shahzaman's in which the King returns home to find his wife betraying him with a slave. The retired army officer's version is about a shepherd who returns home one day, to find his wife in bed with her lover. He picks up his knife – *á la* Shahzaman – and kills them. Before the judge, he defends himself with a simple story: The woman he found in his bed with her lover was not his wife. The woman who was his wife would have never done this to him; it therefore followed that she was not the woman in his bed, and he was not "himself" ("kendisi"; *KK* 171). The shepherd is willing to take responsibility for the crime committed by this other person who has taken over his body. However, he still insists that the couple he killed be seen as two thieves who have broken into his house and made use of his bed. When he has served his time, he goes off in search of his wife in hope that she will help him find his own lost self. The narrator comments (a tongue-in-cheek gesture, again!) that Galip remembers, he has heard or read the story before somewhere but can't remember when and where. Certainly, this story is a variation on the tall writer's story about another writer, and on all previous stories of doubles, substitutes, and look-alikes in the novel, including Galip and Celal. At the end of the story, Galip comments that the retired officer was one person when he began telling the story and became someone entirely different when he finished it. That is, the trauma calls for narrative proliferation and storytelling, for narrating the wound, and for transforming one's imaginary experience into a symbolic one in the process of healing.

Nocturnal Journeys, Doubles, and The Black Book

In his memoir *Istanbul*, Pamuk has written about the appeal of the theme of doubles, look-alikes, siblings, twins and the *Doppelgänger*, variations of which he never tires of exploring (3). The same theme is profoundly dominant in the *Arabian Nights* beginning with the frame tale in which Shahrayar and Shahzaman's stories of betrayal mirror each other and render their respective traumatic experiences indistinguishable – as their names suggest. Many stories that Shahrazad narrates build on the same theme, for instance "The Story of Qamar al-Zaman and Princess Budur," "The Sleeper Awakened," and "The False Caliph." These stories explore various dimensions of the encounter with the double, the imaginary crisis of the ego in encountering sameness, the narcissism involved in the encounter, and the ambivalent feelings of love and hate experienced in this encounter. In "A Very Long Chess Game," one of Celal's newspaper columns in the novel, Pamuk subtly weaves into the narrative fabric the story of the False Caliph to align these existential crises with a specific historical-political crisis – the aftermath of the 1980 coup in Turkey and the period of curfews thereafter. The column/chapter begins with the epigraph "From time to time, Haroun al-Rashid would go around Baghdad in disguise wishing to find out what his subjects thought about him and his rule. So, tonight again …"[9] (*BB* ch. 27). This epigraph alone however, is not sufficient to explain Pamuk's completely original reworking of the *Nights* here. I contend that Pamuk not only borrows the theme of the double from the *Nights* but also explores the master-slave dialectic as a logical extension of this theme to mount a cultural and political critique of dictatorship and oppressive regimes in the history of the modern Turkish Republic.

The False Caliph story in the *Nights* (Lyons 912-28) begins when the restless Harun al-Rashid orders his minister Ja'far and his executioner Masrur to join him on the streets of Baghdad disguised as merchants in search of diversion. They come across a boatman and offer him money for an outing on the river. The boatman objects on the pretext that every night the Caliph Harun al-Rashid appears with his entourage on a boat and has forbidden anyone else to roam around at the same time. The breach would entail death. Harun and his company are intrigued and extremely eager to see the pretender. They introduce themselves as merchants from out of town and bribe the boatman to take them to the scene. In astonishment, Harun witnesses a man who resembles him, is dressed and acts like him, and is also accompanied by men who look like Ja'far, Masrur, and the rest of

---

[9] "Harun Reşit, zaman zaman tebdil ederek Bağdat'ı gezer ve halkının kendisi ve idaresi hakkında ne düşündüğünü öğrenmek istermiş. İşte bu akşam da yine..." (*KK* 299).

his court. He decides to return next evening and follow the pretender until he gets closer to him. The three of them follow the party to an enclosure where they watch the pretender sing verses of lost love, tear his clothes, and fall unconscious. They notice that his body is covered with scars of whipping. Unable to hold himself, Harun orders Ja'far to ask the pretender about his scars. It turns out that the man disguised as Caliph is Ja'far's brother-in-law whose wife, Lady Dunya, grew jealous and left him when he conceded to join Harun's wife, Zubaida, for a party. Since then, he has been staging this theater in hopes to attract the Caliph's attention and to ask for reconciliation with his wife, which Harun executes.

The story is an exploration of the intricacies of the imaginary ego – the ego that traps the subject due to its incompleteness and fascination for the image of the other in the self. The real Harun is fascinated by his double and pursues him relentlessly even to the point of stripping off his royal robe and donning a merchant's clothes as well as obeying the pretender's orders. The story seems to pick on the theme of the master-slave dialectic (an extension of the theme of the double) but falls short at exploring it in depth. Harun is fascinated by his pretender and follows him intently, so much so that Harun becomes the slave and the pretender his master. That is, Harun is never the absolute master, and the positions of master and slave never stable. Harun fears the pretender and orders Ja'far to question him. Similarly, Harun is subject to the pretender's orders in order to satisfy his curiosity and find out what is happening in his household. Certainly, this story resonates with the reversal of the master-slave dynamic in the frame story in which Shahrayar submits to Shahrazad's stories – the slave Shahrazad becoming the master.

A closer look at "A Very Long Chess Game" shows the depth and complexity of Pamuk's use of the *Nights*. The chapter begins with Celal's tongue-in-cheek comment on the 1980 military coup in Turkey, the presumed "transition to Democracy" ("'Demokrasiye Geçiş diye bilinen dönemlerden'"; *KK* 299). Celal informs us that one of his readers gave him a letter that reveals some "mysteries" related to the politics of the coup. We are told that the letter and the "pasha-like grandiosity of its style" ("Paşa üslûbuna") belong to "the dictator who once presided over us" ("O zamanki diktatörümüz"; *KK* 299). The rest of the chapter is that letter.

It is not too difficult to guess that the anonymous dictator is Kenan Evren, the then general and architect of the 1980 coup. In this letter, which he writes to an offspring overseas, he discloses how, on a suffocating August evening, he decided to put on peasant clothes and roam the streets of Istanbul shortly before the curfew he imposed would take effect. Wishing to enjoy the cool sea breeze, he asks a boatman to row him across the Golden Horn. The boatman objects on the pretext that the "Pasha President" ("Başkan Paşamız") goes out in his launch at this time every night, arresting anyone he finds along the way. Intrigued, the real "Pasha President" bribes the boatman and convinces him to row his boat close to the scene. In short, the pretender's launch approaches with searchlights probing every quarter of the city and every inch of the sea. The boatman however, declines to go further on the pretext of the curfew. They return back to the city. Eager to see more, the real "Pasha President" instructs his generals to postpone the curfew by an hour so that he can follow his pretender. The boatman rows closer the next evening but they can only see the pretender step into a fleet of limousines and depart. On the third night, the real president is caught by his pretender's soldiers and queried:

> What was I doing here at this hour? Scared, I explained that there was still time before the curfew; that I was a poor unfortunate peasant staying at a Sirkeci hotel wanting to enjoy a boat tour before I returned to my village. [...] Although he had civilian clothes on, the Pasha looked more like me, and I looked more like a peasant.[10]

The two men mount on the backseat of a bulletproof Chevrolet where the pretender discloses his story: They were classmates at the war college where the pretender's secret jealousy and competition with the real president ensued. The pretender didn't want to be a pale imitation or a second-

---

[10] "Ne işim vardı burada, bu saatte? Sokağa çıkma yasağının başlamasına daha vakit olduğunu söylüyordum telaşla; Sirkeci'de otelde kalan zavallı bir köylüydüm ben, köyüme dönmeden önce son gece bir sandal gezintisine çıkmıştım. [...] 'Sivil' kıyafetler içinde de olsa, Paşa daha çok bana benziyordu, ben de, daha çok bir köylüye" (*KK* 303).

rate shadow to his success; he wanted to be "real." He predicted that the nation would go under the yoke of yet another dictator forty years later who would be this one, now dressed as a merchant:

> 'You!' he said, emphasizing the word.[11] 'After all these years, I realize now with astonishment that you are less real than myself! You, poor peasant!' [...] Inside the real Kayseri peasant clothes my assistant was so proud to put together for me, I felt not so much ridiculous as inauthentic, having been compelled to partake in a dream that was entirely against my will.[12]

To end the competition, the pretender gets expulsed from college and plunges into business where he turns very successful, and having succeeded at elevating himself to the position of a master now, narrates to his captive – the real president – stories similar to this one. The letter concludes this "story" with a comment that "The times when sultans wandered among people in disguise are over; it is a thing found only in the world of books."[13] The writer of the letter (the real "Pasha President") admits that he came across a similar story in a history book in which Sultan Selim, disguised as a dervish, beats Shah Ismail in a chess game. After Selim takes the city of Tabriz at the Battle of Chalderon, the Shah recalls who beat him at chess years ago. The narrator wonders whether the Shah remembers all the moves of the game from so long. For, he contemplates, his pretender must surely remember all the moves in their own game. The letter ends abruptly with a request for a subscription renewal to the chess magazine *King and Pawn*.

---

[11] Freely's translation of this sentence makes the master-slave relationship even more pronounced: "'You!' talking to me as if I were his inferior" (*BB* 314)

[12] "'Sen' dedi kelimenin üzerinde durarak, 'Yıllarca bekledikten sonra, benden daha az gerçek olduğunu bu akşam şaşkınlıkla gördüğüm sen! Zavallı köylü!' [...] Yaverimin gerçek bir Kayseri köylüsü kıyafeti diye övünerek düzdüğü elbiseler içinde, gülünç olmaktan çok, gerçekdışı olduğumu, hiç de istemediğim bir biçimde, bir rüyanın parçası haline getirildiğimi hissediyordum" (*KK* 305).

[13] "Artık padişahların kıyafet değiştirip halk arasına karıştığı dönemler çok geride, yalnızca kitaplarda kaldı" (*KK* 306).

Scholars of the *Arabian Nights* who studied the story of "The False Caliph" in detail have already pointed to its limitations in exploring the theme of the double in comparison to more successful stories such as "Qamar al-Zaman," "The Sleeper Awakened" or "Khalifah the Fisherman" (Beaumont, *Slave* 87, Chauvin 100, Gerhardt 428). Pamuk, instead, complicates the theme of doubles by exploring its hierarchical nature through the unstable power dynamic of the master-slave dialectic. Like the *Nights'* false caliph, Pamuk's pretender compels the real president to strip off his clothes and, consequently, of his power. Pamuk underscores the reversal of positions by presenting a view of the real president (the master) from the position of the other (the slave), thereby first bringing the two at a level gaze (at the back of the Chevy) and subsequently, reducing the merchant-clad Pasha President to the status of the pretender's slave. This theme is further explored at the end when the real President brings an end to the curfew and lifts the martial law; as well as with the reference to the story of Sultan Selim and Shah Ismail and the magazine *King and Pawn*. The incident between Selim and Ismail (like the one between the pretender and the president) is a story of the imaginary ego fascinated and trapped by the image of the other. Disguised as a dervish, Selim beats Ismail in a game and then on the battlefield. Upon reading this story, the real president fears the pending defeat of his pretender and requests a subscription renewal for *King and Pawn* – the desire to emerge from the imaginary relation of the ego to the other and to submit to the symbolic order which as it is here, is never stable and always under threat. The master is never always the master, a fact that is evident in the moment of fear when the real president is caught and interrogated, and even more pronounced in his oblivion to the plotting of his rival. Why else would the story end with the narrator's request for a renewed subscription to *King and Pawn,* other than to reveal his desire to map his pretender's moves? Pamuk imbues all the levels of his story with a closely-knit interweaving of the themes of the double and master-slave reversal in a way that the *Nights*' False Caliph fails to accomplish.

Before I conclude, I would like to briefly return to the end of the chapter on "Love Stories" which I discussed earlier. At the end of that chapter, Galip narrates a story about a lonely columnist whose only excitement in life is to read and re-read Proust's *À la recherche du temps perdu*, to dream of Albertine, and to imagine that he belongs to the world of Proust's novel. The columnist is so wrapped up in his imagination and identifies so deeply with Proust's hero and with Proust himself that he believes he himself wrote the novel. Eventually, he despises those around him because he loves a book they have never read and because he has written a book they can never write. Pamuk does not fail to seize on the opportunity to insert a cultural critique into the story when his narrator connects the habit of reading books to social peace and prosperity. The columnist comments that nobody in "this country" knows who Albertine is, or even who Proust is, which is why the country is in such a wretched state:

> Perhaps when people in this country began to appreciate Proust and Albertine, these impoverished and mustachioed people on the streets would begin to live better lives, perhaps then, they would stop butchering each other the moment jealousy seized them and instead, like Proust, would plunge into fantasies of how they would conjure up their lovers in their mind's eye.[14]

It seems this story gave rise to some ideas Pamuk would develop later for his Peace Prize acceptance speech, which he delivered in Frankfurt in 2005. In it, Pamuk skillfully weaves together his passion for writing as he articulates some sophisticated ideas about literature's capacity to address our most hidden fears in relation to "the other" that is central to one's understanding of themselves. Like the old columnist in Galip's story who takes a moment to analyze the country in which he lives, and the society that surrounds him, Pamuk writes:

> Modern societies, tribes, and nations do their deepest thinking about themselves through reading novels; through reading novels, they are able to argue about who they are; so even if we have

---

[14] "Bir gün Proust'u ve Albertine'i anlayacak birileri bu ülkede çıktığında, evet belki o zaman sokaklardaki bıyıklı ve yoksul insanlar daha iyi bir hayat yaşamaya başlayacaklar, belki o zaman, ilk kıskançlık anında birbirlerini bıçaklayacaklarına, Proust gibi sevgililerinin hayalini gözlerinin önünde nasıl canlandırdıkları üzerine hayallere dalacaklardı" (*KK* 174).

picked up a novel hoping only to divert ourselves, and relax, and escape the boredom of everyday life, we begin, without realising, to conjure up the collectivity, the nation, the society to which we belong. This is also why novels give voice not just to a nation's pride and joy, but also to its anger, its vulnerabilities, and its shame. It is because they remind readers of their shame, their pride, and their tenuous place in the world that novelists still arouse such anger, and what a shame it is that we still see outbursts of intolerance – that we still see books burned, and novelists prosecuted. ("In Kars" 5-6)

Jale Parla argues that *The Black Book* is black because it puts literature on a pedestal higher than that of life (109). Clearly, her argument finds justification in the columnist's words above. *The Black Book* is a dark book also because it cannot break free from the world of literature and constantly turns upon itself and finds itself trapped in the dark hole it creates. The ending of Galip's "love story" befits these implications: The old columnist entrusts his story to a young colleague who decides to pen it down. The old columnist finds it devastating that his lofty love for Proust and Albertine is to be reduced to the taste of common readers who read the paper to gain information for the most serious and equally mundane issues, wrap up fish in the same paper, and then line their garbage cans with it. The columnist's story is eventually written down and it is this story that we, the readers, read in *The Black Book* and I write about now, and you, the reader, read about and so on. At the end of this chapter, the narrator directly comments on *The Black Book*'s spiraling effect that makes the novel another variation on the *Nights*:

Like the real old journalist, the old journalist in the story had a tabby cat. The old journalist of the newspaper column felt devastated when he read that he was ridiculed in a story published in a newspaper column. When the old journalist read the names of Proust and Albertine in the story within that story in the column, he too wanted to die. From the old journalist's endless and bottomless nightmares of the last unhappy nights of his life, lonely journalists, Prousts, and Albertines emerged one by one in the story within the story within the story.[15]

Isn't it these nightmares that give *The Black Book* its color?

Unable to face the grimness of reality and the crude act of reducing the imaginary to the symbolic of language, the columnist dies. Galip's story confirms how allusions to the *Nights* in *The Black Book* circle and coil vine-like through other works which were also influenced by the *Nights*, in this case, Proust's *À la recherche*. Scholars have already written extensively about the extent to which Proust structures and patterns his own *magnum opus* on the *Nights* (Beaumont, "Bedtime Story"; Graham; Jullien; Topping). An interesting moment occurs close to the end of *À la recherche*, which explains the drama of Galip's love story but also throws light on Pamuk's fascination with the *Nights*. Marcel, the narrator, articulates his own obsession with the *Nights*:

> […] when you are in love with some particular book, you would like yourself to write something that closely resembles it, but this love of the moment must be sacrificed, you must think not of your own taste but of a truth which far from asking you what your preferences are forbids you to pay attention to them. And only if you faithfully follow this truth will you sometimes […] find that, by forgetting these works themselves, you have written the *Arabian Nights* […]. (Vol. 4, 524-25)

By forgetting the *Nights*, Pamuk has written the *Nights*. *The Black Book* ends with the memorable "Because nothing can be as astounding as life. Except for writing. Except for writing. Yes, indeed, the sole consolation,

---

[15] "Hikayedeki ihtiyar gazetecinin de, gerçek ihtiyar gazeteci gibi bir tekir kedisi varmış. Köşe yazısındaki ihtiyar gazeteci de, bir köşe yazısında anlatılan hikâyede kendisiyle alay edildiğini görünce sarsılıyormuş. O anlatılan hikâyenin içindeki hikâyede de ihtiyar gazeteci, Proust'un ve Albertine'in adlarını gazetede görünce ölmek istiyormuş. Hikâyenin içindeki hikâyenin içindeki, hikâyenin içindeki yalnız gazeteciler, Proust'lar ve Albertine'ler ihtiyar yazarın hayatının son mutsuz gecelerinin kâbuslarında dipsizlik ve sonsuzluk kuyularından birer birer ortaya çıkmışlar" (*KK* 175-76).

writing."[16] The ending confirms Pamuk's unfailing faith in the power of writing and literature but especially in the power of storytelling to mount critique – personal, political, and cultural. Pamuk's home, then, is the world of storytelling and cultural assessment as much as the city of Istanbul.

Works Cited

Adak, Hülya. Pamuk'un "Ansiklopedik Romanı." Kara Kitap *Üzerine Yazılar*. Ed. Nüket Esen. İstanbul: İletişim, 1996. 275-94.

Afridi, Mehnaz M., and David M. Buyze. *Global Perspectives on Orhan Pamuk: Existentialism and Politics*. New York: Palgrave Macmillan, 2012.

Anadolu-Okur, Nilgun, ed. *Essays Interpreting the Writings of Novelist Orhan Pamuk*. Lewiston, N.Y: Mellen, 2009.

Beaumont, Daniel. "Bedtime Story: Aspects of *The 1001 Nights* in Proust's *Recherche*." *Arabic Literary Culture: Tradition, Reception and Performance*. Ed. Margaret Larkin. Wiesbaden: Harrassowitz, forthcoming.

___. *Slave of Desire: Sex, Love, and Death in* The 1001 Nights. Madison, NJ: Fairleigh Dickinson UP, 2002.

Birkalan, Hande A. "*The Thousand and One Nig*hts in Turkish: Translations, Adaptations, and Issues." *Fabula* 45 (2004): 221-36.

Brendemoen, Bernt. "Orhan Pamuk: Bir Türkçe Sözdizimi Yenilikçisi." Kara Kitap *Üzerine Yazılar*. Ed. Nüket Esen. İstanbul: Iletişim, 1996: 128-41.

Chauvin, Victor. *Bibliographie des ouvrages arabes*. Liege: H. Vaillant-Carmanne, 1902.

Damrosch, David. *What Is World Literature?* Princeton, N.J: Princeton UP, 2003.

Eberhard, Wolfram, and Pertev N. Boratav. *Typen Türkischer Volksmärchen*. Wiesbaden: F. Steiner, 1953.

---

[16] "Çünkü hiçbir şey hayat kadar şaşırtıcı olamaz. Yazı hariç. Yazı hariç. Evet tabii, tek teselli yazı hariç" (*KK* 442).

Eckermann, Johann Peter. *Gespräche mit Goethe in den letzten Jahren seines Lebens*. Ed. Regine Otto. Berlin: Aufbau, 1982.
Esen, Nüket, Ed. Kara Kitap *Üzerine Yazılar*. İstanbul: İletişim, 1996.
Gerhardt, Mia I. *The Art of Story-Telling: A Literary Study of the Thousand and One Nights*. Leiden: E.J. Brill, 1963.
Goytisolo, Juan. "Orhan Pamuk'un *Kara Kitap*'ı." Trans. G. Işık. Kara Kitap *Üzerine Yazılar*. Ed. Nüket Esen. İstanbul: İletişim, 1996: 295-314.
Göknar, Erdağ M. *Orhan Pamuk, Secularism and Blasphemy: The Politics of the Turkish Novel*. New York: Routledge, 2013.
Graham, Victor. "Marcel Proust and the *Mille et une nuits*." *Canadian Review of Comparative Literature* 1 (1974): 89-96.
Gürçağlar, Şehnaz Tahir. *The Politics and Poetics of Translation in Turkey, 1923-1960*. Amsterdam: Rodopi, 2008.
Haddawy, Husain, and Muhsin Mahdi. *The Arabian Nights*. New York, NY: W.W. Norton, 2008.
Hadzibegovic, Darmin, and Orhan Pamuk. Kara Kitap*'ın Sırları: Orhan Pamuk'un Yazı ve Resimleriyle*. İstanbul: İletişim, 2013.
Havlioğlu, Didem. "Border Crossing with *The Black Book*: Overcoming Spatial, Cultural, and Linguistic Distances." *Approaches to Teaching the Works of Orhan Pamuk*. Ed. Sevinç Türkkan and David Damrosch. New York: MLA, forthcoming.
Jullien, Dominique. "Ailleurs ici: *Les mille et une nuits* dans *À la recherche du temps perdu*. *Romanic Review* 79.3 (May 1988): 466-75
Karadağ, Raif. *1001 Gece Masalları*. Vol. 1. İstanbul: Ak, 1959.
___. *1001 Gece Masalları*. Vols. 3-4. İstanbul: Ak, 1961.
Kim, Sooyong. "Master and Disciple: Sufi Mysticism as an Interpretive Framework in Orhan Pamuk's *Kara kitap*." *Turkish Studies Association Bulletin* 17.2 (1993): 23-42.
Kılıç, Engin. *Orhan Pamuk'u Anlamak*. İstanbul: İletişim, 1999.
Lyons, Malcolm C., and Ursula Lyons. *The Arabian Nights: Tales of 1001 Nights*. London: Penguin, 2010.
Mattar, Karim. "Orhan Pamuk and the Limits of Translation: Foreignizing *The Black Book* for World Literature." *Translation and Literature* 23. 1 (2014): 42-67.

McGaha, Michael D. *Autobiographies of Orhan Pamuk: The Writer in His Novels*. Salt Lake City: University of Utah Press, 2008.

Moran, Berna. *Türk Romanına Eleştirel Bir Bakış: Sevgi Soysal'dan Bilge Karasu'ya*. Vol. 3. İstanbul: İletişim, 2007.

Pamuk, Orhan. *The Black Book*. Trans. M. Freely. New York: Vintage International/Vintage, 2006. Trans. of *Kara kitap*. İstanbul: İletişim, 2000.

___. *The Black Book*. Trans. Güneli Gün. New York: Farrar, Straus & Giroux, 1994. Trans. of *Kara kitap*. İstanbul: İletişim, 2000.

___. *Cevdet Bey ve oğulları* [Cevdet Bey and His Sons]. İstanbul: Karacan, 1982.

___. "Dünya Edebiyatı." *Öteki renkler: Seçme yazılar ve bir hikaye*. İstanbul: Yapı Kredi, 2013: 218-20.

___. "In Kars and Frankfurt: Acceptance Speech." Trans. Maureen Freely. Accessed 13 Jan. 2017 <http://www.friedenspreis-des-deutschen-buch handels.de/sixcms/media.php/1290/Orhan%20Pamuk%20Acceptance%20speech%202005.pdf>.

___. *Kara kitap*. İstanbul: İletişim, 2000.

___. "Love, Death and Storytelling." Trans. Maureen Freely. *New Statesman* 18 Dec. 2006-4 Jan. 2007: 34-36.

___. *Other Colors: Essays and a Story*. Trans. M. Freely. New York: Knopf, 2007.

___. *Öteki renkler: Seçme yazılar ve bir hikâye*. İstanbul: Yapı Kredi, 2013.

___. *Silent House*. Trans. Robert P. Finn. New York: Knopf, 2012. Trans. of *Sessiz ev: Roman*. İstanbul: Can, 1983.

___. *The White Castle: A Novel*. Trans. V. Holbrook. New York: Braziller, 1991. Trans. of *Beyaz kale: Roman*. İstanbul: Can, 1985.

Parla, Jale. "*Kara kitap* neden kara?" *Kara kitap üzerine yazılar*. Ed. Nüket Esen. İstanbul: İletişim, 1996: 102-09.

Proust, Marcel. *In Search of Lost Time*. Vol. 6. Trans. A. Mayor, T. Kilmartin, D. J. Enright, and J. Kilmartin. London: Vintage, 1996.

Seyhan, Azade. *Tales of Crossed Destinies: The Modern Turkish Novel in a Comparative Context*. New York: Modern Language Association of America, 2008.

Topping, Margaret. "Les mille et une nuits Proustiennes." *Essays in French Literature* 35-36 (1998-1999): 113-30.

Türkkan, Sevinç. "Orhan Pamuk's *Kara kitap*: (British) Reception vs. (American) Translation." *Making Connections: Interdisciplinary Approaches to Cultural Diversity*, 11.2 (2010): 39-58.

___. "Orhan Pamuk's *Kara kitap* [*The Black Book*]: A Double Life in English." *Global Perspectives on Orhan Pamuk: Existentialism and Politics*. Ed. Mehnaz M. Afridi and David M. Buyze. London: Palgrave Macmillan, 2012: 159-76.

___. "Orhan Pamuk's Novels in German." *Türkisch-deutsche Studien: Jahrbuch*. Ed. Şeyda Özil, Michael Hofmann, Yasemin Dayıoğlu-Yücel. Vol. 7. Forthcoming.

Provincialism in Orhan Pamuk's *Snow* and Turkey's Controversial Political History[1]

Zafer Doğan
Yıldız Technical University

Abstract: *Snow* stands out in Orhan Pamuk's oeuvre as the only novel with an overtly political theme. Revolving around a failed coup attempt, *Snow* sheds light on the conflict between secularist and Islamist powers in Turkish politics as well as on life in a provincial city in the country. In its first section, this essay analyses the two themes of provincialism and Westernisation in the light of socio-political factors that have shaped Turkish politics in the last sixty years. The second section scrutinises Pamuk's political vision in the light of influential political theories developed, among others, by contemporary Turkish thinkers such as Şerif Mardin.

Set in a poverty-stricken, semi-fictional, provincial town, Orhan Pamuk's *Snow* deals with many ever-topical issues of Turkey's recent history such as the tension between East and West, the painful relationship between the common people and the intellectuals, secularism, political Islam and authoritarian state tradition. The conflict between the community and the individual, loneliness and provincialism, love and happiness are but some of the subjects of the novel. The novel, which combines existentialist anxieties with political predicaments in the peripheral province of an already peripheral country, begins with the poet Ka (Kerim Alakuşoğlu)'s journey from Istanbul to the snow-covered city of Kars.

Having published an article without reading it while working as the editor of a magazine towards the end of the seventies, the poet Ka has been forced to seek asylum in Germany as a political refugee because of the military coup of September 12, 1980. Though exiled for political reasons, he leads a simple life, withdrawing from politics altogether. No longer being the carrier of a mission or representing a political identity, Ka grows apart from other political exiles who find him highbrow and snobbish. He retires into his private world. After twelve years in Germany, Ka returns to Istanbul to attend his mother's funeral where he receives a job offer from a

---

[1] Translated from Turkish by Taner Can.

friend to work as a correspondent for a national newspaper to investigate a suicide epidemic among women in Kars. The suicide epidemic has first attracted the attention of a statistician in Ankara. Though published in a local newspaper, the issue does not make it into the national press until the foreign media get interested. In other words, it is only after the centre has been alerted to them that provincials start to take an interest in their own problems. Ka sets out for Kars to investigate issues arising through the possibility of the Islamist party's victory in the soon-to-be-held municipal elections and the non-acceptance of headscarved girls to the Educational Institute, but in fact he has a personal motive for coming to Kars. He has found out that İpek, whom he met in a political group in his university years, is divorced and now runs a hotel in Kars with her father Turgut and her sister Kadife, which revives Ka's hope for her love.

The attraction of his secret love for İpek draws Ka to Kars. There is yet another reason why he comes to Kars: his longing for a romantic childhood dream that is not comprised in his middle-class childhood memories. He can only make this naïve and romantic dream come true by returning to the poorest and forsaken corner of Turkey (Roselli 81). Ka, thus, embarks on a romantic quest for the countryside and nature. Yet, his search will result in disappointment. Within a short time the romantic provincial theme will be replaced by an image of provincial life abundant with violence, foolish and ridiculous fights, and bigotry.

It is not only poverty and desperation that attracts Ka to Kars; he also likes the feeling of loneliness he finds there. Snow is a recurrent image in the novel. The unique shape of each snowflake symbolises Ka's loneliness and his desire to be himself again. Ironically, Ka also wants to overcome loneliness, the reason for his unhappiness. This means he has to mix with others by joining a community and embracing religion. The conflict between Ka's Western, cosmopolitan identity and locality tinted with religion is one of the leitmotifs in the novel. The only thing that Ka knows about Islam is *The Message*, a film starring Anthony Quinn. Ka's presence in Kars is as ironic and alienating as a non-Muslim acting in a film about Islam.

Ka encounters obstacles of politics, violence and poverty in his pursuit of the world's hidden symmetry and love. Religious sects, political groups and the state do not allow the individual, love or creativity to exist. Ka finds himself entrapped in political intrigues in Kars, where he has come in pursuit of happiness, love and his romantic childhood. Ka witnesses a political murder in a café where he meets İpek. An Islamist militant kills the Director of Education Institute for barring girls with headscarf from the classroom. Ka cannot see the murderer's face, but there is a rumour in town that the murderer is a militant called Blue. Blue, rumoured to have fought in Bosnia and Grozny and murdered a television presenter, soon meets Ka, who has come to the city as a journalist.

Another person that Ka's life intersects with is Sunay Zaim. Zaim and his wife run a traveling theatre company. Zaim has been expelled from military high school because of slipping over to Istanbul to perform in theatres and also for staging a secret performance of a political play. He becomes famous for acting Jacobean characters in political theatre companies in the 1970s. His nomination to act Atatürk in a film is the turning point in his career. Discredited by scandals, Zaim sets out to travel through Anatolia with his company to earn his living. His life takes an unexpected turn when he comes across Colonel Osman Nuri Çolak, an old classmate of his from military high school while drinking at a restaurant in Kars. Zaim persuades the colonel, a frustrated man with with no prospects for promotion, to join him in his political ambitions. Sunay Zaim and the colonel organise a military coup, taking advantage of the unceasing snow cutting off the city completely from the outside world. The revolution needs not only weapons but also Sunay Zaim's art as it will start during a performance. It is through his portrayal of Sunay Zaim that Pamuk criticises a common stereotype – the artist who supports militarism and state authoritarianism.

The name of the theatre company, 'Nation,' and the large canvas of characters represented among the audience and actors indicate that the novel unfolds in the form of a national allegory. When religious vocational high school students in the audience are provoked to outbursts by a play, soldiers who are present on the stage as part of the performance open fire at the audience with live bullets instead of blanks. Sunay Zaim's loud voice declares the beginning of the coup on stage: "This is not a play but the beginning of a revolution" (163). The finale of the coup designed by Sunay Zaim also takes place on stage in a performance three days later and is broadcast by a local TV channel. According to the scenario, Kadife, the leader of headscarved girls, shoots Sunay Zaim at the end of the play. Zaim replaces the blanks in the gun with live ones, and Kadife shoots him even though she knows about the live bullets.

Fact and fiction, performance and reality are thus interwoven throughout the novel. This is not simply an outcome of the writer's postmodern black humour. As Michael McGaha indicates, we here encounter two recurrent themes:

> A central concern in all of Pamuk's novels is Turkey's troubled love-hate relationship with the West. Although they differ greatly in their plots, characters and styles, his novels are unified by the constant, obsessive recurrence of two major themes: the problem of identity (how can an individual or a nation remain true to itself while accepting valuable influences from others?) and the problem of representation (Can art truly represent reality? And to what extent is it legitimate for the artist to express his own ideas and personality in his writing?). ("Poetry")

Sunay Zaim's suicide on stage is reminiscent of Beşir Fuat's cold-blooded experimental suicide.[2] Beşir Fuat rejected all kinds of metaphysical thought and held science sacred and above all else, which drew him into a dilemma. A similar predicament befalls Sunay. The only difference is that in his case art takes the place of science. Sunay, seeing art as a sacred transcendental force, substitutes it for reality, which prepares his end.

Trapped in a spiral of violence triggered by the bloody coup on stage, Ka's only aim is to survive and escape to Frankfurt with the woman he loves. To this end, he flirts with political communities in Kars and takes part in some plots that he does not believe in. Ka claims that he has a journalist friend named Hans Hansen, and that an anti-coup declaration could be published in the *Frankfurter Rundschau* newspaper. A secret meeting is

---

[2] Beşir Fuat was an Ottoman intellectual who championed positivist and materialist philosophy, and wrote about science, philosophy and literary criticism. He committed suicide at the age of 35 in 1887. He cut his wrists and recorded his feelings and thoughts on a piece of paper until he lost his consciousness. After this incident, a suicide epidemic broke out among young people in Istanbul.

organised in Hotel Asia to publish the declaration, bringing together all political factions in Kars. Yet, the meting soon turns into a political vaudeville. The love and hate relationship between East and West is expressed in an ironical way through Dostoyevskian dialogues and scandalous scenes. When Ka urges him to sign the declaration, Turgut Bey agrees on one condition – that everyone in the meeting must answer his question: "If a big German newspaper gave you personally two lines of space, what would you have to say to the West?" (273). The discussion among the carnivalesque crowd, laden with black humour and irony, that is caused by this simple but striking question comprises the most vital section of the novel

As the time wears on, the meeting takes on an atmosphere filled with occidentalist clichés. Everyone talks heatedly about how Westerners perceive them, and how Westerners are viewed by the people of this small provincial town:

> "say [...] the first Western man I met in the street turned out to be a good person who didn't despise me, I'd still mistrust him, just for being a Westerner, I'd still worry that this man was looking down on me. Because, in Germany, they can spot people from Turkey just by the way they look. There's no avoiding humiliation except by proving at the first opportunity that you think exactly as they do. But this is impossible, and it can break a man's pride to try" (284)

The relationship between centre and periphery seems to rest on this essential dynamic, what is put here simply as "breaking of pride." It is this feeling of humiliation that leads the provincials to despise everything that the centre stands for, and to embrace everything that is abased by it. One of the young Islamists in the meeting responds to Turgut Bey's question with such reactance: "I'm proud of the part of me that isn't European. I'm proud of the things that the Europeans find childish, cruel, and primitive. If the Europeans are beautiful, I want to be ugly; if they're intelligent, I prefer to be stupid; if they're modern, let me stay simple" (285).

In response to Turgut Bey's question, another speaker describes a dream that he often has, which reveals insights into what it means to be part of a provincial community with all its aspirations, reactions and abasements:

> Pausing from time to time with a shiver, he explained how in this dream he'd been sitting all alone in the National Theatre watching a film. It was a Western film, and everyone in it was speaking a foreign language, but this didn't make him uncomfortable; he somehow understood everything they said. And then, in the blink of an eye, he entered the film itself; it turned out that his seat was not in the National Theatre but in the sitting room of a Christian family. There, before his eyes, was a table laden with food; he longed to fill his stomach, but for fear of doing something wrong he kept his distance. His heart began to race: there, before him, was a beautiful blond woman, and the moment he saw her he remembered that he'd been in love with her for years. The woman was warmer and more gentle than he could ever imagine. She complimented him on his clothes and his manners, kissed his cheeks, and ran her fingers through his hair. He felt so very happy. Before he knew it, she sat him on her lap and pointed out the food on the table. Only then did he realize that he was still a child [...]. It was because he was still a child that she found him so charming. (287)

The dream is a clear reflection of the provincials' reaction to being excluded, which Amin Maalouf terms as "temptation of the precipice":

> It is not so much the sting of poverty which causes their distress as that of humiliation and insignificance, the feeling of not belonging in the world they live in, of being only losers, downtrodden and excluded. And so they dream of ruining the feast to which they have not been invited. (240)

A combination of sexual desire and the aspiration to Westernisation, the dream reveals the anger and longing of late modernisation and provincialism which can find acceptance only as a child.

There is an unbridgeable gap between the experience of modernisation by the West and by the provincial countries at its periphery, respectively. At one end of this gap there is an obsessive love for the West and at the other there are disappointments. It is inevitable that such disappointments turn into reactance, even childish reactance, as in platonic love. Oğuz Atay, one of the Turkish writers that greatly influenced Orhan Pamuk, explains this reactance with a childhood metaphor: "Our childish pride! We immediately take offence when we are not liked. We do everything to clear our names by slandering Westerners. We are just like urchins denigrating children from good families" (28). Reactance is a quality of children or the child-like. Atay parodies the nationalist anger of underdeveloped countries and dilemmas born out of their inadequate adaptation to the modern world: "It seems to me that our nation has remained a child. We still interpret facts and the world according to miracles and myths in a spirit of high seriousness, which any Westerner in his right mind will find amusing" (26).
The dream above in a way sums up the story of platonic, unrequited love between Europe and the Turkey at its fringes. The frustration that the provincial, hopelessly in love with the beautiful blond woman representing Europe, feels illustrates Turkey's collective unconsciousness.

The provincial is not taken seriously as an adult but only found cute like a child. It is a double-edged criticism aimed not only at the province but also at Europe: The main reason for provincial reactance is Europe's unwillingness to share its wealth and grant others a place at the table. Another aspect of this criticism is the Westerners' exclusivist attitude towards provincial people, whom they can only view as ridiculous, bizarre, and incomprehensible, not as equals.

In *Snow*, Pamuk employs all the formal possibilities of a national allegory, as he points out in an interview with Jörg Lau: "I want to describe the condition of people's souls in a city. The city is called Kars and it is situated in the outermost north-easterly edge of Turkey, but it is a microcosm which to some extent stands for Turkey as a whole." The meeting in Hotel Asia shows how permeable the boundaries between the private and public issues are; even sexuality – perhaps the most private human issue – is closely interwoven with national or religious concerns. Pamuk is at pains to show that the conflict between East and West is both a concrete and painful fact and a ridiculous fiction. The crowd gathered at the hotel is drawn into a debate about the West and Westerners. Although most of them have not been to Europe, they talk about Europe with childish naïveté and heatedness. The hotel's name is no coincidence, either. The speeches in the meeting are bristling with Occidentalist prejudices. Both the childishness of the reactions caused by the backwardness of the province and the centre that condemns the province to this kind of reactance get their share of the novel's irony. It is its astute observations about provincialism that make *Snow* a successful novel. Kars can be considered doubly provincial when compared to Istanbul and Europe, which makes it a unique setting. Whereas in *Istanbul*, Pamuk tells the story of a city which has become provincial at the European fringes when its glorious days of the past were over, *Snow* is the story of a town at the periphery of a peripheral country. Ka soon regrets coming to Kars: "[...] first he mused about what a fool he'd been to leave Istanbul for Kars, and then concluded it had been a mistake even to leave Germany and return to Turkey" (179-80). However, he also enjoys "the easy sense of superiority he possessed from knowing he was from Istanbul and Frankfurt" (312). Ironically, this sense of superiority condemns him to remain a stranger in Kars:

> 'For the first time in years, I'm very happy,' said Ka. 'Why shouldn't I believe the same things as you?'
> 'Because you belong to high society,' said Necip. 'People in high society never believe in God. They believe in what Europeans do, so they think they're better than ordinary people.'
> 'I may belong to high society,' said Ka. "But in Germany I'm a worthless nobody. I was falling apart there.' (105)

The author places these complex identity problems between centre and periphery at the heart of the novel with stories set in these three locations. Necip looks down on Ka as a snobbish intellectual from Istanbul, but wants to publish an Islamic science fiction novel he is writing in a classy

Istanbul paper that sells thousands of copies instead of a local one that sells only seventy-five. The question to be examined in this context is what viewpoint the periphery takes to its own periphery in turn? The Turkish sociologist Şükrü Argın's approach brings to the fore another aspect of this issue:

> The gaze of the centre at the province is a bashful one, embarrassed under the gaze of another centre: the West's. That is why Turkish intellectuals are doubly ashamed when in the countryside for one reason or another: on their own account and on account of the Westerners as their own gaze at the province is always already overshadowed by a Western gaze. They are in the position of both the gazer and the gazed at. They are ashamed of what they see because it reveals to them what they look like themselves. (289-90)

How can the paradox be resolved that the centre gazing at the province is itself the peripheral province of yet another centre? Does an intellectual viewing the periphery of their country feel disturbed by the gaze of a third eye, that of a Westerner? As a writer for whom the question of identity has become one of his central themes, Orhan Pamuk naturally confronts these questions obliquely in the novel. Ka is a stranger everywhere, be it in Kars, Istanbul or Frankfurt; therefore he is lonely and exiled everywhere. That he fails to learn German despite living in Germany for years, that he fails to connect to either Germans or immigrant Turks in Germany, that in Kars, he is considered a posh snob from Istanbul while in Istanbul, he is indistinguishable from a stranger – these are all different manifestations of his estrangement and homelessness. On the other hand, people in Kars are not at peace with their own provincialism. There are pictures of the Swiss Alps hanging on the walls of restaurants, teahouses and hotels in Kars, not the local mountains they are so proud of. There is no doubt that Pamuk chose Kars, the easternmost city in Turkey, isolated as it is, as the setting of the novel intentionally. It is one of the poorest and remotest cities in Turkey, which has become part of the cliché of the country that prides itself with extending from Edirne in the remotest west to Kars in the remotest east. It is the capital of provincial life that you can admire from afar but that clamps down on you when you enter it.

For Pamuk, Kars stands as a microcosm representing Turkey allegorically. He criticises not only the province, but also the centre. As the story unfolds, it becomes clearer that it is the centre that construes the province and that is behind the deficiency of the province. This centre is twofold: there is a native centre identified with Istanbul and Ankara and one Western centre identified with Frankfurt. Within this double helix the fates of Kars and the twofold centre intersect. While Turkey is vehemently criticised for its military coups, political violence and oppression of the individual, the higher-level centre is also dealt with. Pamuk's vantage point is not based on that of either side. For this reason, he cannot be situated on either side of a line separating pro-Western and Pro-Eastern perspectives. As an Easterner in the West and a Westerner in the East, Pamuk offers a novel perspective transcending such divisions of identity and discrimination – a perspective based on an attempt to understand each other and to place oneself in each other's place. *Snow* also discusses the possibilities and limits of this novel perspective:

> Here, perhaps, we have arrived at the heart of our story. How much can we ever know about the love and pain in another's heart? How much can we hope to understand those who have suffered deeper anguish, greater deprivation and more crushing disappointments than we ourselves have known? Even if the world's rich and powerful should ever try to put themselves in the shoes of the rest, how much would they really understand the wretched millions suffering around them? (266)

Snow is based on a character who, trying to understand the reasons that lead to misunderstandings, is in the best position to unravel these free-floating and unsteady identities. Ka is a poet in exile. He fits in nowhere. He is the Other in Frankfurt and a stranger in his own country. In other words, he is homeless. Even faith becomes a matter of conflict with the society he comes from. He yearns to be a true believer, but not in the way in which the people in his country believe and practise their belief. Faith is not only a theological problem here, but an existential matter. It is often not possible to have faith as an individual, without becoming part of a collective identity, particularly in the province, where faith is only possible by belonging to certain places or communities.

Membership in a community is considered more important than one's individual personality in provincial life. Individual non-assertiveness and subordination to the community are the key to social harmony where traditional lifestyle and culture are predominant. Ka, however, is yearning to preserve his unique identity like a snowflake while becoming an integral part of the community he is living in. He is aware that this paradox cannot be resolved. Like other intellectuals trapped between traditional and modern values, Ka seeks a relief from the resulting pressure and unhappiness. He is aware that he can only achieve this by embracing the traditional lifestyle, but the modern mind-set he has acquired makes this impossible: "I want to believe in the God you believe in and be like you, but because there's a Westerner inside me, my mind is confused" (100). Seen from this angle, Ka's indecisiveness is due to the question whether it is possible to become an integral part of the community and tradition around him without giving up his individuality. Ka's vacillation also reflects the intellectuals' dilemma of being caught between modernity and tradition.

It is difficult to be a snowflake in the province, to preserve one's personality there that is as unique as the shape of every single snowflake. In his pursuit of individual desires, Ka faces a two-fold dilemma. The first one is that of the communal voice that supresses his own. Ka fails to come to terms with the oppressive, authoritarian and violently political nature of provincial life that makes the individual blurry and does not allow one to live a life without becoming part of the community. On the other hand, he is also aware that the centre, i.e. the West, to which he has a stronger sense of belonging, cannot understand Kars, the province, from afar. He is suspicious of facile, superficial judgements about provincial life: "'I am new to Kars,'" said Ka. "'Even as I come to understand how things work here, I'm beginning to think I'll never be able to make it clear to anyone on the outside.'" (114)

This effort to explain oneself and to understand the other lends *Snow* an optimistic tone. Pamuk is at pains to emphasise the fact that there is not only one conception of the West but many. The inverse is true for the Eastern civilisation. In this respect, the arguments between Ka and Blue read like a polemic against an essentialist, monolithic viewpoint. The occidentalist attitude, represented by Blue in the novel, is as problematic and deficient as the attitude of the West towards Eastern countries. The end of the novel offers a warning to those who, often arrogantly, try to understand the province in a prejudiced, facile manner:

> [...] I turned back to Fazıl and asked him whether he knew now what he might want to say to my readers if ever I was to write a book set in Kars. [...]
> "If you write a book set in Kars and put me in it, I'd like to tell your readers not to believe anything you say about me, anything you say about any of us. No one could understand us from so far away."
> "But no one believes in that way what he reads in a novel," I said.
> "Oh, yes, they do," he cried. "If only to see themselves as wise and superior and humanistic, they need to think of us as sweet and funny, and convince themselves that they sympathize with the way we are and even love us. But if you would put in what I've just said, at least your readers will keep a little room for doubt in their minds."
> I promised I would put what he'd said into my novel. (435-36)

The symmetry between "Ka," "kar" ('snow' in Turkish) and "Kars," the threefold complementariness and simultaneous interwovenness and contrast, create a paradox that is difficult to resolve. What, then, is Ka's situation? His problem arises from his desire to preserve his own unique identity. The similarity between the words "Ka," "Kars" and "kar" ('snow') in Turkish points to a deeper meaning: Ka is a snowflake ("kar tanesi" in Turkish) and Kars a heap of snow. Ka is a snowflake that refuses to be lost among a heap of snow, desiring to assert its distinctiveness.

We fail to acknowledge that feelings of loneliness, our ambitions, sorrows and joys are in fact universal feelings. The things that we have in common outnumber the things that separate us whether we live in Kars, Istanbul or Frankfurt.

Political Representation in Snow

Snow was published in 2002 and raised great interest both in Turkey and abroad. The attention the novel received, particularly in Europe and the USA, was partly due to the atmosphere in the aftermath of the 9/11 terrorist attacks. *Snow* came to be seen as a guide to understanding political Islam in the intensifying debate on political Islam in the post-9/11 USA:

> Although Pamuk had started writing the novel before the extremist arm of political Islam struck the United States in the form of hijacked commercial airplanes crashing into the World Trade Center, with the release of the novel in English translation he became the unofficial interpreter of Islam for the American public. (Seyhan, "Seeing")

The novel animated critical discussions in Turkey as it revolves around a long-standing controversy between Islam and secularism. Politics in the novel appear on two different planes. On the first plane politics are neglected in favour of love and the individual. Even Ka himself can be regarded as not only an apolitical but even an anti-political hero in this respect: "'I'm saying this to you as someone who's spent years as a political exile. Listen to me: Life's not about principles; it's about happiness'" (319-20). Still, *Snow* cannot be called an apolitical text. To better understand the role of politics on this plane of the novel, it is necessary to outline the author's attitude towards politics and the genre of the political novel.

Writing political novels is a risky business. The political discussions presented in these novels may overshadow their aesthetic value. If political events and facts are not filtered by the novel's aesthetics, the work is susceptible to the risk of turning either into a bad propaganda text or into an artificial, forced ghost of a novel. In an interview about *Snow,* Pamuk explains his views about the essential elements of a good political novel thus:

> Contrary to what most people assume, one's politics as a novelist have nothing to do with the societies, parties, and groups to which one might belong – or with a dedication to any political cause. A novelist's politics arise from his imagination, from his ability to imagine himself as someone else. This power not only allows him to explore human realities previously unremarked – it makes him the spokesman for those who cannot speak for themselves, whose anger is never heard, and whose words are suppressed. (*Other Colours* 340)

It has to be examined whether in *Snow* – and in his general attitude – the writer follows his own precepts, which I share. In view of assertions that the novel is a microcosm representing Turkey, its political and historical background have to be examined as well.

The narrativization of political camps in *Snow* reflects the political evolution and changes in power relations that Turkey underwent over the years. Leftists in the novel are described as "terrorists who proudly took responsibility for bombings" (187). Ka deeply regrets his past, seeing it a meaningless pursuit that "he had ruined his life for" (250). In Pamuk's first novels such clear-cut and crude judgements are absent. In his first novel, *Cevdet Bey and His Sons*, political characters are described with respect: "'He's a decent guy!' thought Ahmet, 'After all he's a revolutionary.'"[3] Similarly, the most favourable character in his novel *The Silent House*, published in 1983 – at a time when despite the coup the left still maintained its reputation, at least in the press, the arts and among intellectuals – is the leftist Nilgün. But Pamuk's attitude would change significantly by the time when he wrote *Snow*.

Turkey underwent radical social and political changes during Orhan Pamuk's writing career spanning almost forty years. The religious-political discourse has become dominant both in society and government at the expense of rational, enlightened and universal values. Indirect and intricate reflections of this can be observed in Pamuk's books. However, traces of a

---

[3] "'Namuslu çocuktur!' diye düşündü Ahmet, 'Ne de olsa devrimci'" (*Cevdet Bey ve oğulları* 560).

revanchist attitude are also discernible in *Snow*. In keeping with this, Pamuk says in an interview, "I feel closer to Ka."[4] Through Ka, who can be considered as the author's alter ego, this revanchist attitude is clearly conveyed: "A wave of anger swept over Ka; this took him back to his first political encounters during his bourgeois days in Nişantaşı" (53). This anger prevails throughout the novel. Every novel is ultimately the product of subjective feelings. The problem here is that the novel's revanchist standpoint turns into an obdurate attitude making it difficult for the author to sympathise with and understand others. So much so that even the most tragic events in the novel is a matter of heartless sarcasm for Ka:

> Ka smiled and told him what he'd heard about Tufan, their curly-haired friend from Malatya, who had once written about 'Third World' issues for various periodicals: he'd lost his mind. Ka had last seen him in the central station in Stuttgart, a long pole with a wet cloth tied to the end in his hand, racing back and forth mopping the floor, whistling as he worked. (60).

In this scene, which could have housed a melancholy irony, a cynical attitude backfires instead. The language used to describe the political camps and individuals in the novel is subjective, one-sided. The images used to describe leftist and secular characters and types are associated with wretchedness, ridiculousness, terrorism and violence. For instance, Ka's comrades who fled to Germany as political refugees like himself face an end that is both ridiculous and absurdly tragic. The language used to portray Islamist characters is, on the other hand, very different. It is striking that while the victims of political murders in Turkey (Turan Dursun, Muammer Aksoy, Uğur Mumcu and many others) are frequently parodied and presented as the victims of an absurdly laughable game, their murderers are simply described as "angry young religionists" (305).

Despite all its achievement and brilliance, it seems that *Snow* deserves similar criticism to that which Pamuk himself directed at Vargas-Llosa's novel *Death in the Andes*. In his short but comprehensive text on Third

---

[4] "Ben kendimi Ka'ya daha yakın hissediyorum" (Kırmızı ve Kar 67).

World literature, Pamuk uses the changes over Llosa's writing career to examine the many facets of Third World literature. Pamuk argues that "the reader is left wondering if Vargas-Llosa the modernist has lost his nerve, for he almost seems to have turned himself into a postmodern anthropologist, returning to his native land to study its irrationality, its violence, its pre-enlightenment values, and its rituals" ("Mario Vargas Llosa" 303). Pamuk examines the novel along with the author's political attitude thus:

> Soldiers are the heroes of *Death in the Andes*. There is little effort to understand the Shining Path guerrillas. They figure as representatives of unadulterated irrationality and an evil that borders on the absurd. This has much to do with the political changes that the author underwent as he grew older. As a young man, the modernist Marxist Vargas Llosa was entranced by the Cuban revolution, but as he matured he became a liberal, and in the 1980s, he was scathing about those who, like Günter Grass, said that "all of Latin America had to use Cuba as an example." Half in jest, Vargas Llosa defined himself as "one of the two writers in the world who admire Margaret Thatcher and hate Fidel Castro," adding that "the other writer, more accurately described as a poet, was Philip Larkin."
>
> After reading his account of the Shining Path guerrillas in *Death in the Andes*, it is quite a surprise to read, in one of Vargas Llosa's youthful essays, a tribute to a Marxist guerrilla, a friend who was killed during a "clash with the Peruvian army." One is left wondering whether the humanity in guerrillas is impossible for people like us to see once our own youth has passed, or is it that after we have passed a certain age people like us have no friends who are guerrillas? (306-07)

Why shouldn't the critical framework that Pamuk offers here be used to assess his own novel? The central political issue in *Snow* is political Islam. The image of political Islam presented in the novel and the author's thoughts on this subject are complementary. To understand the presentation of political Islam in the novel, we may draw on a text by Pamuk written before *Snow* about the Sivas Massacre of 1993, in which fundamentalist Islamists burned alive 35 intellectuals and artists besieged in a hotel:

> I would never have thought that the revolt of small towns, outlying neighbourhoods, those shut out, the underprivileged, those not represented in the centre, the humiliated, the unemployed, the despised, that is to say, of desperate provincials would come about at such a scale and with such dramatic methods.[5]

If the perpetrators of the Sivas Massacre represent the provincial, the intellectuals inside the hotel should by this logic represent the centre. However, there are some contradictions in this reasoning: most of those in the hotel who were killed or narrowly survived were intellectuals exposed to state pressure (i.e. exiled, imprisoned, banned from publishing their works). However, the perpetrators of the Sivas Massacre were not underprivileged or shut out. On the contrary, they acted in the name of faith or nation with the conviction that they were the true representatives of the country. That this confidence rested on a concrete reality is attested to by the fact that the people in the hotel were virtually abandoned to their fate despite their hours-long pleas for help to the authorities.

Can the intellectuals in the hotel be indeed considered to represent the centre? And why can the besieged awaiting their death for eight hours not be saved from the hotel? The list of questions could be extended.

It is not a coincidence that Pamuk regards the Sivas Massacre as "the revolt of the provincials." Pamuk's perception of this event is in keeping with the historian and sociologist Şerif Mardin's critical paradigm laid out in a much discussed article titled "Center-Periphery Relations: A Key to Turkish Politics?". His periphery-centre theory enjoyed a vogue especially among those regarding the armed forces as a "ready force" with a political mission as well as among the intelligentsia criticising the bureaucracy-based reform policy of Kemalism. Şerif Mardin advocated a theoretical

---

[5] "[…] küçük kentlerin, kenar mahallelerin, dışarıda kalmışların, imtiyazsız olanların, merkezde temsil edilmeyenlerin, aşağılanmışların, işsizlerin, hor görülenlerin, kısaca umutsuz taşranın isyanının da bu boyutlarda ve bu dramatik yöntemlerle gerçekleşebileceği aklıma gelmezdi hiç" ("Sivas'tan Diyarbakır'a" 403-04).

framework and a political approach that prioritise the people and civil society over the state. This theory would become influential in the period following the 1980s.

The popularisation among intellectuals of Mardin's Centre-Periphery theory in the analysis of Ottoman-Turkish modernisation was concomitant with the rise of civil society. The September 12, 1980 military coup and the deepening of the Kurdish problem in the 1980s led to the questioning of Kemalism, which was a strong tendency among the left. With Marxist intellectuals' drift towards liberal trends in the wake of the coup, the political atmosphere in Turkey took a new turn. Mardin's political theories became influential among the liberal left, which gained prominence in the intellectual climate of the 1980s and the 1990s. The emerging liberal left also influenced Orhan Pamuk, who became known as a writer from the mid-1980s onward. Indeed, Pamuk himself once revealed, "[...] my views may be called left-liberal."[6]

Şerif Mardin's centre-periphery approach takes the division between state and society as its point of departure and regards political history in Turkey as a product of conflict and alienation between secular political elites in the bureaucracy and religiously committed masses. Mardin's ideas, which laid the theoretical foundation for left liberalism opposed to military coups and to a political system under the tutelage of the armed forms, gained strength in the political atmosphere after the 1980s, when the idea of a civil society became popular. Shared by a significant part of the intelligentsia, which included Orhan Pamuk, Mardin's ideas became the intellectual lever for the civil society advocating nationalism on the ideological plane and greater civil participation on the political plane. Without doubt, the opposition based on a civil society contributed significantly to the extension of democratic norms and awareness about human rights in the political atmosphere of state authoritarianism and oppressive nationalism. The rapprochement between the intellectual movement advocating a civil society and the Islamic/conservative segment turned into a hegemonic alliance in time because of the latter's dissident attitude and its significant political power.

---

[6] "[...] sol liberal diyeceğimiz bir görüşte olduğum söylenebilir" (Kırmızı ve Kar 99).

The political power that the civil society gained in the 1990s and the 2000s is only comparable to the power gained in the 1960s by what Doğan Avcıoğlu (*Türkiye'nin düzeni*) called "revolutionary ready forces" ("zinde güçler"), i.e. the reformist army, intellectuals and university students. Although the theory of ready forces assigned a "progressive" role to the armed forces, while the civil society hegemony attributed a democratic attitude to the conservative-Islamic segment, these two camps in fact resemble each other despite the political and ideological differences between them. The most essential aspect of this similarity is that due to the weakness of democratic powers in Turkey and the intellectuals' insecurity about their own capabilities the camps are stuck between mosque and army politics which is neither progressive nor democratic and incapable of independence. The political discourse exhibited in *Snow* bears affinities with the centre-periphery theory. The parallelism between the author's evaluation of the Sivas Massacre as a "revolt of the provincials" on the one hand and the portrayal of Islamist characters in the novel as a force whose members "lay down their lives to oppose the state" (421) on the other are no doubt partly due to this perspective.

The centre-periphery paradigm describes Islamists as a peripheral group opposing the centre, not as struggling for power within the centre. Religion and state are not presented as two intersecting power domains in *Snow* but rather as two separate battlefields. While radical, violent political Islam is parodied, non-violent Islamists are approached with an attempt at empathy. The polarisation between laicists and Islamists as the political backbone of the novel deserves challenging under this aspect.

Despite its appeal the centre-periphery paradigm is problematic in its detachment of Ottoman and Turkish modernisation spanning almost two centuries from its historicist position and its equation of the 1930s, the ascendency of the Kemalist regime, with the 1990s and the 2000s. Interpreting Turkey using the centre-periphery paradigm seems inviting as it agrees with the political background of *Snow* of a critique of republican authoritarianism. This political approach out to criticise an authoritarian centre fails to acknowledge the fact that the supposedly peripheral forces use, in fact, the same authoritarian language as the centre. More importantly, based on this approach the novel presents what is seen as centre and periphery as forces opposing each other, which consciously or unconsciously obscures the fact that the conflict between the two arises because they aspire for the same authority:

> At least as important from a centre-periphery analytic point of view is the assumption that the anomalies of a modernisation undertaken under the leadership of utopian elites alienated from the founding values of society can only be overcome by returning to these values; i.e. the symptoms of modernisation from above can only be remedied by a modernisation from below which agrees with the values of the centre. As pointed out above, this assumption rests on an aberrance which characterises Ottoman-Turkish modernisation, namely on the ideal typification of democratic-reformist circles over the bureaucratic centre. However much the critique of bureaucratic conservatism in the republican era may be based on a democratic positioning, it does not necessarily follow from it that the movement of the periphery towards the centre will pave the way for democracy, that it will put an end to the authoritarian outlook of a modernisation from above. The thesis that top-down modernisation was elitist is as convincing as the argument that bottom-up modernisation is populist and authoritarian. (Açıkel 59)

Orhan Pamuk uses a very prudent and careful language to describe political Islam in the novel. This alone shows that this camp is located not at the periphery but at or near the centre as an important power group. Despite its apolitical protagonists, *Snow* has a hidden political drift resting on a democratic alliance to be created between Islamists and liberalists against military and authoritarian republicanism.

Every democracy depends on a republican government but not every republic has democracy as a corollary. Authoritarian tendencies over considerable periods in the political history of Turkey mostly preferred a regime that gave precedence to the state over human rights and the supremacy of law. This is why liberals, whose social base was weak but who owned hegemonic power, believed that they would succeed by creating an alliance with Islamists, whose social base was strong but who focussed on a share in power rather than on democratic ideals. Through this alliance these liberals intended to change both the Islamists and the authoritarian regime mentality. This tendency among liberal intellectuals, also evinced by Pamuk, forms the political backbone of *Kar*.

It is common to find novels criticised on the basis of the expectation to find objective facts in them, which ignores the aesthetic dimension of literature. It should not be forgotten that the writer always has the liberty to play with reality, stylise and appropriate it to create his/her fictional world. It is of course necessary to differentiate between the writer's fictional license and the quality of the fictional political system set up and of the images used in it. What really needs to be discussed are the writer's images and the representational structures within the fiction, particularly when the novel in question is a political one. When describing Islamist characters *Snow* is careful not to present them as stereotypes:

> He was extraordinarily handsome, but his gracefulness was born of self-confidence. In his manner, expression, and appearance there was nothing of the truculent, bearded, provincial fundamentalist whom the secularist press had depicted with a gun in one hand and a string of prayer beads in the other. (72)

In an interview, Pamuk remarks on this characterisation in the novel as follows; "This may be one of the first books in the world that presents a political Islamist militant as a reasonable person, not as a mad fanatic, but as a reasonable person with understandable passions and reasonable anger" (Kırmızı ve Kar 96).

This attitude is frequently encountered in the novel. İpek comments about Blue, who is hinted at to have committed a murdered: "He's very compassionate, Blue, very thoughtful and generous. [...] He doesn't want anyone to suffer. He cried all night once, just because two little puppies had lost their mother" (364). Responding to criticism of his supposedly friendly attitude towards political Islamists in the novel, Pamuk denied displaying such an attitude; he stated that his country is threatened by both political Islamists and Jacobean Kemalists and that he tries to keep his distance towards both views:

> *There are some very likeable Islamists in your book.*
> I'm not interested in a blanket condemnation of all Islamists as evil, as is often the case in the West. At the same time I am critical of the Islamist perception of the secularists as undignified imitators of the loathed West. I want to destroy the clichés cultivated by both sides. (Pamuk, "Turkish Trauma")

Pamuk explains the intellectual rationale behind this attitude in the novel as follows:

> The lack of understanding that in Turkey the majority of the society unfortunately shows towards, say, Kurdish nationalists or political Islam, the popular media in the West today displays towards Islam in general. Today the West does not understand the anger in the Islamic world just as once Turkey ostracised its own leftists and refused to understand who they were and why they upheld their political ideas. And because of this failure to understand – I have written about this – the West, in my opinion, hands over the anger in the Islamic world to armed, blood-thirsty terrorists. If it understood the Islamists and tried to establish a dialogue with them, the West would become stronger. (Kırmızı ve Kar 97)

What are the boundaries of this effort to understand? Or does this effort to understand include all the political subjects represented in the novel? Is it naïve to reduce all the political polarisations and clashes of civilizations in Turkey and in the world to the question of understanding / not understanding one another? What are we to do with the overt othering in a novel in which the attempt to understand is so prominent? It is possible to extend this list of questions. But it is clear that there is a serious balance problem in *Snow* regarding political representation, be it through identification (Islamists) or estrangement (secularists and leftists). It is therefore hard to call *Snow* a polyphonic novel in the Dostoyevskian sense.

Pamuk's frequently made claim that he regards Dostoyevsky as a model and writes dialogic novels, where the author keerps an equal distance to all sides and discourses needs to be questioned.[7] On a superficial reading, *Snow* does indeed seem to conform to a polyphonic strategy in the Bakhtinian sense. For instance, one of the characters involved in the coup criticises intellectuals, perhaps including the author himself:

> You say you want democracy, and then you enter into alliances with Islamist fundamentalists. You say you want human rights, and then you make deals with terrorist murderers. You say Europe is the answer, but you go around buttering up Islamists who hate everything Europe stands for. You say feminism, and then you help these men wrap their women's heads. [...] As for people like you, you love to trash the army even while you depend on it to keep the Islamists from cutting you up into little pieces. (355-56)

With this passage in mind it could be judged that the author ridicules his own views and refuses to assume an authority over the conflicting discourses, but it should be remembered that these criticisms come from one of the most repugnant characters in the book. How much weight does criticism carry that is uttered by a torturer, a murderer and a member of the paramilitary organization of the state without any depth and with questionable human qualities?

In his *Demons*, written to vehemently condemn nihilism, Dostoyevsky grants the characters he opposes the opportunity to defend themselves instead of facilely condemning them.[8] Perhaps this result was not planned by the author. But in *Snow* the author's attempt to understand certain political

---

[7] Pamuk has repeated this claim on several occasions: "My book has many voices, and I do not comment on them with my personal views. Dostoyevsky was the master of this form of writing. Many of my characters hold ideas which run counter to my own" ("Turkish Trauma").

[8] In his preface to the Turkish translation of Dostoyevsky's *Demons*, Pamuk states as much: "[E]ven though he is angry at leftist liberals and defenders of Westernization, Dostoyevsky cannot help talking about them with true affection at times as he knows from the inside" (Dostoyevski, *Cinler* 12).

subjects is confined to the formal level. The novel tries to question the cliché of "pro-democracy Western seculars" as opposed to "anti-democracy and anti-Western Islamists." Yet instead of keeping a critical distance to both sides, this questioning simply reverses the cliché.

There are other dimensions to the novel that deserve to be discussed. It is an established fact that after the 1980 coup the political left in Turkey was suppressed and the way paved for political Islam as part of the so-called Green Belt Project period. Similar Islamisation projects were also put into practice in the Middle East during the cold war years. Within the framework of the Western world's alliance with political Islam against leftist, reformist liberalism and secular, nationalist currents the West's political decision mechanisms weakened those who may well be closest to the paradigm of modernity that forms the basis of this very civilisation. The secular intellectuals of the region were painfully aware of this. Georges Crom (59-60) deplores the European Powers' preference for supporting archaic structures in modern guise to defenders of democracy and the right of nations to self-determination, a tendency that leads to the rise of dangerous fundamentalism.

Unlike what Pamuk claims in his interviews, secular factions in Middle-Eastern countries are not favoured by the West (or at any rate by its decision makers). In the world of *Snow*, where political Islam occupies a central position, we do not find any manifestations of this fact. In addition, the political fiction of the novel is consistent with the approach of centre-periphery analyses mentioned above. According to those, political alienation in the society can, in contrast to the classically Kemalist view, be redeemed by merging state and religion. The price of such democratisation of the authoritarian republic is the weakening of laicism.

This brings to mind two questions. First, does the abandonment of secularism facilitate the transition to democracy in a country like Turkey whose secular tradition is not as strong as in Europe? Second, is there another way to reconcile secularism and democracy without sacrificing one for the other? The answers that the project of moderate Islam and, on the basis of the centre-periphery paradigm, *Snow* offer to these questions are strikingly similar (that the novel's hero Ka negates politics does not mean that the novel has no political backbone). Therefore, contrary to what Pamuk claims in his interviews, the perception of Islam, state and democracy in the novel is consistent, rather than conflicting, with the prevalent Western perception. The novel's use of facts and fictional elements reinforces this perception.

It is not possible to understand the marginalising language used to portray leftist, secular characters in the novel who advocate modernity if this entails agreement with a pluralist discourse. Moreover, on the fictional plane Islamists are presented as the victims of military coups at the expense of those who suffered the most from them, lost their jobs or were tortured, killed and sent to exile:

> All the hardened political Islamists in the student body had attended the performance at the National Theater, and because they had all been arrested on the spot, the only boys in the dormitory were either raw recruits or else had no interest in politics; but the scenes on television had made them rather giddy, and so – barricading the door with tables and desks and shouting slogans like "God is great!" they'd holed up to wait. One or two of the crazy ones, having stolen a few knives and forks from the kitchen, decided to throw the utensils at the soldiers from the bathroom window and began to horse around with the sole gun in their possession; so the standoff ended in gunfire, with one beautiful slip of a boy – nothing but innocence in his face – falling to his death, a bullet in his forehead." (*Snow* 169-70)

Whether the autonomy and freedom of the author's fiction extend to turning such images upside down is debatable; for neither did the plotters of this coup have such objectives nor did its victims have such a tradition of resistance. What is more important than the question of realism in the novel is why this image is tagged onto a political movement without such a tradition.[9]

---

[9] In her Bakhtinian reading of *Snow*, Didem Uslu states that the above-quoted passage "does not necessarily fit into the scheme of historical realism which [Pamuk] wants to hold fast in his novels" (123). According to Uslu, "Pamuk's imagination must have been working rather 'rowdily' because such a scene can not possibly [have] taken

The novel attacks the cliché that "Westernised seculars are good, Islamists are bad." In an interview published by *La Repubblica*, Pamuk states:

> The media, in general, are not interested in the details of the truth. This is the case with Turkey. Journalists are engrossed by clichés about Islam. For instance, they portray seculars as good and Islamists as bad. But this is not the case! There are laicists who are extremely rightist, even fascist, and Islamists with a liberal tendency similar to European democrats. But it is clichés that people are interested in and that is why clichés hit the headlines. (Qtd. in "Orhan Pamuk ne demek istedi?")

There are quite understandable aspects to this. A large part of the secular movement has an authoritarian, nationalistic attitude towards the Kurdish problem and military coups, which contributes to the fact that the situation is not fully appreciated in the West, as Pamuk claims. The intelligentsia, having struggled with official state policy as represented by the armed forces, coups, bans for many years, have developed a more friendly attitude towards Islamists, even if within the framework of participating with the armed forces in power and authority. The characters and the political world populated by them in *Snow* could partly be read against this backdrop. However, questioning this cliché, the author withholds the diversity that he attributes to the Islamist world view from their opponents. Are we facing a circle which is excluded from the centre or a power struggle within the centre itself? To what extent the political tradition defined as central since the 1950s is dominant in Turkey is all the more open to debate in the 2000s.

Seen from this angle, it is highly debatable whether a book from which disruptions like the Sivas Massacre are absent can be regarded as a microcosm of Turkey.

---

place [...]. [The Army] would not deliberately 'attack' [...] the representatives of Islamic ideology. [...] this is an inconceivable act in Turkey."

Conclusion

That politics dominated critical discussions, whether appreciative or not, on *Snow* was the main reason that obstructed an understanding of the novel. International readers who thought that they could grasp the complex history of Turkey and its region by reading a single novel were as effective in this as Turkish readers who either liked or criticised the novel on political grounds. As a national allegory, *Snow* may convey an idea of current political troubles in Turkey but to what extent it can claim to represent Turkey is highly debatable. On the other hand, the mimetic problems of *Snow* should not prevent us from evaluating the novel fairly.

The novel's impressive achievement in portraying provinciality, love, loneliness, the sense of being a stranger everywhere outweighs the faults that we have been dwelling on. The novel's sound plot and relentless suspense are striking. As in the plays of Henrik Ibsen, elements of black humour created by small details and hints in the dramatic structure create a gripping atmosphere.

The real impact of the novel lies in its treatment of provinciality and of fundamental human concerns such as disappointments created by contempt for the provincial regions and the ensuing hate, loneliness and love. In this respect *Snow* is very successful.

What makes writers and their works important for us are not so much their political ideas and messages than what they evoke in us on the aesthetic plane. From this point of view, *Snow* fulfils the aesthetic requirements of literature. But political novels move on a very delicate and thin line. Those which do not successfully negotiate this run risks such as caricaturising, failing to empathise, getting caught in routines while trying to escape them, unjustly exonerating, helplessly equating everything they treat. Everyone in Turkey who reads *Snow* today and believes in secular, modern and democratic values will blatantly perceive how the political statements made by it have been invalidated in the intervening fifteen years. This is why *Snow* is successful by literary standards but does not possess the same brilliance as a political novel.

Works Cited

Açıkel, Fethi. "Entegratif toplum ve muarızları: 'Merkez-çevre' paradigması üzerine eleştirel notlar." *Toplum ve bilim* 105 (2006): 30-69.

Argın, Şükrü. "Taşraya içeriden bakabilmek mümkün müdür?" *Taşraya bakmak*. Ed. Tanıl Bora. İstanbul: İletişim, 2005. 289-90.

Avcıoğlu, Doğan. *Türkiye'nin düzeni dün, bugün, yarın*. İstanbul: Cem, 1974.

Atay, Oğuz. *Günlük*. Istanbul: Iletişim, 1987.

Crom, Georges. *Doğu-batı: Hayali kırılma*. Trans. Nüvit Bingöl. İstanbul: Ithaki, 2005. Trans. of *Orient-Occident: La fracture imaginaire*.

Dostoyevski, Fyodor Mihailoviç. *Cinler*. Trans. Ergin Altay. İstanbul: İletişim, 2009. Trans. of *Demons*.

Mardin, Şerif. "Türk siyasasını açıklayabilecek bir anahtar: Merkez-çevre ilişkileri." *Türkiye'de toplum ve siyaset: Makaleler 1*. İstanbul: İletişim, 2006. 35-79.

Maalouf, Amin. *Disordered World: Setting a New Course for the Twenty-first Century*. Trans. George Miller. London: Bloomsbury, 2011.

McGaha, Michael. "The Poetry Of Defiance." *Los Angeles Times* 15 Aug. 2004. Accessed 26 July 2009 <http://articles.latimes.com/2004/aug/15/books/bk-mcgaha15>.

"Orhan Pamuk ne demek istedi?" *Mynet.com*. 25 Oct. 2007. Accessed 9 June 2017 <http://www.mynet.com/haber/dun ya/orhan-pamuk-ne-demek-istedi-320838-1>.

Roselli, Bede Greig. "Youth, Masculinity and the Shattering of Sight in *Snow*." *Essays Interpreting the Writings of Novelist Orhan Pamuk*. Ed. Nilgün Anadolu-Okur. New York: Mellen, 2009. 79-97.

Pamuk, Orhan. *Cevdet Bey ve oğulları* [*Cevdet Bey and His Sons*]. İstanbul: İletişim, 1982.

___. "In Kars and Frankfurt." *Other Colours: Essays and a Story*. By Pamuk. Trans. Maureen Freely. New York: Knopf, 2007.

___. *Kırmızı ve Kar*. Interview by Ahmet Hakan Çoşkun. İstanbul: Birey, 2002.

___. Preface. *Cinler*. By Fyodor Dostoyevsky. Trans. Engin Altay. İstanbul: İthaki, 2009.

___. "Mario Vargas Llosa and Third World Literature." *Other Colours: Essays and A Story*. By Pamuk. Trans. Maureen Freely. New York: Knopf, 2007.

___. "Sivas'tan Diyarbakır'a taşranın isyanı." *Öteki renkler: Seçme yazılar ve bir hikâye*. By Pamuk. İstanbul: İletişim, 1999.

___. *Snow*. Trans. Maureen Freely. London: Faber and Faber, 2004.

___. "The Turkish Trauma." Interview by Jörg Lau. Originally publ. in German in *Die Zeit* 14 Apr. 2005. Accessed 20 June 2017 <http://www.signandsight.com/features/115.html>.

Seyhan, Azade. "Seeing Through the Snow." *Al Ahram Weekly* 19-25 Oct. 2006. Accessed 20 June 2017 <http://weekly.ahram.org.eg/archive/2006/817/cu5.htm>.

Uslu, Didem. "A Melancholic Postmodern Mock-Hero in the Middle of Political Carnivalesque Madness: The Journalist-Poet Ka In *Snow*." *Essays Interpreting the Writings of Novelist Orhan Pamuk*. Ed. Nilgün Anadolu-Okur. New York: Mellen, 2009. 111-35.

The Hidden Symmetry in Life-Writing: Pamuk's *Istanbul: Memories and the City*

İnci Sarız-Bilge
University of Massachusetts Amherst

Abstract: This paper explores the interaction between self and urban space in Orhan Pamuk's *Istanbul: Memories and the City*, focusing on the autobiographical characteristics of the text and the ways spatiality is connected to its structure. Two narratives, namely of Pamuk's personal memories on the one hand and of Istanbul's glorious past which in recollection causes a communal sense of post-imperial melancholy, on the other, are juxtaposed in this autobiographical text with a view to constructing a "hidden symmetry" between Pamuk's story and Istanbul's history. Functioning on two narrative levels, this form of autobiography also provides Pamuk with a tool for exploring the formation of his creative identity and his literary sources, both of which are rooted in the "poetic melancholy of lost imperial greatness" of Istanbul. The most succinct expression of this autobiographical form is Pamuk's famous statement: "I have described Istanbul when describing myself, and described myself when describing Istanbul." I argue that the autobiographical design of the book efficiently supports the "hidden symmetry" Pamuk intends to construct between his personal life story and the urban narrative. This conceptualization of life-writing is further supported by the second symmetrical relationship established between Pamuk's past and present selves with a view to construct a coherent identity marked by creativity. Through creative uses of the two symmetrical devices Pamuk incorporates the melancholy of the city into his creative self and fashions himself as the writer of Istanbul.

> The man is only half himself, the other half is his expression.
> – R.W. Emerson, "The Poet"

With the much discussed "spatial turn" in the humanities, spatial aspects and spatialized modes of narrative have recently generated increasing attention in literary studies which branched out to include memory studies and urban studies as well. Rethinking the nature of the relation between self, narrative, and the urban space has also spawned interest in the production and the study of narratives of self-definition under the aspect of the "city." In light of the growing body of scholarship on the relationship between urban spaces and literature, the city is no longer considered a mere setting and a constant source of inspiration for writers and poets, but a form of language, a form of textuality, an agent, or a metaphor in the narrative. Cities also embody certain visions for the authors and help construct identities and images. Paris has been a space of artistic expression and intellectual engagement, for instance, and St. Petersburg has been an inseparable part of Russian identity. Istanbul, with its geographical position etched into the way collective memory is constructed in Turkey, has long been associated with Orhan Pamuk's writing in the network of literary cities. As a matter of fact, the presentation speech for the 2006 Nobel Prize lauded Pamuk for having made "[his] native city an indispensable literary territory, equal to Dostoyevsky's St. Petersburg, Joyce's Dublin or Proust's Paris – a place where readers from all corners of the world can live another life, just as credible as their own, filled by an alien feeling that they immediately recognize as their own" ("Nobel Prize").

Orhan Pamuk has prominently weaved the encounters between the characters and the cityscape, and the intricacies of identity that emerge from these encounters, in various ways into his fictional works from his debut novel *Cevdet Bey ve oğulları [Cevdet Bey and His Sons*, 1982, untranslated] to his last novel (*The Red-Haired Woman*, first published in Turkish in 2016). However, *Istanbul: Memories and the City* (2005, first published in Turkish in 2003), Pamuk's last work on his journey to the Nobel Prize in 2006, primarily dwells on the interaction of self and urban space, which indeed offers a rich territory to explore from multiple angles. It is this encounter that will be approached in this chapter on the ways spatiality and memory processes are connected to the autobiographical structure of the narrative. I argue that the autobiographical design of the book hinges on two parallel, symmetrical structures. The first symmetrical relationship is established between Pamuk's past and present selves with the purpose of maintaining a coherent identity distinctly marked by creativity. The second is constructed between Pamuk's personal life story and the urban narrative progressing through the socio-historical and cultural history of Istanbul. While the demand for self-coherence in autobiography writing explains the first form of symmetry, the concept of *hüzün*/melancholy is the vehicle connecting the autobiographical narrative and the city narrative in the second. It is through these two symmetries that an aestheticized life-narrative, which can also be read as a literary piece, is produced.

Symmetry also proves to be a reflection of and variation on Pamuk's long-term project of "narrating his country into being" as defined by Margaret Atwood ("Headscarves"), that is, narrating himself into world literature as the celebrated author of the city of Istanbul by translating his life-story into an aesthetic narrative tightly anchored in this city. To this purpose, a spatial autobiographical form that stretches the familiar conventions of the genre is supported by a traditional fictional form. Personal memories roughly spanning a twenty-year period between Pamuk's early childhood and his resolution to become a writer in quite a Joycean way are recounted in the easily recognizable genre of the *Künstlerroman*. Pamuk's employment of this literary form as an ancillary to autobiography is particularly telling within the framework of his above-mentioned long-term project because *Istanbul* offers a comprehensive picture of the sources of Pamuk's literary creativity and the motivation behind his authorship, which culminated in international acclaim. In *Istanbul: Memories and the City*, Istanbul as a literary place in Pamuk's fiction transforms into an autobiographical space conditioning the content and organization of this critically acclaimed narrative. The foregrounding of various aspects of the aesthetic significance of Istanbul in world literature determines the nature of Pamuk's self-expression as well. Both Pamuk's personal memories and the communal sense of post-imperial melancholy inscribed in the collective memory are mediated through the city of Istanbul in a symmetrical way.

Towards a Hybrid Autobiography

In *Reading Autobiography: A Guide for Interpreting Life Narratives* (2001), Sidonie Smith and Julia Watson point at the gradual changes in the fundamental concepts lying at the heart of life-writing studies. Framing their overview with reference to the key concepts of "self" and "truth," they identify three approaches which have dominated life-writing studies from the early twentieth century onwards. German philologist Georg Misch's concept of life-writing had a profound impact on the first wave of modern criticism in this field; it defined autobiography as "the description (*graphia*) of an individual human life (*bios*) by the individual himself (*autos*) (qtd. in Smith and Watson 113).

In other words, the first-wave critics were mostly preoccupied with the *bios* of the autobiographer, who was expected to present a truthful life narrative consistent with the biographical facts of a coherent self. Acting as a kind of moralist, the critic evaluated the quality of the life narrated in the autobiography and the narrator's ability to tell that truth (Smith and Watson 123). Life narratives, in this schema, were truthful accounts of "recollected life as transmitted through the unclouded, neutral glass of the *autos* where no significant consideration was given to the questions of self-formation and autobiographical modes of self-expression" (Olney 20-21). As the prevailing notions of a coherent self, truthfulness, and representative power of language were replaced mid-century by the more complex problems of self-representation, second-wave critics shifted their attention from the problematic notion of truthfulness to the modes of self-narrating. The questions of self-formation and self-expression, which according to James Olney were ignored by the first-wave critics, were addressed by the second wave. As a consequence, the understanding of life narratives as processes of identity formation out of subjective experience took hold, accompanied by the reconception of autobiography as an act of creative self-engagement (Smith and Watson 125-28). The problematic of self-representation in life-writing thus opened up was further probed in a third wave in the wake of new theoretical reframings.

Smith and Watson go on to discuss these practical and theoretical interventions that contributed to the fashioning of a third wave of autobiography critics in the past three decades. These theoretical frames, including but not restricted to postcolonial, ethnic, feminist, and queer studies; Lacanian revision of Freudian psychoanalysis, Foucault's emphasis on discourses of identity; and interdisciplinary studies of memory, challenged the concepts of a unified self, authority, authenticity, transparency of language, and truth (133-35). A new emphasis was placed on *graphia*, "the careful teasing out of warring forces of signification within the text itself" (Johnson 5; qtd. in Smith and Watson 137). This paradigm shift in the understanding of life-writing also brought forth a transformation in the perception of the *autos* of autobiographies. For instance, the claim that autobiographical texts reflect reality is no longer a foundational premise of the genre, and the transformation in this premise helped redefine the genre's boundaries on the continuum of fiction and fact. James Olney defined the *autos* as the "'I' that coming awake to its own being shapes and determines the nature of the autobiography and in so doing half discovers, half creates itself" (21). Focusing on *autos* marked the notion of a fictive self who is not accountable for conveying a veritable account of the past. Now the subject matter of autobiography in contemporary life-writing theories is considered to be modes of self-representation, and this self is described by most contemporary critics as fiction formulated in reference to various experiences and processes (Gilmore 68).

Since the shift of critical attention from the *bios* of the autobiographer to the *autos*, autobiographies, or any form of self-telling, have been read as historically and culturally-situated narratives that are also integral to identity formation (Bruner; Eakin). Also, the third wave of autobiography criticism regards autobiography as a non-unified genre which employs various modes of story-telling and narrative media, and as indistinct from fictional or nonfictional literary modes in terms of generic possibilities open to the autobiographer. Established modes of self-narrating are likely to transform, generating new and hybrid forms, generic rules and terms, and new ways of interpreting the self/*autos* that is constructed and narrated in the text.

Among these hybrid forms of autobiography is eco-autobiography. According to Peter F. Perretin, the term denotes "a type of autobiographical text that enables nature or landscape writing to discover 'a new self in nature'" (1). Smith and Watson propose this term for a type of narrative that "interweaves the story of a protagonist with the story of the fortunes, conditions, geography, and ecology of a region and reflects on their connection (and perhaps its failure) as a significant feature of the writing" (268). *Istanbul: Memories and the City*, accordingly, exemplifies such non-traditional, genre-stretching autobiographical texts, providing a spatial reading of the self and life of its author in an urban setting (162). Smith and Watson describe *Istanbul* as a narrative in which the "subjective impressions" of the autobiographer in a city are enmeshed with their "factual counterparts," resulting in a "chiasmic structure" wherein Pamuk describes himself and Istanbul simultaneously. The city in *Istanbul* could be read as an extended self or a site for the self in the process of construction. In this hybrid text combining multiple forms of narrative such as photograph, memoir, and essay to explore the socio-historical and cultural status of an urban environment, Pamuk gives an account of his quest for identity that is concisely embodied in the question "Why am I what I am?" famously posed by Hoja in *The White Castle* (1985) many years earlier. A spatial reading of selfhood, which is the hallmark of this autobiographical text, is borne out with memories from Pamuk's childhood and early adulthood.

Symmetry of the Account

The first prominent aspect of the exclusively autobiographical parts of *Istanbul* relates to a notion that was the centerpiece of theorization in life-writing for a long time, namely autobiographical truth. Pamuk's autobiography opens with a pact between the reader and the narrator of the life-narrative. At the end of the first chapter titled "Another Orhan," Pamuk offers the reader a pact: "[…] dear reader. Let me be straight with you, and in return let me ask for your compassion" (*Istanbul* 8).[1]

With this explicit and immediate pact begins Pamuk's involvement of the reader in his understanding of life-writing. This involvement seems to be constrained by the long-standing convention of truth telling. The "autobiographical pact" as described by Philip Lejeune (*Pacte*) is characterized by the reader's implicit belief that the writer, narrator, and protagonist of an autobiography are one and the same person and by the expectation of a historical truth recounted by the author. Lejeune later revised this paradigmatic description of autobiography: "An autobiographer is not someone who speaks the truth about himself, but someone who says he speaks it" while the pact morphed into "a promise of sincerity" (*Brouillons* 125; qtd. in Regard 20; trans. Regard). What does this promise of sincerity or pledge of honesty entail within the framework of *Istanbul*, a narrative that Pamuk concisely called a combination of *"*an essay about the city" and "an autobiography" ("Art of Fiction")? Does Pamuk's pledge of honesty indicate subscription to the notion of autobiographical truth?

---

[1] "[…] ey okur. Ben sana dürüstlük göstereyim, sen de bana şefkat" (*İstanbul* 16).

Offered very early on in the autobiographical part of *Istanbul*, this pact between Pamuk and his readers appears to be based on an exchange of accurate personal memories for compassion towards memories themselves. However, Pamuk's second critical comment on his understanding of life-narratives brings out the nature of the said pledge of honesty more clearly. It can be argued that Pamuk does not equate honesty or sincerity with the *accuracy* of the memories he shares with the reader: "[…] what is important for a memoirist is not the factual accuracy of the account but its symmetry" (265).

Pamuk thus reveals that symmetry as the touchstone of the autobiographical genre defies and overwrites his initial pact with the reader to exchange honesty for compassion. I argue that the demand for self-coherence in autobiography writing yields to this notion of symmetry in Pamuk's autobiographical narrative. The question of what "the symmetry of the account" corresponds to in the process of writing a life-story remains largely unexplained in the text. Symmetry, in this respect, points at the coherence between the remembered past self and the present self of an individual. This is partly in congruence with the tenets of autobiographical memory.

A fundamental question in autobiographical memory research is whether recollecting past experiences depends on the correspondence of memories to the actual experience or coherence between the memories and the present self (Tulving and Donaldson; Conway et al., *Theoretical Perspectives*; Rubin). In other words, are memories viewed as an accurate reiteration of the original experiences and events in a person's life or do they serve to form a coherent and integrated story of one's life? It is suggested that both are equally important for different purposes; nonetheless, long-term processes such as life-writing that entail building up a continuous discourse are driven by the goal of maintaining a coherent self and presenting it to the addressee, who is the reader of the autobiographical narrative in Pamuk's case. That is, the process of autobiographical remembering is a form of reliving which supports and fits well with the current self-conceptions of individuals and is designed for their particular "needs" and future anticipations (Rapaport 112-13; McAdams 117). As a matter of fact, Pamuk constructs a sensitive and self-conscious child and adolescent throughout the autobiographical parts of his narrative in such a way as to foreshadow his future self predominantly characterized by insight and creativity. The chapters that focus on Pamuk's family life, in particular, impart lengthy descriptions from his childhood that bear the signs of creativity, including the substantial references to the fantasy world: "This was the world I would enter when, out of pure boredom, I pretended to be someone else and somewhere else. It was a very easy escape into this other world I concealed from everyone" (20).

The fantasy world created by young Orhan and "another Orhan" living in another house are the main recurring characteristics of the life script laid out in the autobiographical parts of *Istanbul* to present the reader with coherent links between Pamuk's past and present selves. In harmony with the conventions of the *Künstlerroman*, the past presented to the reader features a child with a heightened sense of aesthetics and an inquisitive adolescent capable of recognizing and internalizing the communal feeling of melancholy that pervades the city:

> On the rowboat with my mother, it seemed to me that the colors of the Bosphorus hills were not reflections of an external light. The judas and plane trees, the wings of the gulls that would flap so rapidly past us, and the half-broken walls of the boathouses – all of them glowed with a dim light that seemed to come from within. (*Istanbul* 55)
>
> "That which I would later know as pervasive melancholy and mystery, I felt in childhood as boredom and gloom" (29).

By displaying the aesthetic continuation of a childhood feeling, boredom, in the form of melancholy and mystery which would later appear in his works, Pamuk, in the second quotation above, directly interrelates his past and present on behalf of the reader. In a comparable scene, he describes his childhood game of creating infinite images of himself using two mirrors facing each other. This game, Pamuk reveals, is "similar to the one [he] would later play in [his] novels" (77). Pamuk, at times, deliberately takes over the reader's task of interpreting these scattered memories as signposts of a past self conspicuously touched by artistic sensibility. A striking example can be found in the chapter titled "The Pleasure of Painting," where

Pamuk explains what sort pleasure he took in drawing as a child (149). A bullet-point list of reasons is prefaced by a note on the shift in focalization from young Orhan to Orhan Pamuk, the fifty-year-old writer of the narrative who thinks "he can explain himself while trying to understand that little kid" (142). Acting as an interpreter between the reader and young Orhan, Pamuk expounds his childhood observations through the sophisticated consciousness of an adult memoirist. Observations such as:

> The world I created through drawing, like the second world I hid in my head, enriched my life; even better, it gave me a legitimate escape from the dusty, shadowy world of everyday life. Not only did my family accept this new habit of mine, they accepted my right to it. (142).

Considering its temporal span, *Istanbul* does not offer a perspective on the present of writing, nor does it focus on the present self of its author. The narrative, rather, comes to a halt with the narrator's announcement of the birth of his artistic self at the age of twenty-two. The personal memories included in the narrative converge upon the underlying motives for Pamuk's journey to creativity as underlined by the *Künstlerroman* structure. In other words, the memories selected for Pamuk's portrayal of his childhood, adolescence, and early adulthood years reveal an artistic sensitivity that confirms his future self.

The goal of retaining a sense of coherence between the past and present selves is not always accompanied by a sense of veracity, thus, it might lead an individual to distort the remembered experience or make up new memories at varying degrees. False memory phenomena also include misremembering the attributes of past selves, such as childhood personality traits, or misremembering the details of events so that the current goals, current self-perception, and beliefs match with the memories of the past (see Newman and Lindsay). In *Istanbul* the demand for symmetry between memory and the self created in the narrative relegates the demand for accuracy to secondary importance in life-writing. Pamuk, indeed, confesses towards the end that he did not abide by his promise of representing the reality and that he distorted his memories or fabricated new ones:

> Later, when reminded of those brawls, my mother and my brother claimed no recollection of them, saying that, as usual, I'd invented them, just for the sake of something to write about, just to give myself a colourful and melodramatic past. They were so sincere that I was finally forced to agree, concluding that, as always, I'd been swayed more by my imagination than by real life. (294)

Correspondence of memories to reality is superseded here by the desire to create a "colorful," or more accurately a "striking" – "çarpıcı" (*İstanbul* 275) – representation of the past in an attempt to validate Pamuk's creative self. False coherence memory here plays the function of creating a meaning that foregrounds the power of imagination, which is the hallmark of Pamuk's present identity as a writer. Hence, this confessional memory holds a predictive function for the future. Interestingly, it also points at the possibility of further memories revised and fabricated with a view to presenting the audience a creative childhood. Indeed, acknowledgement of a false memory is immediately followed by a cautionary note to the reader: "So anyone reading these pages should bear in mind that I am prone to exaggeration" (294).[2] While creating false memories illuminates the autobiographical nature of *Istanbul* driven by the need for coherence between different versions of the self in the past, present, and even future, admitting to false memories throws light on the promise of honesty and the pact with the reader that open the narrative. Pamuk's demand for compassion from the reader is intended for the creative ways he presents his life story following a certain pattern that he calls symmetry, not for individual memories. The hidden symmetry between the past and present selves of Pamuk that allies itself with the *Künstlerroman* concludes in the last sentence of the book and even evokes the seminal text of this sub-genre, *Portrait of the Artist as a Young a Man* (1916): "I'm going to be a writer" (*Istanbul* 368). An unswerving expression of the creative desires, this resolution does signal the beginning of young Orhan's journey to authorship.

---

[2] "Bu yüzden bu sayfaları okuyan okur kimi zaman ölçüyü kaçırdığımı, [...] kendi kuruntularımdan bir türlü çıkamadığımı aklında tutsun" (*İstanbul* 275).

Union of Fate

The sense of continuity, or symmetry, established between Pamuk's past and present selves through an emphasis on creativity is further aligned with a second symmetrical structure. While the first hidden symmetry brings to the fore that Pamuk is going to be a writer, the second symmetry creates a "union of fate" between Istanbul and Pamuk. The city of Istanbul is ultimately portrayed in the book as the repository of meanings and sources cultivating a creative self. The provenance of many of Pamuk's literary themes and tropes that precede and succeed *Istanbul* can be traced in this text, such as the concept of doubles originating in a game invented by young Orhan to escape boredom and an interest in collecting mundane objects, both of which frequently appear in Pamuk's fictional works. In return, by firmly anchoring his self-narrative in the aestheticized history of Istanbul, Pamuk establishes a symmetry between a personal and an urban story/history. The concept of *hüzün*, in this symmetrical structure, serves the technical function of seamlessly juxtaposing the city narrative with a fragmented yet chronological autobiographical narrative. A communal sense of melancholy, or *hüzün,* bleeds into the autobiographical episodes in such a way as to illustrate how a city afflicted with it "made [Pamuk] who he is" (6) and gave him the creative authority to narrate its poetic splendor.

Hüzün, or collective melancholy, is described as one of the defining characteristics of Istanbul and its inhabitants after the collapse of the Ottoman Empire and a sentiment which Pamuk either battled with or appropriated throughout his life. Pamuk's use of *hüzün* in *Istanbul* as a source of literary creativity is adapted from his four lonely melancholic predecessors, the poet Yahya Kemal, the novelist Ahmet Hamdi Tanpınar, the memoirist Abdülhak Şinasi Hisar, and the journalist-historian Reşad Ekrem Koçu. Pamuk unravels the reason why he revisits the origins of this concept in the chapter titled "The Melancholy of the Ruins: Tanpınar and Yahya Kemal in the City's Poor Neighborhoods. " He points at the ways these two twentieth-century Turkish literary figures draw on the works of Gérard de Nerval and Théophile Gautier in exploring the indigenous sentiment of *hüzün* residing in the poor neighborhoods of Istanbul that would pervade the city's dwellers for a long time.

These western travel writers had visited Istanbul and discovered the melancholic beauty in the ruins of a city seventy years earlier, constituting the so-called Western gaze on the city. Juxtaposition of the Western gaze and the literary tradition of Istanbulite writers fed by this gaze allows Pamuk to establish a hybrid understanding of the city and a dual interpretation of Istanbul's past. On the other side of this equation stands Pamuk who conceives of his torn identity as echoing the ambiguity that dominates Istanbul. As the city claims this melancholy-laden ambiguity, Pamuk also learns to embrace it as a constitutive element of his identity.

> Between the ages of sixteen and eighteen, part of me longed, like a radical Westernizer, for the city to become entirely European. I held the same hope for myself. But another part of me yearned to belong to the Istanbul I had grown to love, by instinct, by habit, and by memory. [...] At the same time, the melancholy to which the city bows its head – and at the same time claims with pride – began to seep into my soul. (323)

Istanbul's past and cultural history are engrained in the way Pamuk constructs his own past and present, thus the concept of *hüzün* is narrativized into his life story as a ubiquitous feeling generating and even conditioning his creative identity. The image of the city in the minds of its inhabitants as a space of poverty, ruin, and defeat proves to be a significant determinant in the first instances of Pamuk's attempt at translating this sentiment into art as an adolescent, following the footsteps of Western travelogues and his Turkish predecessors. In other words, Pamuk's understanding of the city was substantially shaped by the inhabitants' unconscious mourning for the glorious past, influencing the process of his mode of expressions from early ages on:

> For the image of the city that Istanbullus have carried with them over the past century is the child of poverty, defeat, and ruin. When I was fifteen and doing my own paintings, it was especially when painting the back streets that I became troubled about where our melancholy was taking us. (264)

As the city's melancholy settles into young Orhan's mode of expression, particularly into his creative endeavors of painting during his coming of age, he learns to accept and embrace this feeling as his own. The feeling of melancholy which initially shows itself as boredom and gloom in childhood, indeed, proceeds from "the poetic melancholy of lost imperial greatness and its historical residue" (256) and blossoms into a productive thread linking Pamuk's life story and Istanbul's history. The interconnectedness of the city and one of its inhabitants, further elaborated by Pamuk as a union of fate (6), exceeds his physical attachment to Istanbul resulting in his living in the same street and even in the same house throughout his life, and infiltrates the structure of the narrative. The text of *Istanbul* forms a complex web of personal memories, urban stories, and history, all of which center on the city of Istanbul. All these constituents are collected, recollected, and textualized in the form of eco-autobiography which does not solely concentrate on the *autos*/I of the narrative, but entertains two centers. While the demand for self-coherence binds past, present, and future selves of Pamuk to creativity, the symmetry between the two centers of the narrative established via the thread of *hüzün* binds these selves to the city of Istanbul, generating a union of fate.

Throughout the text Pamuk writes himself into both the city narrative and the autobiographical narrative using different selves with different functions. His selves as protagonist and narrator of the autobiography and also as the object of the Western gaze are explored in conjunction with his selves as a resident of Istanbul and as an external observer of the city. Multiple subject positions are derived from these identities, such as that of an aspiring artist, a nationally recognized author, a member of the emerging Republican bourgeoisie, and an Istanbulite. These subject positions separately and collectively mark different sections of the book. Pamuk's attempt at narrating himself via multiple selves is accompanied by the presentation of two landscapes, or more precisely, two distinct interpretations of the same landscape of Istanbul, namely the local Ottoman-Turkish perspective on the city and the foreign gaze. The local and Western perspectives are structured palimspsestically rather than sequentially, which at their multi-layered juncture defines Pamuk's hybrid understanding of the city. The dual experience of Istanbul along with Pamuk's dual identity express the similarity that Pamuk intends to invoke between the uniquely complex and contested social, cultural, and historical status of Istanbul and his personal life story. This pattern of similarity, union of fate, builds up throughout the text and finds its most succinct expression in the statement: "[…] I have described Istanbul when describing myself, and described myself when describing Istanbul (265)." As a matter of fact, cultural and political issues and sociological observations concerning the glorious imperial history of Istanbul are directly projected upon Pamuk's autobiographical episodes as well. For example: "It was a long time coming, arriving by a circuitous route, but the cloud of gloom and loss spread over Istanbul by the fall of the Ottoman Empire had finally claimed my family too" (17).

The waning of the wealth of Pamuk's affluent family is put in symmetry with the decline of Istanbul's past glory, both of which result in the same feeling of melancholy. The interconnectedness of Istanbul's history and such autobiographical episodes formed via the thread of *hüzün* relates to a specific period of time spanning the fall of the Ottoman Empire through Pamuk's early adulthood when he resolves to become a writer. One particular episode overtly reveals the symmetrical structure Pamuk intends to fashion between his creative formation and Istanbul's melancholy-stricken past aestheticized through the literary accounts of Western and Istanbulite writers. While he is recounting his first experiences with religion as a child, he briefly digresses with a commentary on military interferences in politics, immediately followed by a note on the necessity of exclusion of this digression from the narrative: "But if I dwell any longer on military coups and political Islam (which has much less to do with Islam than is commonly thought), I risk destroying the hidden symmetry of the book" (183).

This period of military coups in the history of modern Turkey, which also corresponds to Pamuk's adulthood when he made his debut in the literary scene, falls outside of the scope of the so-called symmetry purported to validate how Istanbul made Pamuk who he is. Following the divulgence of a fundamental structural feature of his narrative, Pamuk reprises his childhood perception of religion and his fears of being far away from the collective spirit of the city.

Symmetry as a Memory Filter

Interestingly, in a 2005 interview following the publication of the English translation of *Istanbul*, Pamuk described his narrative as originally a simple juxtaposition of an essay on Istanbul and his autobiography:

> The formula for originality is very simple – put together two things that were not together before. Look at *Istanbul*, an essay about the city and about how certain foreign authors – Flaubert, Nerval, Gautier – viewed the city, and how their views influenced a certain group of Turkish writers. Combined with this essay on the invention of Istanbul's romantic landscape is an autobiography. No one had done this before. Take risks and you will come up with something new. I tried with *Istanbul* to make an original book. I don't know if it succeeds. ("Art of Fiction")

Pamuk evidently does not ascribe any emotional valence to the possibilities and limitations of autobiographical self-expression; neither does he comment on the aesthetic implications of juxtaposing an essay on the "invention of Istanbul's romantic landscape" with an autobiography. However, following his awarding of the Nobel Prize, which associated him with the city of Istanbul, he made a statement on the nature of remembering and forgetting in life-writing with regard to *Istanbul: Memories and the City*. In it he problematized autobiography as a mode of self-representation and made a curious observation about his process of remembering:

> I remember my huge disillusionment when it was finished. Of all the things I had wanted to express about my life, of all the memories that I considered the most crucial, only a few had found their way into the book. I could have written another twenty volumes describing the first twenty-two years of my life, each one drawing from a different set of experiences. It was then that I discovered that autobiographies served not to preserve our pasts, but to help us forget them. ("Orhan Pamuk - Biographical")

It stands to reason that different sets of experiences produce different autobiographical narratives of the same life, thus giving Pamuk's observation about the nature of remembering and forgetting a degree of validity. However, the line drawn between preserving and forgetting memories is indeed ephemeral, given that these two processes are not exact opposites of each other. Autobiographical remembering is often a task-oriented, thus selective process occurring for the most part in the control of the individual who remembers. Pamuk's process of remembering of his personal past and Istanbul's historical past follows a voluntary pattern, as opposed to involuntary remembering with Proustian associations. More importantly, his "formula for originality" relies to a large extent on deliberate and creative aestheticization of a life story through two symmetrical structures functioning simultaneously in the narrative. Writing an autobiographical narrative that hinges on symmetry entails a major memory selection process and significantly restricts the autobiographer. In other words, the overarching framework of symmetry indeed becomes the filter through which an infinite number of possible memories are screened and selected. What Pamuk refers to as "forgetting" is in fact filtering out the memories that do not serve either type of symmetry, with the conclusion that Pamuk's principal goal of describing himself and Istanbul in a symmetrical way necessitated conscious exclusion of certain memories.

This selection process brings the reader back to a pivotal question Pamuk asks in one of the chapters centered on the conceptual and literary frameworks of Western melancholy and its Eastern analogue *hüzün:* "Why have I devoted so much energy to convey to the reader the melancholy I feel in this city where I've spent my entire life?" (220). The autobiographical structure of the narrative that rests on two forms of symmetries fruitfully addresses Pamuk's question. While the "symmetry of the account," the continuity of the creative self, establishes that young Pamuk is going to be a writer, the second symmetry authorizes him to be *the writer* of Istanbul because his fate is inextricable from the history of Istanbul defined by the feeling of melancholy. Not only does a poetic portrayal of Istanbul emerge out of the lengthy representations of melancholy Pamuk devotes so much energy to convey to the reader, but also a portrait of a writer is fashioned in the process who makes peace with this melancholy and incorporates it in his creative self to the point of appropriating it as his own:

> There were times – when every strange memento seemed saturated with the poetic melancholy of lost imperial greatness and its historical residue – that I imagined myself to be the only one who had unlocked the city's secret; it had come to me as I watched through the windows of the Golden Horn ferry, and I had embraced the city as my own – no one had ever seen it as I did now! (256)

Works Cited

Atwood, Margaret. "Headscarves to Die For." *New York Times* 15 Aug. 2004. Accessed 1 Dec. 2016 <http://www.nytimes.com/2004/08/15/books/headscarves-to-die-for.html?mcubz=1>.

Bruner, Jerome. "Life as Narrative." *Language and Arts* 65.6 (1988): 574-83.

Conway, M.A., et al., eds. *Theoretical Perspectives on Autobiographical Memory*. Dordrecht: Kluwer, 1992.

Conway, M.A., J.A. Singer, and A. Tagini. "The Self and Autobiographical Memory: Correspondence and Coherence." *Social Cognition* 22.5 (2004): 491-529.

Eakin, Paul John. *Living Autobiographically: How We Create Identity in Narrative*. Ithaca: Cornell UP, 2008.

Gilmore, Leigh. "Policing Truth: Confession, Gender, and Autobiographical Authority." *Autobiography and Postmodernism*. Ed. Kathleen Ashley, Leigh Gilmore, and Gerland Peters. Amherst: University of Massachusetts Amherst Press, 1994. 54-68.

Johnson, Barbara. *The Critical Difference: Essays in the Contemporary Rhetoric of Reading*. Baltimore: John Hopkins UP, 1980.

Lejeune, Philip. *Les brouillons de soi*. Paris: Seuil, 1998.

___. *Le pacte autobiographique*. Paris: Seuil, 1975.

McAdams, D.P. "The Psychology of Life Stories." *Review of General Psychology* 5 (2001): 100-22.

Newman, Eryn J., and D. Stephen Lindsay. "False Memories: What the Hell Are They For?" *Applied Cognitive Psychology* 23 (2009): 1105-21.

"The Nobel Prize in Literature 2006 – Presentation Speech." *Nobelprize.org.* Nobel Media AB 2014. Accessed 1 Dec. 2016. <http://www.nobelprize.org/nobel_prizes/literature/laureates/2006/presentation-speech.html>.

Olney, James. "Autobiography and the Cultural Moment: A Thematic, Historical, and Bibliographical Introduction." *Autobiography: Essays Theoretical and Critical.* Ed. James Olney. New Jersey: Princeton UP, 1980. 3-28.

"Orhan Pamuk - Biographical." *Nobelprize.org.* Nobel Media AB 2014. Accessed 1 Dec. 2016 <http://www.nobelprize.org/nobel_prizes/literature/laureates/2006/pamuk-bio.html>.

Pamuk, Orhan. "The Art of Fiction." Interview by Ángel Gurría-Quintana. *Paris Review* 175 (Fall/Winter): 2005. Accessed 1 Dec. 2016. <http://www.theparisreview.org/interviews/5587/orhan-pamuk-the-art-of-fiction-no-187-orhan-pamuk.>

___. *Istanbul: Memories and the City.* Trans. Maureen Freely. London: Faber and Faber, 2005. Trans. of *İstanbul: Hatıralar ve şehir.*

___. *İstanbul: Hatıralar ve şehir.* İstanbul: Yapı Kredi, 2003.

Rapaport, D. *Emotions and Memory.* New York: Science Editions, 1961.

Regard, Frédéric. "Topologies of the Self: Space and Life-Writing." *Mapping the Self: Space, Identity, Discourse in British Auto/ Biography.* Ed. Frédéric Regard. Paris: Publications de l'Université de Saint Etienne, 2003. 15-28.

Perretin, Peter F. "Eco-Autobiography: Portrait of Place/Self Portrait." *A/B: Auto/Biography Studies* 18.1 (2003): 1-22.

Rubin, David C. *Autobiographical Memory.* New York: Cambridge UP, 1986.

Smith, Sidonie and Julia Watson. *Reading Autobiography: Guide for Interpreting Narratives.* Minneapolis: University of Minnesota Press, 2010.

Tulving, Endel, and Wayne Donaldson, eds. *Organization of Memory.* New York: Academic Press, 1972.

Provinciality and the City in Pamuk's *Istanbul*

Beyza Lorenz
University of California, Los Angeles

Abstract: In *Istanbul: Memories and the City* (2003) Orhan Pamuk depicts the city as a heterotopia where centers and peripheries are intermingled, where the insiders and the outsiders, the past and the present simultaneously occupy the same space. Throughout *Istanbul: Memories and the City*, Pamuk walks between his home neighborhood, the affluent, westernized Nişantaşı, and the impoverished outlying neighborhoods to cope with the provincialization of Istanbul as it turned from an imperial capital into an impoverished city. I argue that Pamuk reimagines the city, like a collector, by reconstructing it from otherwise seemingly incommensurable elements to create a new whole to cope with *hüzün* – a feeling of collective melancholia offset by the gradual impoverishment and provincialization of Istanbul. The theme of blurred boundaries and heterotopic spaces permeates *Istanbul: Memories and the City* on many levels, including the book's elusive genre, its nonlinear narrative structure, and its depiction of enmeshed social and spatial borders within the city.

In an interview held in 2007, Pamuk stated, "Over the last twenty years, we have witnessed a return to the 18th century Diderot kind of novel, which is a form that combines essays and novels together. Actually, I consider myself a sort of a representative of that 'encyclopedic' novel." Alluding to Mallarmé, Pamuk added, "everything in the world, for the imaginative novelist or imaginative literary person, is in fact made to end up in a book. That's how I see the world as well, because I am a novelist, and I care about the informative, encyclopedic quality of the novel" (interview by Carol Becker, par. 2). A preeminent example of Pamuk's encyclopedic works is his autobiographical memoir, *İstanbul: Hatıralar ve şehir* (2003; *Istanbul: Memories and the City*, 2004). The book covers a twenty-year-long period from Pamuk's birth in 1952 to his decision to become an author in 1972, particularly narrating Istanbul in the 1960s and 1970s and ends right before the 1980s, when Turkey opened to global liberal market economy. *Istanbul: Memories and the City* juxtaposes two stories within this twenty-year time span: the story of a transforming city and the story of

Pamuk's formation as an Istanbul author in the face of melancholic episodes of loss on personal and urban scales. To bridge those two purportedly incommensurate plots, Pamuk works like a collector in the sense that Walter Benjamin explains: "to renew the old world – that is the collector's deepest desire when he is driven to acquire new things" (61). I argue that in *Istanbul: Memories and the City*, Pamuk reimagines the city, like a collector, by reconstructing it from seemingly incommensurable elements to create a new whole to cope with *hüzün* – a feeling of collective melancholia offset by the gradual impoverishment and provincialization of Istanbul. Pamuk forges a new Istanbul landscape by situating himself in a liminal space that allows him to see his hometown simultaneously as an insider and an outsider.

For Pamuk, Istanbul turned into a provincialized city in the wake of two decisive political, social, and economic events that occurred during the second part of the twentieth century: First, Istanbul lost its status as the Ottoman imperial capital when the new Turkish Republic moved the capital from Istanbul to Ankara in 1923. Second, migrants from Anatolian provinces of Turkey started to populate Istanbul. As a result, the social and economic character of the city has irreversibly changed. To reckon with these changes in his hometown, Pamuk reimagines a new spatial configuration for Istanbul by walking between the rich and the poor neighborhoods of the city. During these walks, Pamuk transgresses the boundaries of his home neighborhood – the westernized, affluent Nişantaşı district – and discovers what he views as impoverished outlying neighborhoods. Eventually, during a boat trip through the Golden Horn, Pamuk comes to terms with the overwhelming *hüzün* in Istanbul, and in his own identity, by reconfiguring the city as a space of blurred boundaries where disparate social, historical, and spatial fragments are interwoven as in a Foucauldian heterotopia – counter-sites which are "capable of juxtaposing in a single real place several spaces, several sites that are in themselves incompatible" (25). The theme of blurred boundaries and heterotopic spaces pervades *Istanbul: Memories and the City* on many levels, including its elusive genre, its nonlinear narrative structure, and its depiction of enmeshed social and spatial borders within the city.

The Question of Genre

Pamuk's *Istanbul: Memories and the City* challenges the set boundaries of genre by thematizing the heterogeneity of the narrative. Since the title of the book openly labels the narrative as a memoir, Pamuk was asked in an interview why he wrote his autobiography so early in his life. He hinted that *Istanbul* is primarily a memoir, responding "I want to capture that still crisp freshness of the memory" ("Implementing Disform" 180). However, a closer look at the narrative reveals that it strongly demonstrates the qualities of a *Künstlerroman*, in which Pamuk narrates his transformation from a painter into an author over the course of his youth – the narrative ends at the very point when he decides to become an author.[1] The narrative could well be a *Bildungsroman* in the sense that the book narrates a coming-of-age story (yet another border-crossing experience), at the end of which the protagonist reaches an epiphany by accepting a reality in his life – the heterogeneity in the melancholic landscape of what he calls his hometown. Pamuk's profound concern with Istanbul also makes the narrative a city novel, where the city's transformation acts as a counterpart to Pamuk's discovery of his own identity as reflected in the city space.

Above all, *Istanbul* is a travel narrative with its narrator in endless motion between different parts of the city. Pamuk's constant references to nineteenth-century French travelers links the book to a travel writing archive. He devotes whole sections to travelers including Melling, Nerval, Gautier and to Turkish authors, such as Tanpınar and Yahya Kemal, who have direct intertextual connections with those European writers. Nerval occupies a central position in the network; both Gautier and Tanpınar had remembered Nerval as they walked through Istanbul streets. Similarly, Pamuk emphasizes that he feels the "closest bond" (110) with the Turkish author Tanpınar, who greatly admired Nerval (222). By doing so, Pamuk positions himself in a pantheon of European and Turkish writers to highlight his position concurrently as a resident and a traveler in Istanbul. The

---

[1] Also see Erol's discussion on the chronotope of Istanbul and Laschinger's take on flâneuring and creative economy in Pamuk's narrative. Both authors also argue for the *Künsterroman* characteristics in *Istanbul*.

encyclopedic details, historical notes, and photographs accompanying the text make it a travel narrative in service of foreign and local travelers alike.

Pamuk adopts the gaze of an outsider and this entails consciously assuming a polymorphous identity between East and West. However, his adoption is not a blatant borrowing but a more complex process of metamorphosis; he instead chooses to intermingle, even at times trade places with a European traveler. This theme is particularly prominent in his novel *Beyaz kale* (1985; *The White Castle*, 1990), in which Pamuk merges the identities of a Venetian slave and an Ottoman master in the seventeenth-century Ottoman Empire. The novel derives its plot from a pseudotranslation of a manuscript found by a fictional character, Darvınoğlu (a Turkified translation of "the son of Darwin"). In the novel, the two characters gradually exchange places so that by the end of the narrative, the reader cannot distinguish the characters from each other.[2] In his *Istanbul*, too, Pamuk internalizes European travel accounts by lulling himself into "believing the accounts of Western outsiders are my own memories" (242). A part of this internalization at times morphs into assuming the role of a European in Istanbul: "whenever I sense the absence of western eyes, I become my own Westerner" (288). Pamuk adopts the gaze of a foreigner to decenter himself and his realistic outlook, often not without pleasure. When he starts to paint the city's poor neighborhoods and back alleys at the age of fifteen, as opposed to the open landscape of the Bosporus (where the rich live), not only does he feel "a degree of detachment" but he also leaves himself behind in an ecstatic kind of pleasure (269). This pleasure derives from the imitation of a European painter, Utrillo – a practice that grants him a sense of paradoxical confidence: he would finally find his own style and identity while imitating that of another.

Besides its elusive genre that bridges the characteristics of disparate genres of writing, the book's nonlinear, fragmented narrative structure reproduces its overall concern with heterogeneous spaces. This narrative structure interweaves the story of Istanbul with Pamuk's life story in chapters that seem unrelated at first. However, the chapter organization in *Istanbul* combines fragmental time schemes and thereby allows for Pamuk's life

---

[2] For studies on the self and the other in *The White Castle*, see works by Yazıcıoğlu, and Pittman.

story to run parallel with Istanbul's history. Consider the juxtaposition of the section entitled "The Rich" with the section "On the Ships That Passed through the Bosphorus, Famous Fires, Moving House, and Other Disasters." Both sections talk about the loss of riches in the personal and city scales, respectively. In "The Rich," Pamuk narrates his family's dwindling capital in the second half of the twentieth century (for him, this was one of the "disasters" in his life) and the new rich from among Anatolian landowners taking their place. In a way that parallels this personal history, the subsequent section details the loss of Ottoman heritage and the riches of the city with occasional fires. Similarly, the section titled "Four Lonely Melancholic Writers" is placed strategically right before the chapter titled "My Grandmother." The former narrates the walks of the four Turkish authors in the ruined, outlying neighborhoods of the city to draw inspiration from the Ottoman tradition and European authors at once. This section precedes Pamuk's personal memoirs of his grandmother, a woman who witnessed the transition of Istanbul from the Ottoman to the Republican period, and her struggles to keep up with the privileges that her class provided her, despite the loss of the family fortune over the years. His grandmother epitomizes what the four melancholic writers are searching for: a person who manages to keep up a westernized lifestyle with a touch of Ottoman tradition. The grandmother spends most of her time at home (if not relaxing in her bed) as if to keep her confined world untarnished with the rapidly changing architectural, social, cultural, and economic landscape of the city.

The Question of Provinciality

Pamuk's itinerary in the city reproduces his concern with the changing face of the city in the post-Ottoman period. When Pamuk goes walking through the historic shopping avenue Grand Rue de Pera – subsequently named İstiklal Caddesi (Independence Street) – the "reading machine" in his mind bricolages words to create new wholes:
"SPRINGSALESELAMIBUFFETPUBLICTELEPHONESTAR
BEYOĞLUIPNOTARYALEMACARONIANANKARAMARKET

SHOWHAIRDRESSERHEALTHAPTRADIOANDTRANSISTORS" (319).³

This is when Pamuk stretches the limits of the language to the point that he undermines it. This new configuration combines what had been originally disparate; words and objects that seem to have no relation form imbricated wholes and create a new space, in a way reminiscent of the everyday life tactics mapped by de Certeau, who associates the act of walking and reading to producing new spaces (117).

Pamuk produces these new spaces in the everyday details of city life to surmount a feeling of *hüzün* that he associates with a complex process of political, cultural, and economic impoverishment. In the section titled "To Be Unhappy Is to Hate Oneself and One's City," he combines the words on the billboards as he tries to imagine a "golden age" where "everything was a beautiful whole" as in the works of "western travelers like Nerval, Gautier, and de Amicis." However, he quickly remembers that he loves the city for its lack of purity, which reminds him of *hüzün* (320). For Pamuk, this collective melancholia differs from Lévi-Strauss's *tristesse* because *hüzün* derives from living among the "remains of a glorious civilization" which reminds the Istanbul residents that "the present city is so poor and confused that it can never again dream of rising to its former heights of wealth, power, and culture" (101). While observing the city and its residents, Pamuk forges a new space of incommensurate elements of the past and the present to reckon with his personal identity crisis as a young man growing up in the decaying capital of a former empire: "*Hüzün* rises out of the pain they [Istanbul residents] feel for everything that has been lost, but it is also what compels them to invent new defeats and new ways to express their impoverishment" (103).⁴ This dismal feeling closely relates to a consciousness of being left outside in the world – a sense of provinciality that permeates Pamuk's narrative. In *Istanbul*, Pamuk alludes to the theme of provinciality on two fronts: Turkey's provincial positioning in relation to Europe and Is-

---

³ "BAHARİNDİRİMSELAMİBÜFEUMUMİTELEFONSTARBEYOĞLUNOTERİP İYALEMAKARNASIANKARAPAZARISHOWKUAFÖRSAĞLIKAPTRADYOV ETRANSİSTÖRLERİ" (*İstanbul* 298).

⁴ For other discussions of *hüzün* in Pamuk's works, see Almond, and Helvacioglu.

tanbul's provincialization due to the changing economic and social conditions in the 1960s and 1970s.

To understand Pamuk's references to Turkey's and Istanbul's provinciality, let us start with his self-conscious provinciality as reflected in his home neighborhood. The Nişantaşı neighborhood, one of the beacons of westernization in the Ottoman Empire, is conveniently located in the European side of Istanbul, in proximity to the Grand Rue de Pera, the modern military barracks in Harbiye, and the new sultan palaces along the Bosporus. Since its conception, it has housed bourgeois families, shopping districts, and European-style apartment buildings. It was gradually established in the second half of the nineteenth century, when the physical boundaries of the Ottoman capital started to expand from Istanbul proper (the historical peninsula) toward the northern shore of the Golden Horn and the banks of the Bosporus. The neighborhood developed further when Ottoman elites and foreign ambassadors started to build residences in the proximity of the new Yıldız and Dolmabahçe palaces. The spatial structure of the new Nişantaşı district was perfectly in accord with modern city-planning schemes: wooden mansions with neoclassical façades were located along wide, straight streets that are organized according to a grid system. Later, these residences were replaced with apartment buildings occupied by rich business owners.[5] The Pamuk Apartments, where Pamuk was born and spent his early childhood, were one of the tall stone buildings. Despite being in a quarter of Istanbul most frequently associated with Europeanization, the building stood at the border of Ottoman Istanbul, "at the edge [*kenar*] of a large plot of land in Nişantaşı that had once been the garden of a pasha's mansion" (26). Early in his life, the positioning of the Pamuk Apartments on the "edge" of a space linked to the Ottoman past identifies Pamuk's existence at the border of the European and the Ottoman, in a vulnerable position. In later years, during his adolescence, Pamuk becomes aware of the peripheral position of his birth neighborhood when he realizes that "I did not, in fact, live in the center of the world and the place where I lived was not –

---

[5] For more information on Istanbul's modern urban development, see Çelik's foundational work on the transformation of Istanbul's urban structure in the nineteenth century (for the Pera district, see 64-37) and Akbayar's essay on Nişantaşı in *Dünden bugüne İstanbul ansiklopedisi* (88-90).

this was more painful – the world's beacon" (302). Much later, in his Nobel ceremony speech, Pamuk further broadens his self-perceived provinciality to include Turkey's (and Turkish literature's) provincial position in a EuroAtlantic-centric world.

In his speech at the Nobel ceremony in 2006, Pamuk parallels his marginal position as a resident of Istanbul with the literary provinciality of Turkish literature within world literature. He states, "As for my place in the world – in life, as in literature, my basic feeling was that I was 'not in the centre.' In the centre of the world, there was a life richer and more exciting than our own, and with all of Istanbul, all of Turkey, I was outside it." Pamuk stated in this very speech that "in the same way, there was a world literature, and its centre, too, was very far away from me" (par. 14). At first, Pamuk's references to centers and peripheries in his Nobel speech reveals his consciousness of the recent themes in world literary studies, which seek to map world literature as composed of cores and peripheries.[6] However, the keywords in the speech and themes in Pamuk's larger oeuvre show that his references to centers and peripheries also tap into Turkish literary and cultural archive.

Pamuk's Nobel speech, given in Turkish, comprises keywords that point toward a feeling of provinciality. In the Turkish original of the speech, two synonyms that Pamuk uses for being "outside" are *dışarı* and *taşra*. Although no longer transparent in present-day spelling, both words come from a common root, *dış* meaning "outside, exterior, outer." *Dışarı* refers to the space outside, provinces, and foreign lands. Similarly, *taşra* signifies the outside in the sense of "provinces, the provincial." Pamuk's choice of words hints at the rooted schemes of social organization around the tropes of inside(r) and outside(r), the reflections of which can be observed across a wide range of poetic and artistic expressions.

Walter Andrews and Irene Markoff show that Ottoman Turkish poetry, shadow-puppet theater, and visual arts can be characterized by patterns of compartmentalization and concentricity (e.g., lover and beloved, male and

---

[6] A group of works seeks to map world literature and the cultural, social, and economic relations within according to centers and peripheries. Some prominent examples are Pascale Casanova's *The World Republic of Letters* and Moretti's *Atlas of the European Novel* and *Maps, Graphs, and Trees*.

female, ruler and subjects, nested gardens and neighborhoods). Within these patterns, they argue, the relationships of the insiders and outsiders indicate not only artistic preferences, but also the social structure of ordinary relationships (38).[7] According to this, the notion of the outsider and the insider are completely subjective –an insider in one context can be an outsider in another. Similarly, in modern literature and culture, *taşra* signifies a feeling of being left outside, rather than a geographical position. The literary critic and essayist Nurdan Gürbilek expands on the meaning of *taşra* as self-perception in her seminal essay on modern Turkish literature and provinciality: "for *taşra* to discern itself as *taşra*, it must become conscious of another life denied to it and to its peripheral position in relation to a center, see itself through the eyes of that center, and perceive itself as incomplete and deprived in comparison to that center" (52; my translation).[8] In that case, *taşra* finds its representation in the metaphorical relationship between the center and peripheries. According to that scheme, a place that is not very distant from Istanbul can well be considered metaphorically provincial by being "outside" the urban center and the urban culture that the "center" designates, regardless of its geographical position. The arbitrary organization of the center and the periphery points to a heterotopic relation between the center and the province, as they are interchangeable and intermingled. Pamuk's notion of the outside, or *taşra*, implies a mental rather than geographical distance.[9]

---

[7] Many studies have demonstrated that Pamuk was aware of these social and cultural meanings, as he used the themes of classical poetry in his works. Berna Moran (93-104) draws parallels between *The Black Book* and Rumi's *Mesnevi* and Şeyh Galip's *Hüsn ü aşk* (*Beauty and Love*). Likewise, Brendemoen tracks the Sufi themes in *The Black Book* and Ian Almond explores the role of Sufi tradition in the common theme of sadness in Pamuk's works. Didem Havlıoğlu suggests that a reader who can understand the allusions to Ottoman literature in *The Black Book* will be able to understand the subtexts in the novel (14).

[8] "Taşranın kendisini taşra olarak ayrıştırabilmesi için, kendisinden esirgenmiş bir başka yaşantının, kıyısına itildiği bir merkezin farkına varması, kendisini onun gözüyle görmesi, onun karşısında kendisini eksik, yoksun hissetmesi gerekir" (Gürbilek 52).

[9] Also see the volume edited by Bora, *Taşraya bakmak*, for more discussions on the intermingling of the provinces with the city in modern Turkey.

Many have argued that Pamuk's bourgeois background starkly distinguishes him from the 1980s Turkish authors, who focused on marginalized villagers. Moreover, critics have suggested that Pamuk's postmodernist writing style strikingly differs from the earlier generation of leftist-realist writers.[10] However, I contend that while in terms of writing style Pamuk might differ from the earlier generation of writers, thematically, he continues to write about the tension between the province and the city – a theme that intensely preoccupied his predecessors.[11] Another basic difference between Pamuk and his predecessors is that he sees the provincial in the city. Istanbul in Pamuk's imagination is a heterotopic space where the outside and the inside, the insiders and the outsiders are enmeshed. With his interest in the tension between the center and the province, Pamuk comes from a tradition of authors who have taken issue with border negotiation between the center and the province. We can see this negotiation in a number of Pamuk's novels, particularly in relation to the theme of travel to the outside.

Pamuk's several works involve a travel to the outside. According to Nergis Ertürk a theme of "journey to the *taşra*" is an organizing schema of Pamuk's entire body of work (637). In *Yeni hayat* (1994; *The New Life*, 1998) a character from Germany travels to Anatolia; similarly, in *Kar* (2002; *Snow*, 2004) the protagonist goes to the provincial town of Kars, on the eastern border of Turkey. Even in Pamuk's novels that take place in Istanbul, we witness mobile characters walking back and forth between rich and poor neighborhoods there. In *Kara kitap* (1990; *The Black Book*, 1994) the main character walks through Istanbul streets in search of his lost wife. In *Masumiyet müzesi* (2008; *The Museum of Innocence*, 2009) the protagonist Kemal, a character from the westernized Nişantaşı neighborhood, frequents his lover Füsun's home located in the less affluent, historic neighborhood of Çukurcuma. Likewise, in one of his latest novels, *Kafamda bir tuhaflık* (2014; *A Strangeness in My Mind*, 2014), the street seller Mevlut

---

[10] See Gün 62 and Brendemoen 209.
[11] The interest in the interaction between the center and the provinces cultivated a genre called "Village Novels" (*köy romanları*) throughout the nineteenth and twentieth centuries. For foundational studies on village novels, see Rathbun, and Dino. For a more recent survey of Turkish authors' engagement with Anatolia, see Parla.

earns his living by walking from his poor neighborhood to richer parts of the city, selling various homemade products. In these walks, Pamuk's characters never limit themselves to their home neighborhood, whether rich or poor; instead, they adopt a mobility that represents a constant border crossing experience between different social classes and sections of the city. This constant mobility renders Istanbul a space of heterotopic provincialities where the boundaries between the inside and the outside are rather porous.

In *Istanbul*, what makes Pamuk's journey to the outside within the space of a single city is his simultaneous identification as an insider and an outsider. Pamuk portrays an uncanny journey to the outside without leaving the urban space: while he states "I've never left Istanbul, never left the houses, streets, neighborhoods of my childhood. [...] my imagination [...] requires that I stay in the same city" (5-6), as he walks in the back streets of Istanbul, he also acknowledges that "Sometimes one's city can look like an alien place" (317). Pamuk's walks on the edges of metropolitan Istanbul as a member of the bourgeoisie produce a spatial and temporal displacement comparable to that of a distant journey. Istanbul's backstreets and outlying neighborhoods replace the *taşra* in Pamuk's works.

The narrative organization in *Istanbul* epitomizes this metaphoric journey to the outside. The narrative expands from the inside to the outside: it starts before Pamuk's birth, in his mother's womb, and slowly transitions from his parents' apartment and later into the whole building in which "every apartment seemed like a different country, a separate universe" (17). During his childhood, Pamuk's world gradually stretches as far as the neighborhoods surrounding his home and finally progresses into the surrounding districts, each of which seem like a "distant land" early on in his life (344). The narrative ends with a section in which Pamuk's mother insists that he goes out on the streets in her efforts to convince him to get his degree in architecture instead of idling at home with dreams of being a painter. Pamuk's world expanding to the outside within Istanbul marks the first steps of his realization of the social and economic difference between his birth neighborhood and the outlying neighborhoods surrounding it. Not coincidentally, most of *Istanbul* focuses on Pamuk's childhood and early youth memories. Zafer Doğan's essay on the problem of provinciality in

Snow in this volume brings up the relationship between provinciality and the metaphor of childhood. According to Doğan, the feeling of marginalization in the residents of the province leads to disappointments similar to those in an unrequited love and even to a childish defensiveness against the center on a personal and on a national level. In *Istanbul*, this metaphor of childhood underpins Pamuk's extensive narration of his childhood and early youth memories. The theme of mobility in the narrative depicts a negotiation of the border between this metaphorical, reactive childhood and a mature adulthood that is at peace with its position in the world.

The Question of Capital

Most of Pamuk's recurring childhood and early youth memories revolve around his family's diminishing income and the parallel provincialization of Istanbul. For Pamuk, Istanbul and Turkey, in whole, are located at the margins of the world: "As Istanbul grew even poorer, it lost its importance in the world and became a remote place burdened with high unemployment. As a child I had no sense of living in a great world capital but rather in a poor provincial city" (*taşra kenti*) (246). During his early youth, Pamuk starts compartmentalizing the world between the "happy people" in the outside world and "the rest of the world." He writes, "Happy people in Europe and America could lead lives as beautiful and as meaningful as the ones I'd just seen in a Hollywood film." As opposed to the happy lives, Pamuk and the "rest of the world" were "condemned to live out our time in places that were shabby, broken-down, featureless, badly-painted, dilapidated and cheap; we were doomed to unimportant, second-class, neglected existences" (310), and this applies to people who live in the relatively affluent Nişantaşı neighborhood. In this world organized according to economic and material terms instead of cultural distance, people in Europe and America dominate the "happy" core, whereas those in the rest of the world lead invisible lives, as if confined in a prison. The unimportant residents of a desolate periphery were convicted "never to do anything that anyone in the outside world might think worthy of notice" (310). This world is ruled by inequality: affluence versus poverty, significant businesses versus neglected existences.

Pamuk narrates the provincial poverty and rearrangement of capital both at the urban scale and personal scale: the poverty and backwardness that emerged in post-Ottoman period Istanbul parallel the Pamuk family's decreasing financial means. While Turkey suffers from economic and social marginalization, within Pamuk's personal life an economic dimension of provinciality plays an important role. He mentions several times that his industrialist grandfather, who was born in Ottoman times and who founded a factory that supported the railroad building spree in the early years of the Turkish Republic, accumulated capital, but then his father and uncle spent that capital on failed business ventures. His family's fate gradually intermingled with the fate of the empire as they exhausted their wealth: "It was a long time coming, arriving by a circuitous route, but the cloud of gloom and loss spread over Istanbul by the fall of the Ottoman Empire had finally claimed my family too" (17). The Pamuk family is seized in an encroaching postimperial melancholia that transforms the urban space and everything associated with it. This transformation reveals itself clearly in the encounter between the old Istanbul families and newcomers to the city.

The provincialization of Istanbul involved the replacing of the Ottoman elite with a new wave of wealthy migrants from Anatolia. Starting with the 1950s, a mass migration took place from the rural areas of Turkey into urban centers such as Istanbul due to the rapidly increasing Turkish population, the lack of agricultural opportunities in rural areas, and the attraction of new industrial centers in big cities (Zürcher 269). Those who migrated to the urban centers had great interest in upward social mobility, and some of them gained wealth within a short time. At the same time, families who grew richer in Anatolia were moving to Istanbul as the city gradually became industrialized in the 1970s.[12] This meant that the capital was changing hands from the old Istanbul elite, such as the Pamuk family, to the new migrants who came from outside of Istanbul. Looking out from a bourgeois-Istanbul point of view, Pamuk sees these new families as starkly provincial (*taşralı*) compared to his own family. This new group of people was distinguished from the Istanbul families with their willingness to show

---

[12] See Bali's *Tarz-ı Hayat'tan Life Style'a: Yeni seçkinler, yeni mekanlar, yeni yaşamlar* for a book-length account of the changing face of the Istanbul elite with migrations from Anatolia throughout the second half of the twentieth century.

off their wealth, their "provincial courage" (*taşralı cesareti*), and their "provincial accent" (*taşralı aksanı*) (190). On the other end of the spectrum were the westernized Ottoman elites who failed to capitalize on their inherited wealth because they were reluctant to work with the new rich, the "vulgar businessmen" as they called them (193). Toward the end of the twentieth century, with migrations from Anatolia to Istanbul, the borders between the center and provinces have gradually intermingled. The tension between the center and the provinces was transferred to urban areas as Turkey became more and more provincialized by distancing itself economically, socially, politically, and culturally from the West.

The Question of Space

Pamuk sees Istanbul both as an insider and an outsider and thus perceives the provinciality in the city. While he walks through the city's rich and poor neighborhoods, he acts as a resident of Istanbul and a European traveler at once. Early in the narrative, he declares the affinity between Istanbul and his life when he writes, "Istanbul's fate is my fate. I am attached to this city because it has made me who I am" (6). However, at the height of his identity crisis during his early youth, much like any melancholic person, he hates the city and he remembers thinking, "I've never wholly belonged to this city" (320). Through this double existence as an insider and an outsider, Pamuk highlights a complicated sense of provinciality that blurs the boundaries between the center and the periphery.

The outlying neighborhoods (*kenar mahalle*) play an important role in the way Pamuk and his predecessors sought to perceive the city from a foreigner's perspective. Literally, *kenar mahalle* means "a neighborhood on the periphery," but the phrase also implies a poorer section of the city.[13] The outlying neighborhoods refer to the impoverished sections of Ottoman Istanbul, particularly those outside the wealthy neighborhoods that house westernized buildings made during the nineteenth century. Once more, geographical distance is not the criteria; what makes these neighborhoods

---

[13] *Istanbul*'s translator, Maureen Freely, renders *kenar mahalle* interchangeably, as "poor neighborhoods" and "impoverished neighborhoods" (or, in a few instances, as "outlying neighborhoods").

"marginal" is their social, economic, and cultural distance in relation to what is considered "modern" in mid-twentieth century Turkey. The post-imperial loss embodied in these neighborhoods places them in a spatio-temporal distance to a modernity that left them deprived of their previous status. The keyword *kenar* (margin) thus reflects these meanings better than 'poor' or 'impoverished.' Ironically, the very peripherality of these neighborhoods proves to be spaces of potential renewal for Pamuk and his predecessors, who seek to challenge the boundaries of their set literary traditions and literary marginality. Much like European travelers, the two Turkish authors Ahmet Hamdi Tanpınar and Yahya Kemal wandered through the poor neighborhoods in search of a Turkish national identity. Tanpınar (who also resided in the westernized Pera section of Istanbul) regularly visited the outlying neighborhoods "to accustom himself to the fact of living in an impoverished country, in a city that no longer mattered in the eyes of the world. To explore the poor neighborhoods, then, was to address the reality that Istanbul and Turkey were themselves poor neighborhoods" (246).

These authors were searching for an authentic national literary style: while they were dazzled by the brilliance of French authors, they also sought to create an authentic style of thei own to overcome their perceived provinciality. They saw Istanbul through the eyes of a Westerner in their search for a way to express the *hüzün* of the city. They appropriated an outsider's gaze from European traveler accounts, such as those of Nerval and Gautier, who looked for romanticized views of Istanbul in its "wings" and "poorer quarters" (225). They were vexed by contradictions "to be western and yet, at the same time, to be authentic" (112). They sought to see the city from a foreigner's perspective. These visits to the margins of the city provided Tanpınar, and later Pamuk, with the gaze of a foreigner that stimulated them to cultivate a new approach in literature by combining the two seemingly incommensurate literary traditions: the French and the Turkish. Following their lead, in a section titled "The Picturesque and the Outlying Neighborhoods" Pamuk emphasizes the importance of being an outsider to take pleasure from the exotic features of the city: "To savor Istanbul's back streets, to appreciate the vines and trees that endow its ruins with accidental grace, you must, first and foremost, be a stranger to them."

He adds, "Those who take pleasure in the accidental beauty of poverty and historical decay, those of us who see the picturesque in the ruins – invariably, we're people who come from the outside" (256-57). Being from the richer, westernized section of the city, the best place for Pamuk to be a foreigner in Istanbul is the peripheral neighborhoods: the provinciality, poverty, and backwardness, as well as the exotic character of the city, find their best reflection in its poor neighborhoods.

Not coincidentally, throughout *Istanbul*, Pamuk perambulates the back streets and outlying neighborhoods feeling like a foreigner. He captures a true feeling of foreignness when he goes to the peripheries of the city, where children mistakenly take him and his girlfriend to be tourists who have lost their way in the least westernized, conservative neighborhoods surrounding the Ottoman mosques and bazaars. After hearing the children ask them in English, "Tourist, tourist, what is your name?," they decide to stay away from those neighborhoods, and choose to take refuge in the Museum of Painting and Sculpture, which houses European paintings by French painters such as Bonnard and Matisse, as well as works by Turkish painters who "allowed themselves to be influenced by western artists" (336). The feeling of foreignness in the outlying neighborhoods of Istanbul draws Pamuk and his companion back to a space where they would find westernized acquaintances sheltered in the space of a museum, gazing at them through framed spaces of their paintings.

During his college years, Pamuk begins to frequent Istanbul's backstreets and peripheral neighborhoods like a Baudelarian *flâneur*. He takes these itinerant journeys to escape the uninspiring buildings of the school of architecture where he is a student and to find a way out of his melancholia by aimlessly walking in the streets of Istanbul. His daily journeys in the city streets take him from the familiar to the unfamiliar. First, he walks through the familiar neighborhoods of his childhood, such as those of the westernized Pera and Taksim. Soon after, he goes to the neighborhoods on the banks of the Golden Horn, which "looked fake, like a film set" (344). As opposed to the clean avenues lined with apartment buildings in the "international style" (318) in the modernized neighborhoods such as Harbiye (which takes its name from the military barracks in its vicinity), Pamuk looks for a remedy for his melancholia in the ruins of the older, more impoverished neighborhoods, "which, as they got poorer, seemed older, giving one the impression that middle-class families had been there for thousands of years, changing language, race, religion as the oppressive state required" (345).

A boat ride through the Golden Horn occasions a climactic scene where Pamuk discovers the heart of the city and mitigates his identity crisis. At the end of one of his itinerant walks, in March 1972, Pamuk jumps on a small city ferry on the Golden Horn. Although the boat is a new space for him, he feels at home with the other commuters in it who are busy with their quotidian worries. As the boat starts its short journey, Pamuk looks through the window, as if watching an old movie, and starts seeing the incommensurate times and spaces coming together to create a whole new landscape: hills covered with wooden houses of old Istanbul, cypress-filled cemeteries, shipyards, dilapidated Byzantine churches, Greek neighborhoods, and Ottoman mosques all seem to converge. The boat's engine makes a sound like his mother's sewing machine, as if stitching all these bits and pieces together (347-48). At this moment of epiphany, he asks himself,

> Is this the secret of Istanbul – that beneath its grand history, its living poverty, its outward-looking monuments, and its sublime landscapes, its poor hide the city's soul inside a fragile web? But here we have come full circle, for anything we say about the city's essence says more about our own lives and our own states of mind. The city has no center other than ourselves. (349)

The moving space of the boat marks the center of the city as the mutable center of the Self. Here, social, cultural, and historical hierarchies are suspended; Pamuk's self dissipates in the collective, immediately assuaging his feeling of loneliness and poverty.

The boat journey takes place in a liminal space, the historic waterway of the Golden Horn. Anthony D. King states that boundaries of the city are the key places where the "task of imagining the city" can be executed: "Boundaries mark the space where one thing turns into something else, they exclude as well as include" (3). During this boat journey, the Golden

Horn becomes the ultimate boundary between Old Istanbul, on its southern shore, and the westernized Pera neighborhood on its northern shore. The natural waterway serves as a liminal space that at once connects and separates the two sections of the city. While the southern shore of the Golden Horn housed the Ottoman palace, the Sublime Porte, and grand mosques as well as the old Byzantine churches and Greek neighborhoods, the northern part of the waterway was the section where the foreign emissaries, intellectuals, and Greek, Jewish, and Armenian citizens of the empire led a more westernized lifestyle starting in the nineteenth century. The Golden Horn is a heterotopic space – a space of no place that connects and separates at once. It is a lively passage that people use daily, yet no one dwells there.

But there is more to this liminal space. It is not just the Golden Horn but also the very space of the boat itself, through which Pamuk watches the city like a bricolage of fragments. At the beginning of this journey, when the boat moves, Pamuk immediately feels a sense of "sitting now in the heart of the city" (346). This newly found center (a previously marginal space) provides the observer with a new perspective bridging disparate elements that constitute the imagined space of the city. When Pamuk takes the boat on the Golden Horn, his self quickly dissolves in the collective: "I adapted to my new circumstances [...] I was just another commuter who traveled up and down the Golden Horn on this ferry every day" (346). At the same time, he can watch the city like a film from the windows of the ferry:

> through the ship's clouded, trembling windows, this midday scene seemed, like the Istanbul views I saw in disintegrating old movies, as dark as midnight. [...] At times the sky seemed pitch black, but then, just like a corner in a film that suddenly comes aflame, a cold snow light would appear. (348-49)

The boat scene adeptly shows the paradoxes of being an insider and an outsider in a place where centers and peripheries constantly change: a quotidian insider sitting at the heart of the city and a new outsider watching the city flow like a film in front of his eyes. Pamuk grapples with the melancholy that overpowers the city by coming to terms with this paradoxical existence when he eventually comes "to relax and accept the *hüzün* that gives Istanbul its grave beauty, the *hüzün* that is its fate" (352).

This boat ride comes at an opportune time when the pleasure resulting from painting his girlfriend gradually dissipates, leading Pamuk to seek new inspiration to propel his art. He channels his frustrated energies to the city streets after a break-up with his college love, conveniently nicknamed Black Rose for its associations with black bile, namely melancholia. This channeling of energy reminds of Freud's definition of melancholia: the withdrawal of cathectic energy from the lost object and its diversion to another object to make up for the impoverishment of the ego (245-46). While Black Rose stands for the lost riches and happy memories in a golden age in Istanbul, the streets of Istanbul assume the role of the other object that Pamuk uses to remedy the simultaneous depreciation of his ego and the riches of the old imperial city, now pushed to the margins. He finds his new inspiration in the liminal space that he now occupies: a new Istanbul landscape bricolaged through the lens of the boat window. He finds a consolation in this in-betweenness as an outsider and an insider at once as he comes to terms with the dazzling effects of the simultaneous modernization and provincialization of Istanbul. This new artistic inspiration is ever more powerful than painting the beauties of the city. He instead chooses to internalize the good and the bad, the black and the white, and the happiness and the *hüzün* that empowers the whole city.

Conclusion

Pamuk's liminal insider/outsider perspective of Istanbul (and Turkey) paved the way to two conflicting events: he was acclaimed as a global writer in the world literary scene and he was harshly criticized for his work and political views in Turkey. On the eve of his receipt of the Nobel Prize, he was taken to court for denigrating Turkishness, which placed him in the pantheon of dissident authors in Turkish literature.[14] After he was awarded the prize, columnists and commentators in mainstream media suggested that behind Pamuk's success was that he thought like a westerner, that

---

[14] See Göknar's book-length study for a discussion of Pamuk as a dissident author.

hence he could never be a true Turk,[15] or that he knew how to play by the rules of the world literary market and wrote works that can be easily translated to English.[16]

To what extent does Pamuk's liminal positioning an insider/outsider reflect on his native language in a way that leads him to produce an easily-translatable Turkish? It is not a secret among critics and translators that Pamuk's works read well in English. As Güneli Gün, one of the translators of Pamuk's *Kara kitap* (*The Black Book*) puts it, Pamuk is successful in the world literary market because he was "doing the right thing at the right time" and because "his work translates like a charm" (62). Ease of translation is now perceived as a membership card to a global literature, or a type of literature that Rebecca L. Walkowitz calls "born translated" – that is, works written to be translated from the start and works that internalize translation not only in their language, but also in their narrative structure (4-5).

But translations may not be the only condition to reach the global literary market. Clearly, there are other dynamics that play a decisive role in an author's rise to global fame: among these are the choices made not just by the translator or the author, but by the editors and copyeditors in the process of publishing a book in English. As B. Venkat Mani states, beyond the author and the translator, the literary critic is also one of the important actors that enable distribution and circulation of literary works to a worldwide readership (par. 2). By way of conclusion, I will conjecture that literary-critical trends also contributed to Pamuk's consecration in the world literary scene. With growing interest in world literature in the 1990s, critics sought to challenge the status quo of European universalism by paying attention to marginalized literatures, among which was Turkish literature. The American Comparative Literature Association's (ACLA) "Bernheimer Report" (1993) is telling in this regard. The "Bernheimer Report" sought to remap comparative literature to grapple with a restrictive Eurocentrism. The "Bernheimer Report" advised future generations of comparatists to

---

[15] See Ulagay's column for a summary of the immediate reactions to Pamuk's Nobel Prize in mainstream media.

[16] See Bali's article for an overview of criticisms to Pamuk and a defense of Pamuk's use of literary agents.

study the relations between Western and non-Western cultures in hopes of reaching beyond Europe and Europe's high-cultural lineage. The report drew attention to the theory of "boundaries" and "remapping" by positing that comparatists "now have expanded opportunities to theorize the nature of the boundaries to be crossed and to participate in their remapping" (43). Along the lines of this broadened perspective, Bruce Robbins signaled a change in the conception of world literature when he stated regarding world literature that "we are speaking of a new framing of the whole which revalues both unfamiliar and long-accepted genres, produces new concepts and criteria of judgment [...]" (170). This reframing aimed at shifting the focus of comparative literature and world literature towards a more inclusive world literary canon. It is possible to assume that within a decade of this shift, literary theory's quest to challenge the status quo of European universalism by way of turning its attention to marginalized literatures paved the way for Pamuk's Nobel Prize in Literature. Pamuk's liminal lens through which he depicted Istanbul as a provincial space and his continuous problematization of the metaphorical distance between the province and the "center" conveniently (or coincidentally) dovetailed with a turn-of-the-century transformation in literary criticism.

What better place for Pamuk to showcase his liminal position between East and West, center and the province than his autobiographical narrative *Istanbul*? My goal in this chapter was to show that Pamuk's perspective of Istanbul is not a blatant borrowing of a westerner's perspective, but a culmination of his liminal position at a period of postimperial melancholia. This liminal position surfaces in the ways Pamuk breaks with traditional time and space, as well as the set boundaries of genre throughout the narrative. Rather than follow a chronological or spatial structure, the narration's (and the narrator's) itinerant path brings together incommensurate fragments of memory and space. This view is only possible with Pamuk's personal background, deeply rooted in one of the most westernized sections of the city, Nişantaşı, which provides him with a perspective of an outsider to the poor neighborhoods of Istanbul. By walking in the provincialized neighborhoods, Pamuk decenters his own family origin and departs from the local attachments in the richer quarters of the city. His self-identification of social class is the first step in changing his perspective from the affluent Nişantaşı neighborhood to the neglected backstreets.

Pamuk, like generations of Turkish authors and intellectuals, negotiates his identity at the border between the center and the periphery. Istanbul, for Pamuk, is the best place to challenge the borders because the city comprises both the center and the periphery with its heterogeneous provincialities that range from a geographical organization of urban space to a personal feeling of decentering. In his promenades between his rich, westernized home neighborhood and the poor, outlying neighborhoods, Pamuk discovers a second world where he can see the city through the eyes of a foreigner. In an effort to come to terms with the *hüzün* that overpowers the entire city, Pamuk reimagines twenty-first-century Istanbul as a vast agglomeration of disparate fragments seamlessly sewn together.

Works Cited

Akbayar, Nuri. "Nişantaşı." *Dünden bugüne İstanbul ansiklopedisi*. Vol. 6. Ed. Akbayar et al. Istanbul: Kültür bakanlığı ve tarih vakfı, 1994. 88-90.

Almond, Ian. "Islam, Melancholy, and Sad, Concrete Minarets: The Futility of Narratives in Orhan Pamuk's *The Black Book*." *New Literary History* 34.1 (2003): 75-90.

Andrews, Walter G., and Irene Markoff. "Poetry, the Arts, and Group Ethos in the Ideology of the Ottoman Empire." *Edebiyat* 1.1 (1987): 28-70.

Bali, Rıfat N. *Tarz-ı hayat'tan Life Style'a: Yeni seçkinler, yeni mekanlar, yeni yaşamlar*. İstanbul: İletişi+m, 2002.

___. "Orhan Pamuk ve Nobel edebiyat ödülü üzerine." *Virgül aylık kitap ve eleştiri dergisi* 102 (2006): 62-65.

Benjamin, Walter. "Unpacking my Library: A Talk about Book Collecting." *Illuminations*. Trans. Harry Zohn. New York: Schocken, 2007. 59-68.

Bernheimer, Charles. "The Bernheimer Report, 1993." *Comparative Literature in the Age of Multiculturalism*. Ed. Charles Bernheimer. Baltimore and London: Johns Hopkins UP, 1995. 39-50.

Bora, Tanıl, ed. *Taşraya bakmak*. İstanbul: İletişim, 2005.

Brendemoen, Brent. "Bir Sufi romanı olarak *Kara kitap.*" *Orhan Pamuk'u anlamak.* Ed. and trans. Engin Kılıç. İstanbul: İletişim, 2000. 209-24.

Casanova, Pascale. *The World Republic of Letters.* Trans. M.B. Debevoise. Cambridge, MA: Harvard UP, 2004.

Çelik, Zeynep. *The Remaking of Istanbul: Portrait of an Ottoman City in the Nineteenth Century.* Seattle and London: University of Washington Press, 1986.

de Certeau, Michel. *The Practice of Everyday Life.* Trans. Steven Rendall. Berkeley, Los Angeles, London: University of California Press, 1984.

Dino, Guzine. "The Turkish Peasant Novel, or the Anatolian Theme." Trans. Joan Grimbert. *World Literature Today* 60.2 (1986): 266-65.

Erol, Sibel. "The Chronotope of Istanbul in Orhan Pamuk's Memoir *Istanbul.*" *International Journal of Middle East Studies* 43 (2011): 655-76.

Ertürk, Nergis. "Those Outside the Scene: *Snow* in the World Republic of Letters." *New Literary History* 41 (2010): 633-51.

Foucault, Michel. "Of Other Spaces." Trans. Jay Miskowiec. *Diacritics* 16.1 (1986): 22-27.

Freud, Sigmund. "Mourning and Melancholia." *The Standard Edition of the Complete Psychological Works of Sigmund Freud.* Vol. 14. Trans. James Strachey. London: The Hogarth Press and the Institute of Psychoanalysis, 1957. 243-58.

Göknar, Erdağ M. *Orhan Pamuk, Secularism and Blasphemy: The Politics of the Turkish Novel.* New York: Routledge, 2013.

Gün, Güneli. "The Turks Are Coming: Deciphering Orhan Pamuk's *Black Book.*" *World Literature Today* 66.1 (1992): 59-63.

Gürbilek, Nurdan. "Taşra sıkıntısı." *Yer değiştiren gölge: Denemeler.* İstanbul: Metis, 1995. 42-67.

Havlıoğlu, Didem. "Estetik hafıza olarak telmih: Süreklilik ve başkalaşım." *Monograf* 4 (2015): 10-30.

Helvacioglu, Banu. "Melancholy and *Hüzün* in Orhan Pamuk's *Istanbul.*" *Mosaic: A Journal for the Interdisciplinary Study of Literature* 46.2 (2013): 163-78.

King, Anthony. "Boundaries, Networks, and Cities: Playing and Replaying Diasporas and Histories." *Urban Imaginaries: Locating the Modern*

City. Ed. Alev Çınar and Thomas Bender. Minneapolis: University of Minnesota Press, 2007. 1-17.

Laschinger, Verena. "Flaneuring into the Creative Economy: Orhan Pamuk's *Istanbul: Memories of a City*." *Explicator* 67.2 (2009): 102-05.

Mani, B. Venkat. "A Pact With Books: The Public Life of World Literature." *Global-E Global Studies Journal* 8 (2014). Accessed 23 July 2015 <http ://global-ejournal.org/2014/02/05/vol8iss1/>.

Moran, Berna. *Türk romanına eleştirel bir bakış*. Vol. 3. İstanbul: İletişim, 1994.

Moretti, Franco. *Atlas of the European Novel, 1800-1900*. London: Verso, 1998.

___. *Graphs, Maps, Trees: Abstract Models for a Literary History*. London: Verso, 2005.

Pamuk, Orhan. *The Black Book*. Trans. Maureen Freely. New York: Vintage International/Vintage, 2006. Trans. of *Kara kitap*.

___. "Implementing Disform: An Interview with Orhan Pamuk." Interview by Esra Mirze. *PMLA* 123.1 (2008): 176-80.

___. Interview by Carol Becker. *Brooklyn Rail*. 6 Feb. 2008. Accessed 7 Aug. 2016 <http://www.brooklynrail.org/2008/02/express/orhan-pamuk -wih-carol-becker>.

___. *Istanbul: Memories and the City*. Trans. Maureen Freely. New York: Vintage, 2004. Trans. of *İstanbul: Hatıralar ve şehir*.

___. *The Museum of Innocence*. Trans. Maureen Freely. New York: Alfred A. Knopf, 2010. Trans. of *Masumiyet müzesi*.

___. *The New Life*. Trans. Güneli Gün. New York: Farrar, Straus and Giroux, 1998. Trans. of *Yeni hayat*.

___. "Nobel Lecture: My Father's Suitcase." *Nobelprize.org*. Nobel Media AB 2014. Accessed 1 Mar. 2015 <http://www.nobelprize.org/nobel_prizes/literature/laureates/2006/pamuk-lecture_en.html>.

___. *Snow*. Trans. Maureen Freely. New York: Vintage, 2004. Trans. of *Kar*.

___. *A Strangeness in My Mind*. Trans. Ekin Oklap. London: Faber and Faber, 2016. Trans. of *Kafamda bir tuhaflık*.

___. *The White Castle*. Trans. Victoria R. Holbrook. London: Faber and Faber, 1990. Trans of *Beyaz kale*.

Parla, Jale. "From Allegory to Parable: Inscriptions of Anatolia in the Turkish Novel." *New Perspectives on Turkey* 36 (2007): 11-26.

Pittman, Michael. "Problematizing East-West Essentialisms: Discourse, Authorhood, and Identity Crisis in Orhan Pamuk's *Beyaz kale* [*The White Castle*]." *Global Perspectives on Orhan Pamuk: Essentialism and Politics*. Ed. Mehnaz A. Afridi and David M. Buyze. New York: Palgrave Macmillan, 2012. 63-74.

Rathbun, Carole. *The Village in the Turkish Novel and Short Story 1920 to 1955*. The Hague: Mouton, 1972.

Robbins, Bruce. "Comparative Cosmopolitanism." *Social Text*. Third World and Post-Colonial Issues 31/32 (1992): 169-86.

Ulagay, Osman. "Nobel bizim neyimize?" *Milliyet* 22 Oct. 2006. Accessed 25 Mar. 2017 <http://www.milliyet.com.tr/nobel-bizim--neyimize-/osman-ulagay/ekonomi/yazardetayarsiv/22.10.2006/175316/default.htm>.

Walkowitz, Rebecca L. *Born Translated: The Contemporary Novel in an Age of World Literature*. New York: Columbia UP, 2015.

Yazıcıoğlu, Özlem Öğüt. "Orhan Pamuk'un *Beyaz kale*'si ve *Yeni hayat*'ında ölümü yazmak, 'Ben'i çizmek." *Orhan Pamuk'un edebi dünyası*. Ed. Nüket Esen and Engin Kılıç. İstanbul: İletişim, 2008. 151-62.

Zürcher, Erik J. *Turkey: A Modern History*. London: I.B. Tauris, 2004.

Bridging the Gap between People and Things: The Politics and Poetics of Collecting in Pamuk's *The Museum of Innocence*

Hülya Yağcıoğlu
Zayed University

Abstract: *The Museum of Innocence* revolves around a hoarder figure, Kemal, as its protagonist who obsessively collects objects related to his beloved Füsun and their unfulfilled love. The novel marks a gradual shift from a pathological case of hoarding to a systematized practice of collecting which eventually results in a museum of objects documenting the protagonist's love. As a fetishistic practice caused by an emotional attachment to things, collecting serves to bridge the gap between people and things. Relocated from their commodity scene, or rather "freed from the drudgery of being useful" in Benjamin's terms (*Arcades* 19), the collected objects are reappropriated in an utterly subjective realm. Collections are also reminiscent of personal memories as they encapsulate the lost past. Theoretically based on the writings of Benjamin, Baudrillard and Susan Stewart on the practice of collecting, this chapter will examine the poetics and politics of collecting in *The Museum of Innocence*. Collecting also takes on a cultural significance when the protagonist starts accumulating objects specific to 1970s–1980s Istanbul. Therefore, the museum and the novel are not just testaments to Kemal's love for Füsun but also pay testimony to a specific period in modern Turkish history. In this sense, the novel is a textual museum in its archival representation of material, personal, social, ethical, and cultural values of past culture. Focusing on the emotional value that everyday objects evoke for the characters, Pamuk uses Kemal's collection as a way to understand the entire culture, both in its socioeconomic dimension and in a more spiritual or poetic sense.

Orhan Pamuk's *The Museum of Innocence* is a textual museum which deals with collecting at both a psychological and a sociocultural plane. As a fetishistic practice caused by an emotional attachment to things, collecting serves to bridge the gap between human beings and material objects. In theory, it goes beyond the dominance of the material world of commodities to establish a deeper and more authentic relation to objects, since a collected object is divested of its function and relocated from its commodity scene. The object, then, is reappropriated in an intimate subjective realm to open up endless possibilities for the collector. Disillusioned with the impossibility of intersubjective dialogue, a collector assumes he can establish a more authentic and safer relationship with objects by owning them: "for a collector [...] ownership is the most intimate relationship that one can have to objects. Not that they come alive in him; it is he who lives in them" (Benjamin, "Unpacking" 67). Closely related to nostalgia, collected objects are also reminiscent of personal memories as they defy the transience of time and encapsulate the lost past. The sociocultural dimension of the practice, on the other hand, can be seen in the entire project of "The Museum of Innocence," which is basically a collection of almost-forgotten everyday objects of a specific period. The novel depends on the idea of archival representation and the preservation of culture through collecting, as the collection aims to represent the cultural and personal ethics of this period in modern Turkish history in and through old material objects. This chapter examines both the poetics and politics of collecting in *The Museum of Innocence*, focusing on the personal and then cultural connotations of the practice.

Collecting first appears as a personal endeavor, resulting from the protagonist Kemal's obsessive love for Füsun. In order to deal with the disillusionment of unfulfilled love, Kemal starts collecting mementos reminiscent of Füsun. The catalyst for his impulse is the belief that the material objects can be "palliatives for pain" in the Freudian sense: "We can bear the pain only by possessing something that belongs to that instant [of happiness]" (*Museum* 73). Only by surrounding himself with the objects in the Merhamet Apartments, where he and Füsun first made love, can Kemal find consolation for his heartbreak. Therefore, his relation to the objects he collects is initially that of a patient seeking relief rather than that of a systematic collector. This relation is pathologically conditioned as is evident in his display of an anatomical chart of love pains to show that he too is suffering from physical pain in his stomach, shoulders, forehead, and entire body. While collecting his first pieces, he feels like

> a patient taking stock of his medicines. On the one hand I had a longing for any object that reminded me of Füsun; on the other hand, even as my pain abated under therapy, I longed to run away

from this house and these objects that had both healed me and reminded me of my affliction. (178)

Thus, he resorts to the happiness and relief that the objects bring him in an effort to cope with Füsun's absence, even if that simultaneously perpetuates his suffering. As is usual in fetishism, which involves a mechanism of substitution, collected objects come to stand for the lost object of desire. Kemal transfers his disappointment with and anxiety about human relations to the world of objects, which offers a realm of security.

Similar dynamics hold true for the practice of hoarding on which the novel dwells. Initially, Kemal starts hoarding the objects reminiscent of the times with Füsun from the house where she and her family live, namely the Keskins' house. Hoarding is an urge to accumulate things without a systematized method or an idea of display behind. Toward the end of the novel, Pamuk distinguishes between proud collectors (predominating in the West), who wish to display their objects, and bashful collectors (associated more with the East), who attempt to hide their accumulations. Hoarding is thus presented as an "unmodern disposition" and a shameful practice, caused by an obsessive-compulsive behavior resulting from a psychological wound or past trauma. Like collecting, it serves to create an alternate realm of belonging. In "The System of Collecting," Baudrillard notes that the practice of collecting indicates loneliness and isolation from the world: "It is because [the collector] feels himself alienated or lost within a social discourse whose rules he cannot fathom that the collector is driven to construct an alternative discourse that is for him entirely amenable, in so far as he is the one who dictates its signifiers" (24). Hoarders are outsiders to society – the protagonist feels like "a leper among society's lepers" amid the other hoarders in a meeting of the Lovers of Collectible Objects Association (598). The novel recounts the wretched condition of some hoarders' houses in Istanbul, which contain piles of paper (old newspapers, postcards, photos of celebrities, posters, film tickets, restaurant menus) or heaps of odd objects (old tin cans, medicine boxes, bottles, and so on). These residences reveal how hoarders construct an unconventional discourse with their amassment of literal garbage in their dwelling places. While the practice can be considered as a reflection of the material excess that industrial capitalism has engendered, it also refers to a medical condition arising from a fear of material deprivation. Hoarders have a problem discarding objects because they fail to grasp those objects' real value (or lack thereof). While collecting requires ordering and cataloging, hoarding focuses on simply accumulating things regardless of their worth. In the plethora of collected objects "all kinds of neuroses are neutralized, all kinds of tensions and frustrated energies grounded and calmed" (Baudrillard 11). The intimacy between the hoarder and his hoard substitutes for his lack of intimacy with other human beings.

The novel marks, however, a gradual shift from a pathological case of fetishism (represented by the idea of the shame of the hoarder) to a systematized practice of collecting (represented by the idea of the pride of the collector). This transformation also signifies a self-realization at the end of Kemal's book-length self-quest. Mostly shaped by his love for Füsun, his quest, which he was initially ashamed of, eventually becomes a source of pride and self-fulfillment in and through his collection. Collecting becomes a way of possessing experiences for Kemal, who is a figure of modern man – an "isolated individual, starved of all but sterile experiences" (Abbas 228). Only by collecting, by becoming an anthropologist of his life, can he render his "starved" life meaningful. Similarly, Pamuk posits in *The Innocence of Objects* that the first collectors were motivated to create a new identity and thus secure a new future for themselves, rather than preserve the traces of the past.[1] Kemal's collection is not just an exposition of the past; it embodies his entire life and exposes his real self. He devotes his life to understanding the magic and secret of objects, and they finally become the substitutes of his unfilled life.

> The singular object never impedes the process of narcissistic projection, which ranges over an indefinite number of objects: on the contrary, it encourages such multiplication, thus associating itself with a mechanism whereby the image of the self is extended to the very limits of the collection. Here, indeed, lies the whole mir-

---

[1] "[T]he first collectors did not set out to preserve the traces of a past life, but to fashion for themselves a new identity – and a new future to go with it" (46).

acle of collecting. For it is invariably *oneself* that one collects. (Baudrillard 12)

In line with what Baudrillard posits above, one can argue that Kemal collects himself as much as he collects Füsun. The intimacy between collector and collected object lends itself to displacement of the distinction between the self and the material. It is, then, not surprising at all that in the end, Kemal becomes a living museum piece himself, moving to the attic of "The Museum of Innocence." Collecting, therefore, is a practice in which the boundaries between the self and the world of objects are gradually eroded.

Nostalgia is another defining characteristic of collecting, as the practice becomes the ultimate way of evoking the past. Memories are embedded in collected objects which preserve and display specific moments in Kemal's past. For the protagonist, such "mementos preserve the colors, textures, images, and delights as they were more faithfully, in fact, than can those who accompanied us through those moments" (73). Characters' emotions are related to corresponding objects, which then become objective correlatives of evoking sentiments in the narrative. Pamuk believes that "objects are essential parts of the countless discrete moments in novels, as well as the emblems or signs of those moments" (*Naïve* 110). For example, as relics of their first lovemaking in the Merhamet Apartments, Kemal displays Füsun's floral batiste handkerchief as a sign of their compassionate caresses, a crystal inkwell and pen set to illustrate "the refinement and the fragile tenderness [they] felt for each other," and Füsun's belt as a sign of their melancholy (30). "The Museum of Innocence," in a sense, is a museum of the mind – it consists of souvenirs of Kemal's personal past.

As Rheims observes, "a phenomenon often associated with the passion of collecting is 'the loss of all sense of the present'" (qtd. in Baudrillard 15). Collecting is thus an apt distraction for the protagonist, since it helps him escape his current misery. The objects work as souvenirs of the past, "as emblematic of the nostalgia that all narrative reveals – the longing for its place of origin" (Stewart 23). "Irreplaceable mementos of a lost world," collected objects are the concrete evidence of his blissful memories with Füsun. The novel starts with the description of a moment of ultimate happiness in the past: "It was the happiest moment of my life, though I didn't know it. Had I known, had I cherished this gift, would everything have turned out differently? Yes, if I had recognized this instant of perfect happiness, I would have held it fast and never let it slip away" (3).[2] The protagonist's nostalgia for the past goes hand in hand with his quest for "innocence" as the past happiness is regarded as the lost Garden of Eden. According to Stewart, "the nostalgic's utopia is prelapsarian, a genesis where lived and mediated experience are one, where authenticity and transcendence are both present and everywhere" (23). Collected objects evoke both the lived and mediated experience for the protagonist as they are testimonies of the past. The past, however, is always "a prelapsarian ideal" as Stewart suggests, and while constructing his museum, Kemal simultaneously deconstructs and reconstructs his personal past. It may not be surprising, then, that after reading hundreds of pages of the story of the protagonist's suffering, his last words "reimagine" his life as a happy one: "Let everyone know, I lived a very happy life" (532).

Museum objects are aimed at evoking Kemal's memories rather than accurately recording specific moments in his life. The past is thus mnemonically restructured in his collection. This also suggests the idea of the "innocence of things," as he proposes that his collection should be viewed as exempt from the spatial and temporal limitations of the outside world. Related to phantasmagoria and memory of his deep sentiments, they are almost transcendental rather than explicit and worldly. Collections digress from and displace real time, as time is translated into a system of collecting, which ultimately serves to abolish time (Baudrillard 15). Kemal wishes to convey "the feeling of being caught in a dream" in his museum in order to create a feeling of being outside time. This sense of timelessness can be found in the Keskins' residence, which will later house the collection. The protagonist expects the museum visitors to feel how the Keskins' pos-

---

[2] In the original Turkish version of the novel, "happiness" is repeated as many as five times in the first four sentences: "Hayatımın en mutlu anıymış, bilmiyordum. Bilseydim, bu mutluluğu koruyabilir, her şey de bambaşka gelişebilir miydi? Evet, bunun hayatımın en mutlu anı olduğunu anlayabilseydim, asla kaçırmazdım o mutluluğu. Derin bir huzurla her yerimi saran o harika altın an belki birkaç saniye sürmüştü, ama mutluluk bana saatlerce, yıllarca gibi gelmişti" (*Masumiyet* 11).

sessions, "especially all these broken, rusting clocks and watches that haven't worked for years [...] seem to exist out of time, how they have created among themselves a time that is theirs alone" (286). Just like the stopped watches, the space emerges as a realm of arrested time. The big clock on the wall, for instance, reminds them not of the passing of time but of its continuity and stillness. Kemal also recounts Aristotle's distinction between the "present" (single indivisible moments) and Time (the line connecting those moments we call the present) (287). Although Time itself is painful as its linearity suggests an ultimate death, these separate moments, which are encapsulated in the individual objects, are evoked in the museum. This seems in line with Bergson's idea of *la durée*, according to which time is indivisible, mobile, and constantly flowing; past, present, and future flow and progress, thus producing each other. "In the collection, time is not something to be restored to an origin; rather, all time is made simultaneous or synchronous within the collection's world," writes Stewart (151). An underlying idea of spatializing and materializing the temporal pervades the museum, as Kemal envisions it as a place where the visitors lose all sense of time and where "Time is transformed into Space" (510). So, he longs for an eternal present through his collection removed from anxieties about time.

> The miniature does not attach itself to lived historical time. [...] the metaphoric world of the miniature makes everyday life absolutely anterior and exterior to itself. The reduction in scale which the miniature presents skews the time and space relations of the everyday lifeworld, and as an object consumed, the miniature finds its "use value" transformed into the infinite time of reverie. This capacity of the miniature to create an "other" time, a type of transcendent time [...] negates change and the flux of lived reality [...]. (Stewart 65)

The suspension of time relates to the still life of objects, which freeze the flow of time, especially in the museum, in the Keskins' house and Merhamet Apartments. Kemal's meditation on the objects in these places is always atemporal; as Stewart notes, "miniature time transcends the duration of everyday life in such a way as to create an interior temporality of the subject" (66).

For Baudrillard, collecting is based on the collector's desire and passion, so the time of the collection is "the a-temporality of the unconscious" (244). In their evocation of human memories and emotions, collected objects transcend their materiality. "The power of things inheres in the memories they gather up inside them, and also in the vicissitudes of our imagination, and our memory [...]" (*Museum* 324). While emotional experiences are stored in them, things are animated and almost imbued with souls. Kemal the collector recounts that the Chinese believed that things had souls (378) and feels "like a shaman who can see the souls of things, [and] feel their stories flickering inside [him]" (512). Pamuk refers to the idea of anthropomorphism of objects in *The Innocence of Objects* as well: He recounts how he sometimes feels as if the objects in his room talk to each other, how he is reminded that objects have souls (75, 83). No longer inert and mute, collected objects are vitalized for the collector. They become fetishized entities, awakening "feelings of humility, respect, and reverence" in Kemal's museum, which becomes "a place of worship like a mosque" (*Museum* 519).

This brings us to the cultural connotations of the museum project. Although the collection is related to the protagonist's personal history, it is at the same time composed of cultural artifacts and daily objects used in the second half of the twentieth century in Istanbul. So, Kemal is similar to Benjamin's ragpicker who "collects and catalogues everything that the great city has cast off, everything it has lost, and discarded, and broken" (*Arcades* 348). In these worthless objects that are bound to be thrown away he finds a means of evaluating the past and understanding history. Benjamin's ragpicker "makes a selection, an intelligent choice; like a miser hoarding treasure, he collects the garbage that will become objects of utility or pleasure when refurbished by Industrial magic" (*Arcades* 348). In a similar vein, Kemal's collecting practice focuses on the refuse and detritus generated by an ordinary middle-class family. Such a collection would bring out the personal hi(stories) of everyday people rather than the official histories dictated by public museums. According to Pamuk, the past might be encapsulated in the objects of everyday life, the loss of which may signify the loss of culture. The rationale behind the museum, then, is to nostalgically preserve the everyday life of ordinary people through material objects as they are the sole records of the vanishing past: "Now the only way I could ever hope to make sense of those years was to display all that I had gathered together – the pots and pans, the trinkets, the clothes and the paintings – just as that anthropologist might have done" (*Museum* 496).

Every single object in Kemal's collection "becomes an encyclopedia of all knowledge of the epoch, the landscape, the industry" (Benjamin, *Arcades* 204). The novel, just like the museum, is an anthropological document that also preserves the manners and ethical values of the time against the threat of cultural change. Across the span of the novel, one can see the drastic social and cultural transformations that radically change the world the author knows. The Westernization process of Turkey in the 1970s–80s creates a breach between the old Istanbul and the new one, leaving Kemal out of tune with his times: "I had become suspended in one age while the rest of humanity lived in another" (*Museum* 501). Kemal's mother also notes, "that old world is gone, anyway. Everywhere you look it's all parvenus from the provinces" (468).

> Sometimes the passage of time would be marked by seeing a building torn down, or discovering that a little girl had become a high-spirited, buxom woman with children of her own, or I'd notice that some store to which my eyes had grown accustomed had been boarded up, and I would feel anxious. When I saw, at around this time, that the Şanzelize Boutique had closed, I was pained not only at the loss of my own memories, but equally by a sudden feeling that life had gone on without me. In the window where Sibel had spied the counterfeit Jenny Colon handbag nine years earlier, coils of Italian salamis were now hanging, and wheels of hard yellow cheese, as well as the European brands of bottled salad dressings, the pastas and soft drinks just entering the Turkish market. (*Museum* 440)

The entrance of Western commodities – Italian salamis, European pastas, and soft drinks – into Turkish markets was an important indicator of the loss of cultural values in the 1980s. Before the 1980s, the importation of Western commodities was strictly banned in Turkey. The liberalization of foreign trade at the time was significant in terms of the integration of the country into the capitalist world of the West. The objects in the museum belong to an endangered precapitalist Turkey. The museum not only exhibits Füsun's personal objects but also some consumer products and daily objects of the time such as china dogs, lottery tickets, phone tokens, empty medicine bottles, soda bottles, and receipts. Another example is the display of a bread loaf bought from a grocer: "Its function is sentimental, but also documentary, a reminder that millions of people in Istanbul ate no other bread for half a century (though its weight did vary) and also that life is a series of repeated instances that we later assign – without mercy – to oblivion" (*Museum* 192). Pamuk's endeavor is to preserve and exhibit these daily objects of consumption, which have shaped not only people's everyday lives but also their spiritual lives for years. And yet, although the museum pieces are highly culture- and period-specific, they are neither local nor artisanal productions: When Kemal sometimes finds objects such as the saltshakers, lighters, and ashtrays similar to the ones in the Keskins' house in other parts of the world, he does not hesitate to buy them for his collection. Therefore, it is unimportant whether the objects are industrially reproduced consumer goods in capitalist circulation, for even such consumer goods can be the parts and parcels of our daily lives.

The Museum of Innocence "is not simply a story of lovers, but of the entire realm, that is, of Istanbul" (*Museum* 525). Above all else, Kemal attempts to create a miniature version of the city with the museum which will encapsulate the period through the objects of a past culture. Such objects are engendered vis-à-vis the drastic changes in the cityscape, which directly reflect on people's everyday lives. The function of the museum is to recall that world in order to resist change. After Füsun's death, even the city itself becomes a museum for Kemal, reminding him of Füsun's memory.

As one of the so-called "repositories of those things from which Western Civilization derives its wealth of knowledge, allowing it to rule the world" (*Museum* 73), the museum also has a political dimension in the novel. Most public museums of the West have been designed as nationalist projects promoting states' power and wealth. In traditional museums, one can see the representation of history as a transmission of "spoils" of ages to the present, totally divorced from the environment in which they were produced. In this sense, it may even be "barbaric" – as Benjamin asserts, "there is no document of civilization which is not at the same time a document of barbarism. And just as such a document is not free of barbarism, barbarism taints also the manner in which it was transmitted from one owner to another" ("Theses" 256). Adorno also links the museum with Western civilization and modernity, and sees it as "a metaphor for [...] the anarchical production of commodities in fully developed bourgeois society" (93). As such, the museum has been an important site for Western modernity specifically in regard to the relationship between tradition and the present.

On his visits to Western museums after Füsun's death, Kemal concedes that museums abroad are essentially based on power and pride. That is, any collected object, if preserved and displayed in a museum, can be a source of pride rather than of shame. Conversely, his project may be seen as the antithesis of Western museums: "What Turks should be viewing in their own museums are not bad imitations of Western art but their own lives," muses Kemal (525). His museum will have not only a local but also a personal twist, as it will be based on personal life stories of Turkish people, which are as important as any other history. In Pamuk's latest museum catalogue, *The Innocence of Objects*, "A Modest Manifesto for Museums" emphasizes the importance of personal museums, which recount personal stories rather than collective ones, to better understand the human condition (54–57). The author advocates museums in which states are replaced with individuals and history is replaced with stories. In an interview, Pamuk asserts that his museum is not related to power but to intimacy:

> [I]n my novel, where Kemal collects the teacup, cigarette butts, bedroom door handle and other items of Füsun's, he is building a museum not to power, but to the intimate experience of love, to an individual life. My point is that, whatever a life is made of, its dreams and disappointments, is worth taking pride in.

> In building my own museum in Istanbul, I am very close to my character Kemal. I don't want to exhibit power, but express my interiority, my spirit. A museum should not be flags – signs and symbols of power – but intimate works of art. It should express the spirituality of the collector. ("Talk")

This reminds us of Benjamin's juxtaposition of museums and private collections – as opposed to "the death" of the objects in museums, private collections are the places where objects "get their due" ("Unpacking" 67).

Collecting is not just a thematic focus but also a narrative mode in Pamuk's novel. The boundaries between the novel and the museum blur as they both present detailed expositions of the material world in terms of their representational power and of archival quality. For Pamuk, novels "form a rich and powerful archive – of common human feelings, our perceptions of ordinary things, our gestures, utterances, and attitudes. Various sounds, words, colloquialisms, smells, images, tastes, objects, and colors are remembered only because novelists observe them and carefully make note of them in their writings" (*Naïve* 130). While museums preserve objects, novels preserve "customs, attitudes, and ways of living" and "nuances, tones, and colors of language" (130, 132). The museum-like quality of the novel also lies in its evocation of the past as a resistance to forgetting. *The Museum of Innocence* is an archive of the minute details of that world, an almost nostalgic safeguard against the loss of the cultural past. Although they employ different mediums, both museums and novels record the actual facets of human lives. Pamuk's experiences in writing the novel and founding the museum go hand in hand:

> At the same time, I was also writing a novel, as well as keeping an eye out for items in secondhand shops, flea markets, and the homes of acquaintances who liked to hoard things. I was looking for objects that could have been used by the fictitious family whom I imagined to be living in that old house from 1975 to 1984 […].
>
> Intending to use them in my novel, I was imagining situations, moments, and scenes suited to these objects, many of which (such

as a quince grater) I had bought on impulse. Once, when browsing in a secondhand shop, I found a dress in a bright fabric with orange roses and green leaves on it, and I decided it was just right for Füsun, the heroine of my novel. With the dress laid out before me, I proceeded to write the details of a scene in which Füsun is learning to drive while wearing that very dress. (*Naïve* 121–22)

As such, the author constructs the plot out of the objects, and imagines situations and scenes suited to the objects he has been collecting. In "Telling Objects: A Narrative Perspective on Collecting," Mieke Bal examines collecting as a narrative mode and asks: "can things be, or tell, stories?" (99). The power of things in telling stories likewise rests on the foundation of *The Museum of Innocence*. The representation of collected objects often surpasses the plot and characters in the novel, becoming not only a process by which a narrative is told but also the narrative itself, as Bal suggests. So, collecting arises from a human urge to tell stories, in a different way than employing words or "other conventional narrative modes" (Bal 103).

Pamuk collects fragments, parts and details of the outside world to create a unified entity: the novel as a collection. This metonymical awareness in the author's novels suggests that not only totality but also meaning itself is created out of the accumulation of fragments. The novel sets up a representational universe in which metonymical parts can still stand for the whole.

The collection also precedes the narrative. After years of collecting, the protagonist decides that he needs an annotated catalogue which relates the details of the story of each and every object in his collection: "the line joining together these objects would be a story. In other words, a writer might undertake to write the catalog in the same form as he might write a novel" (*Museum* 512). That is why the distinctions between the novel and museum blur in this novel-like museum and museum-like novel. There are eighty-three museum displays corresponding to eighty-three chapters of the novel. Moreover, references to the novel and museum go hand in hand ("My story will revisit all these episodes, as will the exhibit" [45]), and the reader is addressed together with the museum visitor in many places. Indeed, the reader becomes yet another museum visitor, who observes the objects of Kemal's life with attention and care. Reading the novel is like walking around a museum, looking at objects and listening to their stories/histories. All these further bring to attention the materiality of "the novel," which is also an object, a fetishized thing. The novel includes a Nişantaşı map; it can even be used as a ticket for the real-world Museum of Innocence. It is both a collection of the novelist's imagination and a collectible item itself.

Pamuk writes:

> When we stand before an object or a painting in a museum, we can only guess, with the help of the catalogue, how the piece fitted into people's lives, stories, and worldviews – while in a novel, the images, objects, conversations, smells, stories, beliefs, and sensations are described and preserved as an integral part of the daily life of the period. (*Naïve* 130)

Indeed, a museum normally is a place in which authentic art objects or real artifacts from the past are displayed, so the power of any museum has to do with its representation of reality. "The Museum of Innocence," conversely, takes its power from fiction, which is an imaginary and subjective construction of reality. In this sense, Pamuk does not distinguish between the real world and the world of fiction, as any fictional world can be as significant as real life. Therefore, the idea of founding a museum based on a novel, which is already based on the writer's fantasy, blurs the distinction between fiction and reality.

The visitor in a normal museum is a detached observer who makes the connections himself, whereas in Pamuk's novelistic museum, the connections have already been set up within the narrative. Thus, the novel is much more than a catalogue – it tells the story of museum objects. Whereas a normal reader envisions a fictional world in which things and people are situated in an imaginary setting while reading a novel, Pamuk establishes this fictional world through the museum, which becomes the crystallization of that very setting. And yet, does not each novel also belong to the reader in the sense that it is up to him to construct a truly personal interpretation of the fictional world? Although Pamuk mentions the pride of the reader when s/he "correctly" visualizes the images the writer suggests in a novel

(*Naïve* 126), that pride actually seems to belong to the novelist, who takes full credit for determining the coordinates of that world.

This brings us finally to the idea of the novelist as a collector. There is a link between "the relation of the writer to the image and the collector's relation to the object: the writer possesses experience through the image, the collector through ownership of the object" (Abbas 229). The writer and collector have much in common with regard to selecting, collecting, and ordering the world of objects. For Benjamin, this analogy is embodied in the figure of ragpicker: The solitary figure of the ragpicker, who is concerned with "the refuse of society in the streets," resembles a poet. With regard to his experience as a collector-novelist, Pamuk says that he wrote *The Museum of Innocence* not only by "finding, studying, and describing objects" but also by "trolling the shops for objects that the novel required, or having them made to order by artists and craftsmen" (*Naïve* 122). In Pamuk the writer-collector, one can see a reflection of protagonist Kemal and a hoarder/collector. The refuse of the industrial society gives the hoarder/ragpicker/poet/writer a way to evaluate the past and understand history. So, the novelist is yet another collector in his accumulation, juxtaposition, and conservation of the visual "relics" in a novel, with their smells, textures, and color.

In sum, the collecting practice in *The Museum of Innocence* has been discussed as a psychological and cultural experience, problematizing personal and social relations with the material world. On the personal level, the protagonist/collector builds up a truly private relationship by collecting simple objects in a middle-class house in order to defy the values of his bourgeois class. On the cultural level, on the other hand, there is an attempt to display these simple, everyday life objects used by Istanbulites in the second half of the twentieth century. Pamuk uses Kemal's collection as a way to understand the entire culture, both in its socioeconomic dimension and in a more spiritual or poetic sense. *The Museum of Innocence* may also be read as a fictional collection of objects or "textual museum," as it heavily depends on the description of material objects. In this sense, the author acts like a collector, displaying objects and putting them into interaction with their surroundings and with people and their emotions. The reader, just like a museum visitor, reads the novel with attention to individual artifacts, observing the fictional collections the writer as a collector/curator has produced.

Works Cited

Abbas, Ackbar. "Walter Benjamin's Collector: The Fate of Modern Experience." *New Literary History* 20.1 (1988): 217–37.

Adorno, Theodor W. "Valéry Proust Museum." *Prisms*. By Adorno. Trans. Samuel and Shierry Weber. Cambridge, MA: MIT Press, 1981.

Bal, Mieke. "Telling Objects: A Narrative Perspective on Collecting." *The Cultures of Collecting*. Ed. John Elsner and Roger Cardinal. London: Reaktion Books, 1997. 97-116.

Baudrillard, Jean. "The System of Collecting." *The Cultures of Collecting*. Ed. John Elsner and Roger Cardinal. London: Reaktion, 1997. 7-25.

Benjamin, Walter. *The Arcades Project*. Trans. Howard Eiland and Kevin McLaughlin. Cambridge, Mass.: The Belknap Press of Harvard UP, 1999.

———. "Theses on the Philosophy of History." *Illuminations: Essays and Reflections*. Ed. Hannah Arendt, Trans. Harry Zohn. New York: Schocken, 1969. 253-64.

———. "Unpacking My Library: A Talk about Book Collecting." *Illuminations: Essays and Reflections*. Ed. Hannah Arendt, Trans. Harry Zohn. New York: Schocken, 1969. 59-69.

Bergson, Henri. *Time and Free Will: An Essay on the Immediate Data of Consciousness*. Trans. R.L. Pogson. London: G. Allen, 1921.

Foucault, Michel. "Texts/Contexts: Of Other Spaces." *Diacritics* 16 (Spring 1986): 22-27.

Pamuk, Orhan. *The Innocence of Objects: The Museum of Innocence*. Trans. Ekin Oklap. New York: Abrams, 2012. Trans. of *Şeylerin masumiyeti*.

———. *Masumiyet müzesi*. İstanbul: İletişim, 2008.

———. *The Museum of Innocence*. Trans. Maureen Freely. New York: Vintage, 2009. Trans. of *Masumiyet müzesi*.

———. *The Naïve and the Sentimental Novelist*. Charles Eliot Norton Lectures. MA: Harvard UP, 2010. Trans. of *Saf ve düşünceli romancı*.

——. "A Talk With Orhan Pamuk: Caressing the World With Words." Interview by Nathan Gardels. *Huffington Post*. 18 Mar. 2010. Accessed 15 Dec. 2016 <http://www.huffingtonpost.com/nathan-gardels/a-talk-with-orhan-pamuk-c_b_353799.html>.

Pearce, Susan M. *Museums, Objects, and Collections*. Washington, D.C.: Smithsonian Institution, 1993.

Stewart, Susan. *On Longing: Narratives of the Miniature, the Gigantic, the Souvenir, the Collection.* Durham: Duke UP, 1993.

The Quest for Home and Identity:
Modernity and Innocence in Pamuk's *The Museum of Innocence*

Gönül Eda Özgül
Bahçeşehir University

Abstract: Orhan Pamuk's novel *The Museum of Innocence* tells the story of an impossible love which can be read as a modern individual's quest for a home and identity in a modernizing non-western society. This essay examines the way these two categories are constructed in the novel and analyzes the memory regime that it produces with the aim of laying bare the novel's discourse on modernity and the modernization process in Turkey. Ironically, the novel adopts a critical stance with regard to this process, but in the final analysis it fails to move beyond the limited and selective perspective of the modernizers. Due to its portrayal of home and identity as unified categories, its adoption of a nostalgic memory regime which maintains the past – and the present, for that matter – as closed categories, and its tendency to define Turkish identity by lack – of modernity – the novel produces an Orientalist view of Turkey.

A museum of innocence implies a world where innocence belongs to the past. The word 'innocence' conventionally denotes a state which, once lost, can never be regained. That's why speaking of innocence gives rise to a nostalgic regime of memory according to which the past is a closed and finished category. Similarly, most conventional museums are founded on an understanding of an unchanging past and contribute significantly to the production of the prevalent nostalgic view of time. Yearning for innocent past times comprises a strong vein in the literature and cinema of Turkey. Orhan Pamuk's novel *The Museum of* Innocence, first published in Turkish in 2008, invokes, even joins this vein as a postmodern appropriation of this theme of nostalgia for innocence. This essay examines the memory regime produced in *The Museum of Innocence* and analyzes the way home and identity are conceptualized in it with the aim of laying bare the novel's discourse on modernity and the modernization process in Turkey.

The novel tells a tale of impossible love, a theme very common in Eastern literature and in the popular Yeşilçam cinema, which inherited it from literature. Kemal, a well-educated man from the upper[1] class, goes to a boutique to purchase a gift for his girlfriend Sibel where he comes across Füsun, his distant lower class relative, who has grown to be a beautiful woman, and is quite taken with her. Despite his impending engagement to Sibel, who has completed her education in France and comes from a rich family like his, Kemal frequently finds excuses to see Füsun, who works in the boutique because she didn't succeed in the university entrance exam, and eventually starts secretly meeting her. Even though he falls in love with Füsun, he goes through with the engagement, because he believes he should marry into his own class. He intends to keep seeing her after his engagement, but Füsun disappears. Soon Kemal's love for her turns into a passion and he starts spending all his time among the objects she has touched in the apartment where he and Füsun used to meet secretly. Finally he breaks off his engagement to Sibel. Following the death of his father, Kemal's mother receives a letter of condolence from Füsun's family and when Kemal goes to the address on the letter he finds out Füsun is married to Feridun, a young man who aspires to make films. Nevertheless, just to be close to Füsun, Kemal starts visiting the house where she lives with her husband and her parents every night, stealing an object from the house each time with the hope that these objects will bring him a sense of closeness to her, a habit he maintains for years. Following her separation from Feridun, Füsun agrees to marry Kemal under certain conditions, including that they make a trip to Europe before the wedding. During this trip, Füsun crashes the car into a tree and dies, leaving Kemal heavily injured. It's after his recovery that Kemal establishes a museum of objects that belonged to Füsun which he's collected over the years, the museum that gives the book its title. He also asks the author Orhan Pamuk to write his story, and following a narratorial shift in the novel, it is revealed that what the reader holds is the very book Pamuk wrote at Kemal's request. It's worth noting that in 2012 Pamuk actually opened a real-world Museum of Innocence in Istanbul, as mentioned in the novel.

---

[1] Historically, in contrast to the formation of classes in European societies, there has not been a distinctive aristocratic class in Turkey. Since the nineteenth century, in the absence of an aristocracy, the uppermost layer in Turkey's class structure comprised capital owners and bureaucratic elites.

The novel is an allegory of the relationship between different classes that have been affected in different ways by the modernization process in Turkey. Everyday life and material culture in Turkey in the period between the 1970s and 2000s; class distinctions and the differing views of different classes on issues related with modernity; the question of identity and ideas about masculinity, femininity and the position of women in a modernizing society are some of the themes that are addressed in the novel.

The Museum of Innocence can be read as the quest of an upper class individual in a modernizing non-western society for a home and an identity. In this society, not only is the way home is imagined altered in the process of modernization, but also have forms of oppression, violence, and exclusion peculiar to modernity laid the grounds for a state of homelessness. In this respect, even though it brings forth a new understanding of home, modernity can be considered a quest for a home that seems to have vanished into thin air. The loss of home in Turkey is closely related to the identity crisis that emerged during modernization, since one of the main principles of Turkish modernization has been a self-imposed resignation from being "oneself." This is a common theme in the novel and related to the concept of innocence; it is also a common theme in the world of thought of the late Ottomans, which expresses an understanding of modernization as complete Westernization (Mardin 14).

In accordance with this, in the first section of this essay, the homes in the novel will be analyzed as an allegory of "modern" Turkey, and the way "home" is defined in the novel will be evaluated. In the second section, the identity crises of the novel's characters will be considered in relation to the modernization process and the novel's way of looking at the past will be problematized. With his obsession with the past and symbolic relationship with objects that finally lead him to establishing a museum, Kemal holds a contradictory position within the modernized and modernizing class that he belongs to, a point of rupture of the social texture, since modernity has always been defined as a break with the past both in the West and in Turkey: a break with the "dark" Middle Ages and a break with and salvation from the "dark" Ottoman age, respectively. It can be stated in Barbara Johnson's deconstructive terminology that *The Museum of Innocence* deals not only with the "difference between" classes, but also the "differences within" each class (x). Still, it needs to be addressed whether Kemal's way of looking at the past converges with that of his class after all, since they both suffer from conceptualizing the past as a finished category. This conceptualization results in the absolutization of the past, in other words, the past is cast in a fixed form with an unchangeable meaning. Indeed, the view of time as a neutral, homogeneous and stable category is one of the defining traits of modernity, as this time conception necessarily arises from modernity's ideal of progress, order and control. It has far-reaching consequences, including that it contradicts, even renders illusionary, modernity's own acclamation of freedom. Nostalgia, Kemal's way of dealing with the past and the memory regime employed in *The Museum of Innocence* as a whole, is the epitome of this modern conception of time, because it is the expression of a yearning for a past that is completed and left behind. It is remarkable that while modernity does not favor remembering, nostalgia, by viewing the past as a dead category, enables both looking at the past and detaching oneself from it, which latter is modernity's desire. This essay aims to show the restraining nature of such a view of the past, as opposed to an understanding of it as an unfinished and open category, always in a state of flux, of re-imagination and re-construction. Hence, it's one of the main arguments of this essay that the regime of remembering put forth not only by the novel's characters, but also by the novel as such, objectifies the past as a homogenous and frozen category.

Another remarkable theme of self-contradiction forming one of the pillars of the novel is modern Turkish women's sexual liberation, which seems unrealized yet despite the embracement of the secular discourse of modernity. Thus, modernity brings forth an identity crisis regardless of whether it is labeled "false" or "incomplete" (the adjectives it most frequently takes on in the context of Turkey) and whether it is examined by means of its effects on the level of the individual, class or nation. The analysis of the novel's regime of remembering and the way home and identity are constructed in it will help to illuminate the work's discourse on modernization in Turkey.

In this process there have been enormous changes in the legal and social structures of Turkey, as well as transformations in the conceptions of home, identity and language, resulting in radical changes in the ways of seeing and thinking. Modernization in Turkey has always been hand in hand with Westernization, so much so that the two terms can be said to have become synonymous. During the Tanzimat period (1839-1876) the determining question was "what to import from the West;" following the establishment of the Turkish Republic (1923) practically all non-Western constituents of social structure, culture and, perhaps more importantly, language, were disposed of as part of a vast development program. State politics in present day Turkey still bear the traces of this program based on the equation of progress with adopting Western values and Western institutions. Completely breaking with the past and building a "new" home and identity have been the ultimate goal of Turkish modernization. Modernity is defined as a break with the past in the West, too, however, Turkish modernization differs from that in that it involves a radical desire to become the other. The process of modernization and of forming nation-states in the West involved constructing closed and absolute national identities (Bauman 20-22); Turkish national identity, additionally, has been built on Westernization, in other words, the sources of Turkish selfhood lay in another home.

As one of the main themes of the novel, innocence is taken as being oneself, not an imitation, preserving one's essence. Thus, Kemal's quest for innocence can be read as the quest of the modern Turkish upper class individual for a home and identity. Different classes portrayed in the novel represent different attitudes towards modernity. In the course of modernization Turkish elites took on the role of pioneers and educators in whose view the masses that form the lower class needed to be modernized. In the Turkish context, dualities of upper vs. lower class, urban vs. rural, western vs. eastern have always been closely related to the master duality of modernity vs. tradition. *The Museum of Innocence* is one link in the long chain of Turkish novels that deal with these deep-rooted themes. From the first Turkish novels written in the second half of the nineteenth century, when the modernization process gained momentum, to the novels of our day "how to modernize" has been one of the main questions of Turkish literature. Yet, despite their different ways of dealing with the issue of modernity, neither the first Turkish novelists, including Ahmet Mithat Efendi and Recaizade Mahmut Ekrem, nor modernists such as Ahmet Hamdi

Tanpınar and Oğuz Atay or those considered postmodernists like Orhan Pamuk have offered a comprehensive critique of modernity as Western authors did, especially after the 1950s. It is always the mistakes of the modernization process that are dealt with, but never modernity itself, a general tendency among Turkish intellectuals.

The objective of this essay is to address critically Pamuk's vision of these issues as it manifests itself in *The Museum of Innocence*. To this aim, the ways home and identity are conceptualized and the memory regime is created in the novel will be analyzed, which will lay bare its way of dealing with modernity.

Home and Nostalgia

The following discussion of the novel's treatment of the concept of home is grounded on the belief that modernity brings forth a certain understanding of home and that there is a close relationship between the concepts of home, identity and memory. The concept of home is closely related with belonging and identity; its possible meanings cover a broad spectrum ranging from physical homes to the communities and nation-states that one belongs to. In its modern sense it is constructed and "imagined" in isolation from the "outside" world which enables it to be qualified with the illusion of security.

Home also provides the self a sense of continuity since the past that is preserved in it provides the grounds for the imagination of the self. The loss of memory leads to a crisis of identity, and the loss of identity is closely related with the loss of memory. According to Bachelard home is "one of the greatest powers of integration for the thoughts, memories and dreams of mankind" (6). For him, because home enables one to imagine, it is an area in which reality and fiction are intertwined. Memory can also be conceptualized as a home that is both comforting and disturbing, which turns it into an *unheimlich*, or uncanny, category. Since remembering is one of the fundamental conditions of identity formation, memory is a home in which one finds comfort; but at the same time, since remembering is a process through which one encounters others (because individual and social memories are intertwined) and the past with its injustices and inequalities, it is a source of pain and discomfort. The analysis of the way home is imagined in *The Museum of Innocence* will also provide an analysis of the novel's regime of memory.

The construction of home varies in different regimes of memory. Modernity can be defined as the quest for a unified, coherent and orderly home that is shaped according to the ideals of individualism, progress, unification and order in which differences are eliminated through assimilation and exclusion. The imagination of home as a unified and coherent category turns memory into a homely area where one finds comfort, whereas an uncovering of its unhomeliness would pave the way for a questioning of the existing social conditions. The quest for home is also a quest for identity. The novel, by taking the reader on a journey to different neighborhoods of Istanbul such as Nişantaşı, Fatih, Boğaziçi and Çukurcuma presents the discussions on modernization in Turkey and represents space as an element that effectively determines individuals. The homes that Kemal, the protagonist of *The Museum of Innocence*, resides in reflect the differing views of different classes on modernity and can be read as different memory-spaces and identity-spaces. They can also be seen as ontological centers through which the perspective of the author regarding modernity and modernization refracts. In this refraction, each home has different functions as an element of the novel's plot and in terms of the discourse of the novel on modernity and modernization in Turkey. This paper aims to unearth these functions.

The quest for a home, such as that undertaken by Kemal, is the modern subject's answer to a situation of homelessness which arises because modernity seeks detachment from the past, a past that makes home possible. According to Kracauer, this situation, which he calls "transcendental homelessness," is a result of the hegemony of the capitalist *ratio* which is detached from reason and based on abstraction (75); in Adorno's view, "[t]he house is past. The bombing of European cities, as well as the labour and concentration camps, merely proceed as executors, with what the immanent development of technology had long decided was to be the fate of houses" (39).

In non-Western societies homelessness results not only from modernity but also from the concomitant adoption of an alien culture and the resulting identity loss. According to Konuk, Turkey's relationship with the West is determined by its position as a post-imperial state; "Its ambivalent relationship with the West is not the outcome of anticolonial struggle but of an empire in decline" (256).

The home in Nişantaşı where Kemal lives with his parents represents the modern elite's perspective on modernity in Turkey; the flat at the Merhamet Apartments in Teşvikiye – a *lieu de mémoire* or memory place in the form of a storehouse of commodities considered outmoded by Kemal's mother – represents what is excluded by modernity; Fatih Hotel, a non-place that is paradoxically more homely for Kemal than the home in Nişantaşı, represents the period before the "false" modernization process in Turkey; the old Bosphorus yalı (sea-side mansion) in Anadolu Hisarı that Sibel's family uses as a summer home is a space of shelter that is curative for Kemal rather than a space of desire and it represents both the destruction of the Ottoman past and the change of power during this transformation period; Füsun's family house in Nişantaşı Kuyulu Bostan Street represents classes and things that are situated at the margins of modernity but aspire to the upper-class life-style and values; Füsun's family house in Çukurcuma which Kemal visits for nearly eight years because for him it preserves the city's pre-modern essence; and finally the house in Çukurcuma, transformed into a museum, in which Kemal finds a real home, represents nostalgia for the past. Thus all these different places represent different ways of experiencing modernity and different forms of memory and identity in Turkey. Kemal's story that unfolds in these different spaces represents the quest for a home and identity of a modern individual questioning the values of his class and certain aspects of modernity in a non-western society.

Various neighborhoods of Istanbul appearing in the novel are already laden with ideological significance. The pro-modernity perspective in a modernizing society and the adoption of Westernization by the privileged class are reflected in Nişantaşı, "home" of this class. Nişantaşı, home to orchards and countryside cafés in the 1780s, transformed into a site of attraction for members of the dynasty and high state officials in the second half of the nineteenth century after the Ottoman dynasty moved, in parallel line with efforts to modernize/westernize, first from Topkapı Palace in the Ancient Peninsula to Dolmabahçe Palace and then to Yıldız Palace closer to Pera (Beyoğlu), the pioneering district of westernizing Istanbul. The members of this elite class had mansions and palaces built in that district. After the 1930s, apartment blocks started to fill the area but it preserved its characteristic of being the home of the upper classes. In the 1950s, the wave of migration from the rural areas of Turkey to the cities gave rise to slums in Beyoğlu; in the 1970s, Beyoğlu was no longer the home of wealthy non-muslim merchants and business men, but of the lower classes. This transformation resulted in Nişantaşı taking over some of the functions Pera served until then and turned it into a place where western products were exhibited in its multifarious brand shops.

The modernization/westernization movement was initiated and led by the Ottoman dynasty in the eighteenth century. In the following century, in the absence of a civilian middle class analogous with the bourgeoisie formed in Europe following the French Revolution and the Industrial Revolutions, the role of the modernizers in the Ottoman country was taken over by the bureaucratic and military elites (Mardin 177). They increasingly gained power, especially after the Tanzimat Reforms (1839), which paved the way for the establishment of Western style institutions including secular and military schools (Mardin 178). Many of these bureaucrats and military men underwent western style education in these institutions and some, in Europe. Forming a significant part of the new upper class they maintained their educative role after the proclamation of the Turkish Republic at the beginning of the twentieth century. This is reflected in the relationship between Füsun and Kemal, who assumes the role of her educator from the very beginning. Their relationship is initially one between master and pupil: Kemal gives mathematics lessons to Füsun, who wants to take the University Entrance Exam soon. This is meaningful because mathematics provides the grounds for Enlightenment thought. That the first gift that Kemal gives Füsun is a ruler reflects the modern understanding's glorification of rationalism. Kemal later teaches Füsun how to drive, the automobile being a symbol of modernity in that it is a modern technological product that promotes individualism by providing the freedom to travel alone. Although Kemal, coming from the upper-class, questions the views of his own class, he seizes the educative role the modern elites adopted in Turkey.

Modernizers tended to regard the past as a "dark age" – a term directly borrowed from Western literature on modernization – and the reforms realized in the course of the formation of the modern nation-state (among others, the abolition of the Caliphate, the banning of certain traditional, especially religious, styles of dressing – for instance by the "Hat Law" – and of religious zawiyah and dervish lodges, the change of the time and calendar system and the adoption of the Latin alphabet) were a result of the understanding that the West should serve as a model in all areas of life.

Although in the novel the upper classes embracing modernization are criticized for turning out to be cheap copies of the West, the fact itself that Turkish society is depicted as falling short of western standards presents these standards as the ultimate measure of society and thus only underscores the central position of the West. Kemal's family and upper-class friends who have enjoyed a western style education, imitate the western lifestyle, go to knock-off western restaurants, purchase western products – one of them even hires a western actress to play in a local commercial – are portrayed in the novel as imitators and their efforts seem to fall short of achieving complete modernity. But ironically, with this the novel itself sets western modernity as an ideal. This is problematical, firstly, because it reproduces an ethnocentric – in this case Eurocentric – and Orientalist perspective and secondly, because it defines the west as a homogeneous entity.

This perspective is most clearly seen in the comparisons between the West and the East constantly brought up in the novel. The most remarkable of these involve sexual relations; the protagonist, who criticizes Sibel as un-modern for being uncomfortable about "making love before marriage," praises Füsun for being different: "'[Sibel]'s not as modern and courageous as you are…'" (67). Similarly, European men and women are portrayed as capable to stay in a room together in a civilized manner without engaging in sexual relations, whereas Turkish men and women can't "stay in that room for long without succumbing to temptation" (117), because they can't avoid considering how other people would view their being closeted together, in other words, they can't think and behave as individuals, and thus, as themselves. Comparisons between the East and the West are encountered even in the description of insignificant details: "A kilim hung on the wall in the way Europeans hang a painting" (134). In another instance, Turkish bourgeois are depicted as European wannabes who purchase all the latest household appliances imported from the West, but can't operate them properly (171-72). As in these examples, such comparisons always position the West as the superior side setting the standard by which the inferior Eastern side is to be measured. This centralization and idealization of the West not only serves to reproduce centuries-old Eurocentric views of time, history and modernity, it also entails violence to Europe itself, since the ascription of a singular, unified and homogeneous identity disregards the differences within it. Thus, besides collapsing the differences within them, establishing hierarchical oppositions between all entities under its gaze is the essential characteristic of Orientalism, which emerges as the novel's prominent discourse. One of the principle dogmas of Orientalism for Edward Said is "the absolute and systematic difference between the West, which is rational, developed, humane, superior, and the Orient, which is aberrant, undeveloped, inferior" (300).

The novel's Orientalist perspective also affects the relations between upper and lower classes and between rural and urban districts. The lower classes in the novel appear to be more modern than the upper classes in certain respects: a striking example is that Füsun is not tied down by the virginity taboo, while upper class women still attach great importance to it even as they argue against it. In modern Turkey, it ironically was the upper class which supported the status quo. With Turkey's international and EU politics in mind, Erdağ Göknar argues that "Pamuk has allowed us to see another irony of our age: no longer are religious traditionalists reactionaries of change, but, in a curious inversion, patriotic secularists are" (38). However, for Pamuk, the society in general lacks the modernity of its Western model.

In the nineteenth century the Ottoman society's self-image took the shape of a reversed self-image of colonialist Europe with its self-universalizing discourse and historicist perpective which views non-western societies as underdeveloped. As this Eurocentric discourse gained acceptance among the intellectuals of the declining Ottoman Empire, for many Ottomans the West became synonymous with power (Mardin 15).

Pamuk's novel fails to go beyond this intellectual heritage and reproduces the problematic binary opposition between the East and the West, defining Turkish society by lack with regard to its "original."

The virginity taboo as a sign of this absence of modernity is one of the fundamental themes in the novel. In the chapter titled "A Few Unpalatable Anthropological Truths," the moral code regulating sexual relations between a man and a woman in Turkey is portrayed and the consequences of such a relationship before marriage are presented as anthropological truths (82-87): One result might be marriage in order to save the woman's honor (83); or if the girl is under age her father could "take the philanderer to court to force him to marry her" (84); if a modern upper class couple intends to marry, premarital sexual relations are acceptable in their circle, but they still need to remain unmentioned (83). Although these are mostly manifestations of the patriarchal structure of the society, they are attributed in the novel to not being modern enough. That the values of a society which have social, cultural, historical, religious and traditional foundations are presented as absolute anthropological truths reflects an understanding of home (society) as a unified and homogeneous entity. Neglecting the multifarious sources of this taboo and attributing it to lack of modernity ignores the differences within Turkish society and between it and other cultures. In the novel, the desire of women to keep their virginity until marriage is represented as a consequence of the traditional oppression in society, but it may well be a woman's free choice based on her beliefs and values. Equating keeping one's virginity with blind submission to an overbearing tradition throws the idea of free will into crisis. In fact, the identification of women as passive carriers of tradition reproduces the oppressive and homogenizing understanding prevalent in patriarchal societies.

The flat at the Merhamet Apartments in Teşvikiye filled with outmoded objects by Kemal's mother is a memory-space from the very beginning: containing objects that belong to their common past, it first becomes Kemal and Füsun's love nest, later a space where Kemal goes to wait for Füsun to come, then a space where he goes to remember the times he spent there with Füsun and lastly a space of a collection of objects that Kemal stole from Füsun's house in order to fill in her lack. This is a place reserved only for remembering, but the objects that are stored in this home are detached from their context. Kemal, rather than making these objects part of his life, goes to that past that has been frozen in order to remember. Rolf Tiedemann discusses Walter Benjamin's understanding of history thus:

> the historian should no longer try to enter the past; rather, he should allow the past to enter his life. A "pathos of nearness" should replace the vanishing "empathy" (I°, 2).[2] For the historian, past objects and events would not then be fixed data, an unchangeable given, because dialectical thinking "ransacks them, revolutionizes them, turns them upside down" (D°, 4); this is what must be accomplished by awakening from the dream of the nineteenth century. (935)

Since Kemal, rather than allowing "the past to enter his life," "enters the past" himself in the flat at the Merhamet Apartments, these past objects detached from the present time exist as fixed data for him. This kind of remembering, rather than making the reader question the present time, freezes the past at a certain point in history and thus produces nostalgia.

The Merhamet Apartments were built by a rich old man who had controlled the sugar black market during the First World War. Probably in order to compensate for his past misdeeds, he decided to distribute the income the apartment generated to the poor, but thereupon his two greedy sons had him declared incompetent and took possession of the apartments. "Merhamet" ("mercy") is a notion excluded by the modern capitalist system since it does not yield profit. The objects in the flat at the Merhamet Apartments represent a past that is not merely useless, but also an obstacle in the way of progress. Similar to the concept of mercy which has become obsolete in the modern capitalist system, these objects don't have a place in that system either, because they do not exist by their exchange-value or use-value, but through their symbolic value. Like the

---

[2] Tiedemann refers to Benjamin's early drafts (listed under "First Sketches" in the Works Cited) of *The Arcades Project* and uses Benjamin's own numbering system in this quotation.

rich old man who acts against capitalist logic by refusing to gain profit, Kemal, by choosing to be in this memory-space among objects that only have symbolic value, turns his back on the values of his own class and on modernity as detachment from the past, thus drifting apart from his former social circle. But because these objects representing the past in the way of progress are captured in this memory-space, the threat that they pose for the current society is eliminated by their detachment from the present time. The attempt to detach and freeze the past in a chamber serves only to render it ineffective in the present. The past can be a means to rethink the present time only if it is brought into the present as a disruption in the familiar order of time.

In Kemal's quest for identity, the flat at the Merhamet Apartments constitutes his first relationship with the past and the objects of the past. What turns this place into a home for Kemal is that it is full of memories and a place for remembering. In order to find his identity, Kemal begins by remembering the past that has been labeled as "junk" and learns to cherish that past. Füsun as Kemal's distant relative is also a figure from Kemal's past; thus different stages of Kemal's relationship with Füsun can be read as different stages of Kemal's relationship with his own past. Füsun, coming from a lower class and being a part of Kemal's childhood, represents, according to the typical modern conception of progress, an earlier stage of modernization, a "dark age" that the modern elites strive to leave behind. Pursuing a relationship with this past causes one to be labelled "reactionary" and Kemal's relationship with Füsun is not approved in the modern circles that he comes from, so in order to be closer to Füsun he needs to get away from his family and friends.

Sibel takes Kemal off to the Bosphorus yalı in Anadolu Hisarı to cure his love for Füsun which she refers to as an illness. These mansions were built in the Bosphorus mainly by the Ottoman elite. Mostly destroyed by fire and antique dealers (27), they are the last remnants of a powerful ancient empire and remind the residents of the city of the times when the empire was powerful, but also confront them with its loss.[3] Indeed, Kemal

---

[3] In Pamuk's autobiographical *Istanbul: Memories and the City* (published in Turkish in 2003) the last remnants of the past in the city are one of the reasons for the feeling of *hüzün*, or melancholy, that characterizes the whole city.

and Sibel move into the yalı with the hope of mending their broken relationship amidst "the vestigial presence of a vanished Ottoman culture" (282). Paradoxically, these remnants of the old empire do not only remind one of power, but also of its loss. Thus the place where Sibel takes Kemal to make him forget the past becomes a painful reminder of it. The Bosphorus yalı in Anadoluhisarı is, in the words of Kemal's mother, in "dreadful shape" (90), and problems such as "the rusty water that poured from the old taps, the dankness of the ramshackle kitchen, the yalı's leaks and drafty cracks" (273) represent the destruction of the Ottoman Empire and the following inability to restore Turkey to its former power. The Bosphorus yalı turns into a metaphor of the identity crisis in Turkey caused by the power shift resulting from the modernization process. It is the lost power that has been mourned for and the dichotomy of modernity and tradition that creates Pamuk's melancholy, or *hüzün*, which shows up at this point: false modernization ruined what was pure, which with a proper modernization would have been avoided. It is implied by the novel that if the process of modernization had been successful, if the society had managed to duplicate the "original," then it would be possible to forget that this was a process of duplication, and the feelings of failure, guilt and lack would be avoided. This implication arises from the association of the problems of Turkish society with incomplete or false modernization; according to this view, proper modernization would have prevented these problems. As manifested in the transformation of the seaside mansions from signs of power to signs of its loss, the problem of modernization is established in the novel as one of power, which overlooks the deficiencies of modernity itself.

When Sibel goes to Paris with one of her friends, Kemal stays alone for some more time at the yalı and two weeks before Sibel's return he moves to Fatih Hotel because of his desire to be with Füsun's ghost that he has encountered previously in such poor neighborhoods of the city. A hotel is a non-place as defined by Marc Augé, where one's identity does not matter and where thus differences are eliminated since one exists only as a customer:

> a person entering the space of non-place is relieved of his usual determinants. He becomes no more than what he does or experiences in the role of passenger, customer or driver. [...] he tastes for a while – like anyone who is possessed – the passive joys of identity-loss, and the more active pleasure of role-playing. (Augé 103)

Kemal feels more at home in this place than in his home in Nişantaşı and the Bosphorus yalı. For Kemal, the non-place of the hotel turns into a place providing him with clues about his identity rather than the "joys of identity-loss." Kemal realizes much later that his days at the Fatih Hotel were full of happiness rather than painful:

> Sometimes I felt that my happiness issued not from the possibility that Füsun was near, but from something less tangible. I felt as if I could see the very essence of life in these poor neighborhoods, with their empty lots, their muddy cobblestone streets, their cars, rubbish bins, and sidewalks, and the children playing with a half-inflated football under the streetlamps. My father's expanding business, his factories, his growing fortune, and the attendant obligation to live the "elegant European" life that befit this wealth – it all now seemed to have deprived me of simple essences. As I walked these streets, it was as if I was seeking out my own center. (292-93)

Despite his class Fatih is more homely for Kemal, mostly because it is a place that has not turned into an imitation of the West and lost its "essence." In contrast to Nişantaşı that has always been upper class, Fatih is mainly the home of the lower class, muslim segments of society that remain distant to modernity. In these poor neighborhoods modernization did not affect everyday life as deeply and there is still a resemblance of the past. Kemal finds these neighborhoods and the identity they offer him more "real" than the knock-off Western identity of his own class.

After the death of his father Kemal returns to his home in Nişantaşı and fills in for his lack: his death makes Kemal realize the resemblances between himself and his parent (he notices one more time that their big toes are identical) and he happily takes the deceased's place, sitting in his chair, drinking the Yeni Rakı half-finished by him:

> With the death of my father, it wasn't just the objects of everyday life that had changed; even the most ordinary street scenes had become irreplaceable mementos of a lost world whose every detail figured in the meaning of the whole. Because coming home now meant a return to the center of that world, there was a happiness I could not hide from myself, and my guilt was even deeper than that of a man whose father had just died. (312)

His father's death signifies the end of Kemal's childhood and his transition to adulthood. He is happy to remember his lost childhood, but also feels guilty about taking his father's place. This is a step in Kemal's quest for his identity; it appears that in order for him to gain his identity, his father had to die. The significance of this supersedence becomes especially obvious in the contrasting ways in which the father and the son choose to act about their respective love affairs with lower class women. Kemal's father refrains from breaking the codes of his class and keeps his affair secret and his dignity intact, while Kemal goes against class codes and abandons his fiancée and his sphere to be with his lover, despite the warnings of his mother and his friends. He visits Füsun's family house in Çukurcuma for nearly eight years, turning into a member of her family. These visits denote Kemal's withdrawal from his own class and its values. Since his father represents modern upper class values, in this case the death of the father – which is usually equated with an oedipal revolt and a break with tradition – signifies a radical break with modernity. Kemal finds his own identity only when he detaches himself from the class that he was born into.

Füsun's family house in Nişantaşı Kuyulu Bostan Street represents the lifestyle and views of classes living on the margins of modernity. Like Füsun and Aunt Nesibe, these people aspire to the more modernized upper class. Füsun's father Tarık Bey never actually wants his sixteen year old daughter to enter the beauty contest, he is the one who decides to move from Nişantaşı to Çukurcuma and who first proposes to marry off Füsun to cure her of her heartache and save her honor. After Tarık Bey's death, which can be read as the death of tradition, Füsun's desire to modernize gets a chance to materialize. This is reflected in the transformation of her conditions for continuing to see Kemal. Before her father's death, Füsun had said that she wouldn't leave Kemal on two conditions: that he would never lie to her again and that he would come to her family's house for supper bringing with him her lost earring and the tricycle that both of them rode as children (116). After her father's death the conditions are thus: Füsun wants to meet all of Kemal's friends and family once she is officially divorced from Feridun; she wants Kemal's mother to come to their house to seek permission for their marriage from Aunt Nesibe; she wants to tour Europe with Aunt Nesibe and Kemal and buy her trousseau from Paris; she wants "a big, beautiful wedding at the Hilton, like everyone else" and, lastly, she wishes to wait with sexual relations until after marriage (626-28). After her father's death, Füsun starts to transform into a "modern" woman and her wishes and desires imitate those of the upper-class. The desires repressed by the law of the father return after his death. For Kemal, his father's death provides the grounds for finding his identity; the death of Füsun's father transforms that "innocent" girl who can be herself without considering others' thoughts into a woman who imitates upper class habits.

According to Kemal, the "defining property" of Füsun's family house in Çukurcuma "was its timelessness" (394). What enables him to make this judgment is the house's position *outside of the modern world*. For Kemal, Çukurcuma and the home there represent the past that the rich neighborhoods lost through modernization and westernization. Kemal finds his home in this "innocent" past rather than the present time and its loss of identity. Kemal's desire to transform the home in Çukurcuma into a museum is a consequence of his desire to live in the past that has become a home for him, to substitute Füsun's absence with the objects that remind him of her and to tell his individual story to others so that it becomes a story to "take a pride in" rather than a story "to be ashamed of" (711). The distinguishing characteristic of Çukurcuma is that it is located between Fatih, the space of tradition, and Nişantaşı, the space of modernity.

Dellaloğlu argues that the decision to construct the museum in this district can be read as a proposal for a cultural armistice (107).

The home in Çukurcuma from the very beginning resembles the museum-homes of the European bourgeois class of the nineteenth century with all its knickknacks, clocks and decoration. The objects and bibelots in this home signify their aspiration to the modern bourgeois life:

> The bibelot is an imitative object, a decorative cliché whose models are so variegated and mismatched as to defy all notions of authenticity or restitution. The bibelotized interior points to a failure to make oneself at home in one's own life and times. In this sense, home turns into its opposite, homesickness. (Maleuvre 118)

Füsun's home in Çukurcuma represents the homesickness of its residents who cannot feel at home in a modernizing society. As in this house, bibelots generally exist in pairs reflecting the homogenization of society (home) in modernity which eliminates singularities and differences, but they also provide those living in this home with a sense of homeliness and belonging.

The choice of a museum as home reflects the homelessness that modern societies could not overcome, since "the museum represents the absence of a place" (Maleuvre 75). So the question of belonging is answered by attachment to a place that it is impossible to belong to. This is a reflection of an understanding of history as the opposite of individual memories, and thus a place that is bereft of history is the most suitable home for the modern individual. Kemal finds his home and identity in the most unhomely place of a museum, in a frozen reality, a frozen past that is captured and detached from the present time.

Identity and the Past as a Stage of Childhood

The Museum of Innocence could be read as an allegory of the crisis of identity in Turkey caused by the process of modernization. The eponymous innocence is defined in the dictionary ("Innocence") as "the state, quality, or fact of not being guilty of a crime; lack of guile or corruption, purity;

and a person's virginity," and in the novel it has all those meanings, but it also signifies an answer to the question of identity: Being yourself without considering what others think about you.

The idea of innocence endorsed by the novel shows a close affinity to the view that the current stage of the modernization process in Turkey corresponds to the childhood stage of the development of the West. This view is based on a teleological understanding of history according to which all societies go through the same stages on their course to modernity. This understanding has paved the way for colonization and ethnocentrism – in this case Eurocentrism – which regard cultures and societies at a supposed childhood stage as "primitive" compared to the mature western societies. The perspective on Turkish modernization adopted in *The Museum of Innocence* reproduces this Eurocentric, historicist understanding: Füsun as a representation of Kemal's lost childhood is a kind of child in his eyes. In contrast with upper class women, Füsun is uncorrupted and more free; such romantic and essentialist conceptions provide the grounds for attributing to her a purity associated with childhood. In the novel, the past, as a time of innocence, is conceptualized as the childhood of society before modernization and westernization ruined everything. Kemal identifies Füsun's family house in Çukurcuma, Fatih Hotel and the museum with innocence because they conserve the past and traditions better than the places where the upper classes reside. The West itself and the uncorrupted lower classes are attributed originality by the novel and thus idealized. The whole structure of the novel is founded on dichotomies such as modern-traditional, east-west and original-copy; this structure is manifested in the fact that all the characters, classes and places in the novel are defined by means of their degree of modernization/westernization. Another clear manifestation of this dichotomous structure is the association of the upper classes and their places with imitation as opposed to the association of the lower classes and their places with an uncorrupted essence. Furthermore, most of the novel's plot follows the course of its main character's journey from one pole of this set of hierarchical dualities to the other pole: From being with Sibel to being with Füsun and from living in Nişantaşı to residing in Çukurcuma. Idealization – in this case defined by originality –

is a necessary consequence of dichotomous structures as they always function by the elevation of a superior pole over its inferior other.

Modernization in Turkey is characterized by self-rejection and a desire to become "the other." Turkish society, placed at the periphery with the West as the center, was reconstructed with that center/original as a model. In this imitation process, a diversity of identities was suppressed in order to construct a unified and homogeneous identity through "Turkification." Ironically, the model for this supposedly genuine Turkishness was derived from the nationalistic currents of Europe.

The novel creates a contrast between collecting and commodity fetishism. The collector who dreams of a better world is unhappy with the one he lives in and this exactly defines Kemal's situation. Kemal, as a collector, turns his back on the values of his own class and constructs his "happiness" through collecting. Thus, collecting, as viewed by Walter Benjamin, becomes a critical act. Benjamin defines the collector as "the true resident of the interior":

> He makes his concern the transfiguration of things. To him falls the Sisyphean task of divesting things of their commodity character by taking possession of them. But he bestows on them only connoissseur value rather than use value. The collector dreams his way not only into a distant or bygone world but also into a better one – one in which, to be sure, human beings are no better provided with what they need than in the everyday world, but in which things are freed from the drudgery of being useful. (*Arcades* 19)

But the collector also tries to create a miniature world to live in where he is in control:

> What is decisive in collecting is that the object is detached from all its original functions in order to enter into the closest conceivable relation to things of the same kind. This relation is the diametric opposite of any utility, and falls into the peculiar category of completeness. What is this 'completeness'? It is a

> grand attempt to overcome the wholly irrational character of the object's mere presence at hand through its integration into a new, expressly devised historical system: the collection. And for the true collector, every single thing in this system becomes an encyclopedia of all knowledge of the epoch, the landscape, the industry, and the owner from which it comes. It is the deepest enchantment of the collector to enclose the particular item within a magic circle, where, as a last shudder runs through it (the shudder of being acquired), it turns to stone. (*Arcades* 204-05)

In this way the critical act of collecting turns into a tool of controlling the world and thus helps to construct the collector's self as powerful. According to Baudrillard, "the object pure and simple, divested of its function, abstracted from any practical context, takes on a strictly subjective status" (8). Thus, the objects Kemal collects and then exhibits in the museum function as a means of establishing his subjectivity. This brings into view one of the major dichotomies that *The Museum of Innocence* relies on, that between the subject and the object. This is closely related to other dichotomies that lie at the foundation of modernity and play a significant role in the novel, such as those between individual and collective, genuine and fake and East and West.

Despite the antagonism in the novel between collecting and commodity fetishism, the objects that Kemal collects are also fetish objects for him. According to Freud, the fetish, which is "a substitute for the woman's (mother's) penis that the little boy once believed in" (152-53) is "a token of triumph over the threat of castration and a protection against it" (154). Modernization in Turkey has meant a castration of society through the definition of home and identity according to a western model. The upper classes in the role of modernizers played an important role in this, but as a part of that society they were also the objects of castration. In the novel, the modern upper classes fetishize commodities which in turn serve as a substitute for modernity. Although Kemal is aware that this substitute, rather than making up for the lack of modernity, reminds one of it, he also fetishizes objects that compensate for Füsun's lack so that his passion for her is diverted to these objects. While the upper classes fetishize objects representing modernity, Kemal fetishizes objects that remind him of his past, which is how they provide a protection for him against the castration that his class went through. When he decides to open a museum where he can exhibit his individual story through these fetishes, by gaining control over them he gains control over his own story and thus avoids being defined by others. He escapes the threat of castration by the West through the adoption of modern individualism. He is aware of the problems that modernization poses for his class, but in order to avoid them he chooses to act as an individual, thus distinguishing himself from his class. In the final chapter of the novel, there is a narratorial shift: Orhan Pamuk as a character takes over the role of the narrator from Kemal, however, this doesn't bring along a shift in attitude towards the central issues of the narrative such as modernity, westernization, individualism etc. Indeed, in *The Innocence of Objects* (the catalogue of the museum) the author Pamuk argues for a museum in which the individual creates his/her own meanings instead of the conventional museums in which objects signify collective and/or national meanings (*Innocence* 55). Kemal's (and also Pamuk's) desire for a museum of individuals is also related with this issue, but trying to escape the commodity fetishism of his class Kemal gets caught up in another type of object fetishism, that of belongings invested with personal meanings. Furthermore, trying to avoid the idealism of the nation-state, Pamuk gets caught up in another type of idealism, one that glorifies individualism.

In the modern capitalist system, the value of things is based on their exchange value, on how much they are worth. In the novel, different classes have differing views regarding the value of objects. The flat at the Merhamet Apartments is full of objects that are not used anymore and considered as junk in the capitalist system; but for Kemal and Füsun these objects are reminders of their childhood and the times that they spent together. When Füsun diasappears, Kemal fills her lack with her belongings and caresses them at the flat at the Merhamet Apartments, which contrasts with the habits of the modernized upper classes, who are presented as treasuring the exchange value of objects. When Kemal buys Sibel a Jenny Colon bag as a gift, she tells him that she cannot use it because it is fake and asks him to return it. Later, when talking with Sibel at the engagement party, Füsun says:

> "For me, it's not in the least important whether something is or isn't a European product. And it's not in the least important to me either if a thing is genuine or fake. If you ask me, people's dislike of imitations has nothing to do with fake or real, but the fear that others might think they'd 'bought it cheap.' For me, the worst thing is when people care about the brand and not the thing itself. You know how there are some people who don't give importance to their own feelings, and care only about what other people might say" […]. (197)

Füsun's remarks are critical of Sibel, who values objects for their exchange value, but also of Kemal, who despite his love for Füsun, gets engaged to a woman from his own class, because he cares "only about what other people might say." In the novel, being innocent is associated with being yourself without regard to others' thoughts, and Turkish modernization represents the loss of innocence. The argument of false modernization, which has been an important theme in literary works in Turkey beginning with the first novels, underlies this association. The upper classes in the novel cannot escape being copies of the West, and this is why they are not innocent. European style restaurants are described as places that "wished to give their customers a subtler illusion of being in a European city" (14). The Fuaye, for instance, with its name meaning 'lobby' "reminded one of being on the edge of Europe" (14).

In the beginning of the book, the German model Inge is to act in commercials for Meltem Soda. Behind that choice lies the yearning for Europeanness. All the questions that Kemal asks Inge are concerned with what she thinks about Turkey and Istanbul; he is humiliated to hear from her that it is not hard to become famous in a country with only one television channel, and pleased when she praises Turkey for being way ahead of Europe with respect to advertising (40-41). This dialogue presents further evidence that the interiorized European gaze is a constitutive element of Turkish identity. On the other hand, for Kemal, the museum is an area of innocence where the "essence" of things can be seen, where he can be himself without regard to what others think. The typically modern reliance on clearcut dualities such as the novel's copied vs. original, pure and innocent leads to the idea that there is a pure Turkish identity that is stable, homogeneous and unified, but also to a rigid understanding of modernization tied to a pure and unified European culture and identity.

Conclusion

The Museum of Innnocence makes the reader conscious of its form through techniques of reflexivity such as addressing the reader, shifting narratorial roles in the last chapter, young Orhan Pamuk and his actual family members entering the narrative as guests at Kemal and Sibel's engagement party and characters from Pamuk's other works appearing in the novel. Pamuk himself opened a museum in Çukurcuma in real life which is modelled after Kemal's fictional one. All this pushes the limits of intertextuality and blurs the distinction between fiction and reality.

However, the novel cannot escape absolutism and essentialism for several reasons. First of all, it creates coherent pasts for coherent selves and constructs unified and integrated identities for its characters from different classes. Secondly, in order to escape from the hegemony of institutions and structures in a society, it absolutizes the category of the individual. And lastly, it produces a unified historical discourse by idealizing the past as an age of innocence. Thus the reader's formal consciousness raised by the novel is simultaneously undermined by its Orientalist discourse; consequently, the novel fails to fulfill the promise of its formal design as metafiction which otherwise would serve to convert the reader's formal consciousness into a critical awareness of his/her own ideological context.

In the novel, the past is absolutized along with the individual's story. The individual is regarded as "innocent" in contrast to the structures and institutions of society and thus the monumentalization of the nation by official histories is replaced by a monumentalization of the individual. Although the novel tells the story of ordinary individuals, attributing innocence to them eventually results in their exemption from responsibility and guilt, as they exist outside of history. Individuals are characterized as innocent as a result of a centralist understanding of power according to which collective structures such as institutions and nation-states have power while individuals are merely its objects. The definition of individuals as powerless in the face of collective structures frees them from responsibility and establishes them as innocent.

The Museum of Innocence is an attempt to remember in a modernizing society detached from the past, but the regime of memory in the novel prevents remembering from turning into a transformative and critical act because such a past has ceased to constitute a threat to the present time; instead, it is domesticated within the walls of a museum by nostalgia.

The novel's world-view is a modernist one, because although false modernization is criticized on many levels, the problems of modernity itself are not addressed. What's more, the Western criteria for being modern are absolutized by characterizing home and identity in Turkish society as lacking modernity. This absolutization of a Eurocentric model for modernity is founded on a progressivist understanding which demands that all societies go through identical stages of development. This has served as the very justification for the colonization of "underdeveloped, non-European" nations in history. Consequently, Pamuk's Orientalist, anthropological view marginalizes Turkish society. The novel cannot escape a historicist, nostalgic understanding of home and identity, because it accepts the main principles of modernity such as progressivism, individualism and rationalism unquestioningly as it fails to escape the dualisms and absolutism of modernity.

Works Cited

Adorno, Theodor W. *Minima Moralia: Reflections on a Damaged Life*. 1951. Trans. E.F.N. Jephcott. London, New York: Verso, 2005.

Augé, Marc. *Non-places: Introduction to an Anthropology of Supermodernity*. Trans. John Howe. London, New York: Verso, 1995.

Bachelard, Gaston. *The Poetics of Space*. Trans. Maria Jolas. 1964. Boston: Beacon, 1994.

Baudrillard, Jean. "The System of Collecting." *The Cultures of Collecting*. Ed. John Elsner and Roger Cardinal. Second ed. London: Reaktion, 1997. 7-25.

Bauman, Zygmunt. *Identity: Conversations with Benedetto Vecchi*. Cambridge: Polity, 2004.
Benjamin, Walter. *The Arcades Project*. Ed. Rolf Tiedemann. Trans. Howard Eiland, Kevin McLaughlin. Cambridge, Mass., London: The Belknap Press of Harvard UP, 1999.
___. "First Sketches." *The Arcades Project*. Ed. Rolf Tiedemann. Trans. Howard Eiland, Kevin McLaughlin. Cambridge, Mass., London: The Belknap Press of Harvard UP, 1999. 825-68.
Dellaloğlu, Besim. "Nişantaşı ile Fatih'in imkânsız ortalaması Çukurcuma." *Monograf: Edebiyat eleştirisi dergisi* 7 (2017): 100-08.
Freud, Sigmund. "Fetishism." Trans. J. Strachey. The Complete Psychological Works of Sigmund Freud. Vol. 21. London: Hogarth and the Institute of Psychoanalysis, 1927. 147-57.
Göknar, Erdağ. "Orhan Pamuk and the 'Ottoman' Theme." *World Literature Today* 80.6 (2006): 34-38.
"Innocence." *Oxford Dictionaries*. London: Oxford UP. Accessed 16 Aug. 2015 <http://en.oxforddictionaries.com/definition/innocenc e>.
Johnson, Barbara. "Opening Remarks." *The Critical Difference: Essays in the Contemporary Rhetoric of Reading*. London, Baltimore: Johns Hopkins UP, 1985. ix-xii.
Konuk, Kader. "Istanbul on Fire: End-of-Empire Melancholy in Orhan Pamuk's Istanbul." *The Germanic Review: Literature, Culture, Theory*. 86.4 (2011): 249-61.
Kracauer, Siegfried. *The Mass Ornament: Weimar Essays*. Trans. Thomas Y. Levin. 1963. Cambridge, Mass., London: Harvard UP, 1995.
Maleuvre, Didier. *Museum Memories: History, Technology, Art*. Stanford, California: Stanford UP, 1999.
Mardin, Şerif. *Türk modernleşmesi*. Makaleler 4. Ed. Mümtaz'er Türköne, Tuncay Önder. İstanbul: İletişim, 2007.
Pamuk, Orhan. *The Museum of Innocence*. Trans. Maureen Freely. London: Faber and Faber, 2009. Trans. of *Masumiyet müzesi*.
___. *The Innocence of Objects*. Trans. Ekin Oklap. New York: Abrams, 2012. Trans. of *Şeylerin masumiyeti*.
Said, Edward. *Orientalism*. New York: Vintage, 1979.

Tiedemann, Rolf. "Dialectics at a Standstill." 1988. *The Arcades Project*. By Walter Benjamin. Ed. Rolf Tiedemann. Trans. Howard Eiland, Kevin McLaughlin. Cambridge, Mass., London: The Belknap Press of Harvard UP, 1999. 929-46.

A Novel Like a Well:
A Girardian Reading of Pamuk's *The Red-Haired Woman*[1]

Elif Türker Gümüş
Doğuş University

Abstract: This essay argues that even though Orhan Pamuk's *The Red-Haired Woman* appears to treat the East-West divide based on the stories of patricide by Oedipus from the West and the filicide of Sohrab by Rostam from the East, a deeper concern of the novel is the ancient father-son conflict. Drawing on René Girard's analysis of mimetic desire, a possible biographical background to the novel's proliferation of parent-son conflicts is explored on the basis of Pamuk's Nobel Lecture and other writings.

> "Something resembling a well… Once you're in it, you'll only go deeper and deeper… But I'll listen. Now it, later I, will be on top. Until one drowns."
> – Ahmet Hamdi Tanpınar, "Yaz Gecesi"[2]

Let us recall the epigraph of *Öteki renkler*,[3] the book of essays billed by Orhan Pamuk as that in which he reveals the most about himself:[4] The epigraph is a line from the eighteenth-century poet Ghalib Dede or Shaykh Ghalib (Galip Dede or Şeyh Galip in modern Turkish spelling), which reads, "Wear any color, but don't reveal your true color."[5] This epigraph is the golden rule that governs Pamuk's writing. Still, I believe readers can track the author down as, while taking on every color, he also appears in what probably is his own color. Otherwise he wouldn't be writing at all. In

---

[1] This is an extended version of the essay "Orhan Pamuk Kuyusu" published in the online magazine *t24.com.tr/k24*, along with an English translation by Yasemin Gürkan. The present text is based on this translation.

[2] "Kuyu gibi bir şey… Bir kere takıldın mı derine, daha derinlere gideceksin… Bununla beraber dinleyeceğim. Şimdi o, biraz sonra ben üste çıkacağız. Böylece boğulana kadar."

[3] *Other Colors* is partially a translation of *Öteki renkler*.

[4] "[…] heyecanlansam bile çoğu zaman hiç renk vermiyorum. Bu kitap renk verdiklerimdir" (Pamuk, "Önsöz" 22).

[5] "Her renge boyan da renk verme."

his Nobel Lecture titled "My Father's Suitcase" he defiantly explains his reasons for writing:

> I write because I have an innate need to write! I write because I can't do normal work like other people. I write because I want to read books like the ones I write. I write because I am angry at all of you, angry at everyone. I write because I love sitting in a room all day writing. I write because I can only partake in real life by changing it. I write because I want others, all of us, the whole world, to know what sort of life we lived, and continue to live, in Istanbul, in Turkey. I write because I love the smell of paper, pen, and ink. I write because I believe in literature, in the art of the novel, more than I believe in anything else. I write because it is a habit, a passion. I write because I am afraid of being forgotten. I write because I like the glory and interest that writing brings. I write to be alone. Perhaps I write because I hope to understand why I am so very, very angry at all of you, so very, very angry at everyone. I write because I like to be read. I write because once I have begun a novel, an essay, a page, I want to finish it. I write because everyone expects me to write. I write because I have a childish belief in the immortality of libraries, and in the way my books sit on the shelf. I write because it is exciting to turn all of life's beauties and riches into words. I write not to tell a story, but to compose a story. I write because I wish to escape from the foreboding that there is a place I must go but – just as in a dream – I can't quite get there. I write because I have never managed to be happy. I write to be happy.

When we put all of these reasons together it seems possible that Orhan Pamuk reveals his true color, don't you think? The defiant voice is heard when Pamuk, about to describe his feelings on reading the writings from his father's suitcase, wants "to change the *subject/mood*" (my emphasis).[6]

---

[6] The Turkish original is: "Ben de benzeri bir müzik işlevi görecek ve sevilecek bir-iki söz ile konuyu değiştireyim!" Maureen Freely's translation on *Nobelprize.org* reads,

Dante Gabriel Rossetti: *Regina Cordium* (red chalk). 1860.
Source: Wikimedia Commons.

Part of *The Red-Haired Woman*,[7] Pamuk's most recent novel, deals with the issue of refusing to reveal. After the book's release, topics of debate surrounding the novel included the father-son dynamic and the East-West divide. I don't want to argue against these views, but I reserve the right to find them incomplete. As a matter of fact, why should I hide that I find these comments superficial? Let me explain: The novel revolves around a situation faced by fifteen-year-old Cem, who dreams of becoming a writer but ends up an engineer, during his time digging wells in the town of Öngören to make money for his education after his father walks out on his family. This incident, which occupies Cem's mind all through his life, turns out to lay the ground for his undoing.

The narrative alludes to the stories of Oedipus on the one hand and Rostam and Sohrab on the other. Given the degree of Pamuk's novelistic craft,

---

"Let me change the mood with a few sweet words that will, I hope, serve as well as that music."

[7] An English translation of the book is to be published in 2017.

the obvious manner in which these two underlying stories represent the West and the East, respectively, and point to a father-son conflict should raise one's suspicions.

The novel's fictional structure in the manner of a spiral that deepens as the narrative progresses has the Red-Haired Woman at its center. Her character forms a triangular structure with the father-and-son relationship. A schematic representation will make my case more convincing, and for that I'll get some help from philosopher René Girard, whose anthropology offers the most effective schema for such a structure.

In his *Deceit, Desire, and the Novel: Self and Other in Literary Structure*, Girard looks at literary texts in accordance with how desire is positioned in a specific work. Narrative is organized around the question whether an object is the source of the desire for it or not. When a subject desires an object because another subject desires it or when, to desire an object, a subject needs another subject to desire it as well, Girard's model of "mimetic desire" can be used to describe the result. According to this model, the subject desires the object by mediation: Works with a hidden object of desire and highlighting the subject are romantic, whereas those in which a mediator for the desire exists and the subject desires the object through such mediation are novelistic. Girard uses the term "triangular desire" to describe and schematize novelistic works. The verteces of this triangle-like structure are formed by the subject, the object of desire, and the mediator, respectively. Here, the mediator is the key. Girard proposes two types of mediators:

> We shall speak of *external mediation* when the distance is sufficient to eliminate any contact between the two spheres of *possibilities* of which the mediator and the subject occupy the respective centers. We shall speak of *internal mediation* when this same distance is sufficiently reduced to allow these two spheres to penetrate each other more or less profoundly. (9)

According to Girard, "The hero of external mediation proclaims aloud the true nature of his desire. He worships his model openly and declares himself his disciple" (10).

This can be applied to *The Red-Haired Woman* as follows: When Cem, who suffers from fatherlessness, begins digging wells with Master Mahmut, he is captivated by his master's fatherliness, attention and affection; he is happy to be his apprentice and submits to his master's authority. The type of mediation we have here is external. The object of desire, on a surface level, is drawing water out of a well. But let's dwell on this a little longer. It will be helpful to think over the psychological connotations of the "well" metaphor. Since the story of Oedipus is insistently present in the text, exploring the image of the "mother" may be worthwhile. The suspicion that the concepts of "mother" and "well" may be connected leads us to the Jungean archetype of "the mother." C.G. Jung (15) cites the deep well among the many symbols of the mother archetype. That means that the object that makes up the desire vertex of the triangle between Mahmut and Cem may be "the mother." But since Cem respects the authority of Mahmut the mediation is external. Cem has successfully completed the phallic stage, described by Freud as the developmental phase in which the male child regards his father as a rival for the possession of the desired mother and feels the wish to kill him. This situation leads to the boy's fear of being castrated by the father in retaliation. When this psychosexual stage is not completed successfully the boy is left with an Oedipus complex.[8]

Although Cem overcomes the Oedipus complex by bowing to the authority of Mahmut, his father's replacement, Cem's true object of desire is something else: namely to write. We are given no clue as to whether Cem's father also has the desire to write. We know that Orhan Pamuk's father used to write from the author's Nobel Lecture, but that's a different story – for now. But even though we do not know whether Master Mahmut, the hero of external mediation, desires to become a writer or not, we do know there is something that stimulates Cem's desire and makes him see Mahmut as his rival, thus creating internal mediation, which tightens the

---

[8] Girard himself, despite what he refers to as his "anti-Freudianism," has pointed out the affinity of his theory of mimetic desire with Freudian thought: "From a Freudian viewpoint, the original triangle of desire is, of course, the Oedipal triangle. The story of 'mediated' desire is the story of this Oedipal desire, of its essential permanence beyond its ever changing objects" (186-87, n. 1).

spiral and deepens the well: we know that Mahmut tells religiously themed stories at nights. When Cem reciprocates for these exemplary tales by telling the story ofOedipus, his aim is the same as his master's. Cem by internal mediation puts on his weapons and threatens his master with stories of his own in order to protect his territory – on a subconscious level, of course. For this to happen on the conscious level, internal mediation needs to manifest itself more sharply. For Cem to regard Mahmut as his rival the two need to have a shared object of desire, which would be the Red-Haired Woman.

Cem's submission is replaced by rivalry when he finds out that Master Mahmut, despite a ban, has been to the tent show to watch the Red-Haired Woman in her very impressive portrayal of the tragedy of "Rostam and Sohrab" from Ferdowsi's tenth-century Persian epic *Shahnameh* and even has chatted with her. The spheres of mediation are now intersecting. For Cem, Mahmut has become a rival that needs to be eliminated. But Girard says that the "person who hates first hates himself for the secret admiration concealed by his hatred" (11). This is exactly what happens to Cem. When his master, to whom he has assigned the role of a "father," turns into his rival and when Cem thinks he has eliminated that rival, he is massively ridden with guilt (85, ch. 21).[9] Although this guilt at times diminishes, it never really goes away. It even jeopardizes Cem's only desire in life: "But could such a conscienceless person who left his master to die at the bottom of a well be a writer?" (91, ch. 22).[10]

To fully apprehend what he has done, Cem starts to study the stories of Sohrab and Oedipus. These stories are explored in such detail in the book that Pamuk has been criticized for it (see, for instance, Ergenç). He leaves nothing unexplored, meticulously going from Freud's writing on *The Brothers Karamazov* to Sophocles' *Oedipus Rex* all the way to Ferdowsi's *Shahnameh*. Apparently, "Rostam and Sohrab" from that epic is dwelt upon because Rostam's unwitting killing of his son Sohrab presents an inver-

---

[9] Page, chapter and part numbers refer to the Turkish edition of the novel.
[10] "Ama ustasını kuyunun dibinde ölüme terk eden vicdansız bir kişi yazar olabilir miydi?" All translations from the novel were prepared for this volume from the Turkish original, *Kırmızı Saçlı Kadın* (2016).

sion of the story of Oedipus. Such love for detail is hardly is without a deeper meaning.

Gustave Moreau: *Oedipus and the Sphinx.* 1864. Source: Wikimedia Commons.

The second part of the novel deals with Cem's life as it unfolds at a rapid pace. In addition to the stories that he sets out to explore, we follow Cem as he evolves into a typical, highly educated, well-to-do business man. As is frequently emphasized in the novel, there is no escape from destiny, so when Cem is contacted about construction work in the town of Öngören, events unfurl fast and the knots tied in the novel start to emerge in this part. Sırrı Bey, whom Cem encounters at his father's funeral, is the owner of the house where Cem slept with the Red-Haired Woman, Gülcihan. Sırrı is an acquaintance of Cem's father, and Cem also finds out from Sırrı Bey why the Red-Haired Woman was looking at him as though they already knew each other: it is because Gülcihan is the ex-lover of Cem's father.

Thus another instance of internal mediation emerges as the Red-Haired Woman, Master Mahmut and Cem's shared object of desire, is on a deeper level actually Cem and his father's shared object of desire. Moreover, the story of Oedipus, which Cem has been exploring for years, has indirectly become part of his own life. But this too is a cloak for the real issue. Avid readers of Pamuk's fiction are always watchful for this kind of trap; this is not the crux of the matter yet.

Cem finds out that he has a son with the Red-Haired Woman. He goes to Öngören to see this child, who has filed a paternity case. This part of the novel is narrated as though Cem hasn't been able to see his son Enver. However, we, the readers, are almost sure that Serhat, supposedly Enver's friend, is actually Enver himself. We learn from Cem's conversation with Serhat (alias Enver), that Enver writes poetry. Thus we're presented with yet another object of desire. And so we find ourselves back where we started with a twist: Whereas at the beginning of the book, writing was an object of desire shared by Master Mahmut and Cem, from this point on, it's an object of desire for Enver and Cem. We sense that this will end in a murder, but we cannot tell whether it will be as in the story of Oedipus, studied by Cem for a lifetime, where the son kills his father or as in "Rostam and Sohrab," where the father kills his son. "When I get mad at you I feel like blinding you," Enver tells his father at one point (170, ch. 43).[11] Here we're given a hint as to the story's ending and, yes, eventually Enver ends up killing Cem in self-defense by shooting him in the eye with his own gun. The mythical Oedipus, on learning that he killed his father and that the woman he married is his mother, blinds himself. In *The Red-Haired Woman*, the son kills his father, as in the Oedipus story, but doesn't blind *himself*, but his father, thus killing him.

One of the best ways of underscoring the fictional nature of the events is to leave a narrative gap in the text, and Pamuk does that with a single sentence. Hiding his real identity, Enver goes to his house with Cem. They ring the doorbell but no one answers although inside the lights are on. When later on we find out that the person accompanying Cem that night was Enver, a discrepancy in the novel's time scheme is created when the angry son says, "Somebody rang the doorbell just now when I was writing a poem, I didn't answer" (167, ch. 43).[12] Through this blurring of planes of reality the fictional character of the text is underscored.

In the last part of the novel the story is narrated by the Red-Haired Woman. She recaps the story from her point of view to be written down by Enver. This is the most important part of the entire text, because here additional information as to the novel's title is presented. I don't think that Pamuk's choice of the word "kırmızı" instead of "kızıl" for the original title, *Kırmızı saçlı kadın*, is a lapse as Ergenç suggests.[13] The reason is rather that "kızıl" doesn't convey the artificiality/fictionality expressed by "kırmızı." At the beginning of her account, the Red-Haired Woman prides herself that red is not her hair's natural color, but a choice (175, pt. III). In

---

[11] "'Sana kızdığım zamanlar aslında seni kör etmek geliyor içimden' [...]."

[12] "'Demin kapım çalındı, şiir yazıyordum, açmadım.'"

[13] Both words mean "red," "kızıl" is normally used to refer to hair.

my opinion this alludes to the fictional nature of her narrative. Her unnatural hair color, enforced by the choice of unusual vocabulary, inconspicuously places the woman's account among the multitude of stories like those of Oedipus, Sohrab and Hamlet alluded to in the book, and to the conflicts between master, father and son. The fictional woman urges Enver to write down his father's – and ultimately her own – story. Enver complies and writes the novel that we hold in our hands.

Thus we are presented with two more triangles of desire. The first is is that Enver, while writing the book, desires his mother through internal mediation by his father. That he gives his account of his parents' relationship in the voice of his father as a first-person narrative is hard to ignore. The Red-Haired Woman tells how her son "used to take his mother's hands and kiss them with respect like a lover" (194, pt. III).[14] She adds that Enver wants to read the books read by Cem: "He would read them like his father and, grasping his father's thoughts as he read them in his youth, put himself in his place."[15] When we contrast Enver's thoughts during his settling of accounts with his father on the priority of images over words (170, ch. 43) with what Cem, talking about his school days, says about the vacillation of the priority between the two (10, ch. 1), we cannot argue that Enver is really walking in Cem's shoes. Quite the opposite; using the power of writing, Enver has managed to make his father think like himself. At this point we may consult Girard's statement that "[i]n the quarrel which puts him in opposition to his rival, the subject reverses the logical and chronological order of desires in order to hide his imitation. He asserts that his own desire is prior to that of his rival; according to him, it is the mediator who is responsible for the rivalry" (11). This explains Enver's attempt to attribute his own ambitions to his father Cem.

We can push this a little further and say that Cem, Cem's father and Enver are amalgamated into each other. It can't be coincidental that Cem's words about his father – that his neck and chest "had a very special smell

---

[14] "[…] annesinin ellerini tutar, bir sevgili gibi onları saygıyla öperdi."
[15] "Babası gibi onları okuyacak, babasının gençliğinde ne düşündüğünü anlayarak, kendini onun yerine koyacaktı."

(the smell of cheap soap and bicuits)" (134, ch. 34)[16] – are also used by the Red-Haired Woman about her son, Enver: "[…] I once again noticed with happiness that his neck smelled of a mixture of cheap soap and biscuits, just as in his childhood" (194, pt. III).[17] And this completes the cycle of the Oedipus complex in the book.

Rostam mourns Sohrab (from Persian *Shahnama* manuscript).
Source: Wikimedia Commons.

Let's return to the beginning when we stated that the well stood for the mother archetype. This secures the place of Enver, the novel's scribe, within the Oedipus complex. The novel thus gains coherence. But the Red-Haired Woman's and the novel's last words once more underscore that the object of desire at issue is writing: "Don't forget that your father *actually* [*aslında*] wanted to be a writer as well" (195, pt. III; my emphasis).[18] Now let's look at the novel's first sentence: "*Actually* [*Aslında*] I wanted to become a writer" (9, ch 1; my emphasis).[19] In my opinion, the fact that the word "actually" [*aslında*] appears at both the beginning and the end, be-

---

[16] "[…] çok özel bir kokusu olan boynuna ve göğsüne (ucuz sabun ve bisküvi kokusu)[…]."
[17] "[…] boynunun tıpkı çocukluğunda olduğu gibi ucuz sabun ve bisküvi karışımı bir kokuyla koktuğunu mutlulukla bir kere daha fark ettim."
[18] "'Unutma, *aslında* baban da yazar olmak istemişti'" (my emphasis).
[19] "*Aslında* yazar olmak istiyordum" (my emphasis).

sides serving to amalgamate the characters of Cem and Enver, clearly indicates that the novel "actually" aims to discuss something else.

I contend that Pamuk reveals his true color with the novel's last sentence. He had declared in "My Father's Suitcase" that his father had given him several notebooks in a suitcase. This makes Pamuk uneasy. "My *real* [*Asıl*] fear, the *crucial* [*asıl*] thing that I did not wish to know or discover, was the possibility that my father might be a good writer" (my emphases)[20] is how Pamuk confesses the reason for his uneasiness. What is rendered as "real" and "crucial," respectively, in this translation is "asıl" in the original text – the same "asıl" ("actual") from which the form "aslında" ("actually") in *The Red-Haired Woman*'s first and last sentences discussed above is derived. This connects the novel's father-son relationships to Pamuk's treatment of his relationship to his own father in his Nobel Lecture.

Ilya Repin: *Ivan the Terrible and His Son Ivan on November 16th, 1581*. 1885. Source: Wikimedia Commons.

---

[20] "*Asıl* korkum, bilmek, öğrenmek bile istemediğim *asıl* şey ise babamın iyi bir yazar olması ihtimaliydi" ("Babamım bavulu"; my emphases).

In a way, Pamuk's dad is stripped of his role of being a father and turns into a mediator. The son expresses his dissatisfaction with this rivalry with these words: "Because even at my advanced age I wanted my father to be only my father – not a writer" ("My Father's Suitcase"). There is of course an explanation for this. Pamuk is angry at his father, even jealous of him. From beginning to end of his lecture, Pamuk compares himself with his father. According to this comparison, Gündüz Pamuk is a happy person, Orhan Pamuk is unhappy. Whereas Gündüz Pamuk is full of life and enjoys crowds and fun, Orhan Pamuk enjoys being alone and patient. Moreover, Gündüz Pamuk is a father who often leaves his family to travel to other countries. And yet the son adds: "I had to bear in mind that when he was living with us, my father, just like me, enjoyed being alone with his books and his thoughts – and not pay too much attention to the literary quality of his writing." I feel that here the son's emphasis on "just like me" is very important. This emphasis apparently aims at showing "that his own desire is prior to that of his rival," as Girard puts it in his above-quoted statement. Consider the following passage that occurs when Pamuk turns to the connection between his father's suitcase and the Nobel Prize:

> Twenty-three years before my father left me his suitcase, and four years after I had decided, aged 22, to become a novelist and, abandoning all else, shut myself up in a room, I finished my first novel, *Cevdet Bey and Sons*; with trembling hands I had given my father a typescript of the still unpublished novel, so that he could read it and tell me what he thought.

With these words Pamuk actually underscores that long before his father gave him the suitcase he had decided to become a writer, that he had succeeded in what his father probably didn't dare to, namely shutting himself up in a room and coming out of it four years later with a novel. And when he is presenting the outcome of this success to the "mediator" he is challenging, Pamuk's hands tremble, even though he insists that his father always supported him. Upon reading his son's first novel, his father "tells him lightly" ("öylesine söyleyiverdi")²¹ that one day Orhan Pamuk will win the Nobel Prize. However much the son insists that his father made that remark to encourage him, that something "said lightly" becomes a reality one day requires a different kind of comparison. Just as for Enver and Cem in *The Red-Headed Woman* writing is a shared object of desire, this situation suggests that a similar desire is shared by Gündüz Pamuk and his son. Even though Orhan Pamuk always speaks of his father with kindness and respect, he doesn't hide the frustration he used to feel whenever his father went away. Just like Cem.

As a typical Orhan Pamuk reader, I became suspicious when I read that Cem takes his father's "tiny old suitcase" ("babamın küçük eski bavulu[...]" [14, ch. 2; my translation]) with him when he goes to Öngören. What Gündüz Pamuk gave to his son was also a "small, black, leather suitcase." All we have at this point is that the suitcase in both cases is small and previously owned by the father, which is not enough as proof but enough to raise one's suspicion. In his essay "Babam" ["My Father"] in the autobiographical *Manzaradan parçalar* [*Fragments of the Landscape*, untranslated], when telling of Gündüz Pamuk, Orhan Pamuk also seems to talk about Akın Çelik, Cem's father. "Not once did my father scowl at me, scold me, give me a flick" (16; my translation).²² Cem says the same about his father: "Then I'd miss my dad who never yelled at me and who never scolded me" (27, ch. 6).²³ This is not enough to prove my point either. In

---

[21] "[B]abam, bana ya da ilk kitabıma olan güvenini aşırı heyecanlı ve abartılı bir dille ifade etti ve bugün büyük bir mutlulukla kabul ettiğim bu ödülü bir gün alacağımı öylesine söyleyiverdi" ("Babamın bavulu").

"[M]y father expressed his confidence in me or my first novel in an overly excited and exaggerated language and said lightly that one day I would win the prize that I accept today with such great happiness" ("My Father's Suitcase"; translation prepared for the present volume).

Maureen Freely, whose translation of "My Father's Suitcase" is quoted elsewhere in this essay, renders this passage somewhat differently: "[M]y father resorted to highly charged and exaggerated language to express his confidence in me or my first novel: he told me that one day I would win the prize that I am here to receive with such great happiness."

[22] "Babam bir kere bile bana kaşını çatmadı, bir kere bile beni azarlamadı, bir fiske bile vurmadı" ("Babam" 16).

[23] "O zaman bana hiç bağırmayan, beni hiç azarlamayan babamı özlerdim."

the same essay, Pamuk recalls how when he was very little his father taught him how to swim in Heybeliada. When his father moves away the child worries and shouts, "Dad, don't leave!" Pamuk continues in a chagrined voice, "But he would leave us. He'd go to faraway places, to other countries, to corners we didn't know" ("Babam" 19; my translation).[24] When Cem learns of his father's demise, he recalls a similar moment: "Once, when I was seven, my mom, me and my dad went to Heybeli Beach to swim. To teach me to swim, my mom would place me in the water holding my belly and I would desperately struggle to swim towards my father standing three steps away from us. Just as I was getting close, he would take a step backwards to make me swim a bit longer and learn faster, and eager to catch up to him, I'd yell, 'Dad, don't leave!'" (133-34, ch. 34).[25] But just like Pamuk's father, Cem's father too has a habit of disappearing.

Orhan Pamuk loves his father's scent, just like Cem. These are Pamuk's works: "As a child, I loved climbing on [my dad's] lap, lying next to him, smelling his unique scent and touching him." ("Babam" 19; my translation).[26] And these are Cem's: "he was pulling my head towards his neck and his chest, to the very point on his neck that I'm looking at now, which had a unique scent even at sea (the smell of cheap soap and biscuits)" (134, ch. 34).[27]

Looking at the evidence so far, we can now claim a certain parallelism between Cem's father and Pamuk's father. But is there a deeper meaning to this? To my mind, the following situation emerges from the link between

---

[24] "'Baba beni bırakma!' diye bağırırdım. Ama o bizi bırakırdı. Uzaklara, başka ülkelere, başka yerlere, bilmediğimiz köşelere giderdi" ("Babam" 19).

[25] "Yedi yaşındayken bir kere annem, ben, babam Heybeli Plajı'na denize girmeye gitmiştik. Yüzme öğreneyim diye, annem beni karnımdan tutarak suya bırakıyor, ben de üç adım ötede ayakta duran babama doğru can havliyle debelenerek yüzüyordum. Tam babama yaklaşmışken o biraz daha yüzeyim ve çabuk öğreneyim diye bir adım geri atıyor, ben ona yetişme heyecanıyla 'Baba, gitme!' diye bağırıyordum" (133-34).

[26] "Küçük çocukken onun kucağına çıkmayı, onun yanına yatmayı, benzersiz kokusunu koklamayı, ona dokunmayı çok severdim" ("Babam" 19).

[27] "[...] denizde bile çok özel bir kokusu olan boynuna ve göğsüne (ucuz sabun ve bisküvi kokusu), işte şimdi baktığım boynunun tam bu noktasına başımı yaslıyordu."

Enver and Akın by way of scent: Orhan Pamuk would normally have this novel written by "the novelist Orhan," just as in his previous novels. However, probably being averse to placing the issues he discusses too close to his own biography, he had a fictional "son" by the name of Enver write *The Red-Haired Woman*. Thus the similarity between Cem and Pamuk doesn't exceed an acceptable measure, and in a way Pamuk outdoes his father by blending Cem's ambition to be a writer with Gündüz Pamuk's similar ambition. In this manner Pamuk "takes revenge" on his father, about whom he feels a permanent disappointment, no matter how often Pamuk dwells on his gratitude to his parent. My claims are based on Orhan Pamuk's words about himself: "[...] I try to take my own revenges, but often I do that in my own special way so that that the reader doesn't recognize it and mistakes revenge for beauty" ("Ne kadar hayattan ne kadar intikam?" 27).[28]

In *The Red-Haired Woman*, Orhan Pamuk hides underneath the tumult of the stories of Oedipus and Sohrab the desire to become a writer. Basing the relationships between a subject and a mediator on that desire, he weaves these relationships around the same tumultuous stories, and by constantly altering the personages in the verteces of the Girardian triangle he digs the well of his fiction deeper. The well is a significant element which illustrates the novel's fictional structure.[29] To draw water from the bottom of this well one needs to try a little. Pamuk would never let his readers reach the water inside the well that easily because, though he may have written his novel in just fourteen months, it had been brewing in his mind for almost thirty years ("Orhan Pamuk: Romanım Araf'ta geçiyor"). After all, it is Orhan Pamuk, the author of *The Black Book*, *The New Life* and *My Name is Red* that we're talking about.

---

[28] "[...] ben kendi intikamlarımı almaya çalışıyorum, ama çoğu zaman bunu son derece kişisel bir yolla yapıyorum, öyle ki okur bunu fark etmiyor ve intikamı güzellik sanıyor" ("Ne kadar hayattan ne kadar intikam?"27).

[29] Pamuk has stated that for thirty years he thought of the novel's title as *The Well* ("Orhan Pamuk: Bizi terk eden bir babayla büyüdüm").

Works Cited

Ergenç, Ahmet. "Orhan Pamuk ve yarım kalmış bir kuyu masalı." *t24.com.tr/k24* 22 Feb. 2016. Accessed 25 June 2017 <http://t24.com.tr/k24/yazi/orhan-pamuk-ve-yarim-kalmis-bir-kuyu-masali,589>.

Girard, René. *Deceit, Desire, and the Novel: Self and Other in Literary Structure*. Trans. Yvonne Freccero. Baltimore and London: Johns Hopkins UP, 1965. Trans. of *Mensonge romantique et vérité romanesque*. 1961.

___. *Romantik yalan ve romansal hakikat: Edebi yapıda ben ve öteki*. Trans. Arzu Etensel İldem. İstanbul: Metis, 2013. Trans. of *Mensonge romantique et vérité romanesque*.

Jung, C.G. *Four Archetypes: Mother, Rebirth, Spirit, Trickster*. Trans. R.F.C. Hull. Princeton, NJ: Princeton UP, 1970.

Pamuk, Orhan. "Babam" ["My Father"]. *Manzaradan parçalar: Hayat, sokaklar, edebiyat [Fragments of the Landscape: Life, Streets, Literature]*. By Pamuk. İstanbul: İletişim, 2010. 15-20.

___. "Babamın bavulu: Nobel konuşması." *Nobelprize.org*. 7 Dec. 2006. Accessed 28 May 2017 <http://www.nobelprize.org/nobel_prizes/literature/laureates/2006/pamuk-lecture_tu.html>.

___. *Kırmızı saçlı kadın: Roman*. İstanbul: Yapı Kredi, 2016.

___. "My Father's Suitcase: Nobel Lecture." Trans. Maureen Freely. *Nobelprize.org*. 7 Dec. 2006. Accessed 29 May 2017 <http://www.nobelprize.org/nobel_prizes/literature/laureates/2006/pamuk-lecture_en.html>. Trans. of "Babamın bavulu: Nobel konuşması."

___. "Ne kadar hayattan ne kadar intikam?" *Manzaradan parçalar: Hayat, sokaklar, edebiyat [Fragments of the Landscape: Life, Streets, Literature]*. By Pamuk. İstanbul: İletişim, 2010. 26-27.

___. "Orhan Pamuk: Bizi terk eden bir babayla büyüdüm." Interview by Çınar Oskay. *Hürriyet Kelebek* 30 Jan. 2016. Accessed 2 July 2017 <http://www.hurriyet.com.tr/orhan-pamuk-bizi-terk-eden-bir-babayla-buyudum-40047198>.

___. "Orhan Pamuk: Romanım Araf'ta geçiyor." Interview by Gülenay Börekçi. *Habertürk Pazar* 7 Feb. 2016. Accessed 25 June 2017 <http://www.haberturk.com/yasam/haber/1191922-orhan-pamuk-romanim-arafta-geciyor>.

———. *Other Colors: Essays and a Story*. Trans. Maureen Freely. New York: Knopf, 2007.

———. "Önsöz." *Öteki renkler: Seçme yazılar ve bir hikâye*. 1999. İstanbul: İletişim, 2011. 15-22.

———. *The Red-Haired Woman: A Novel*. New York: Knopf, forthcoming. Trans. of *Kırmızı saçlı kadın*.

Türker, Elif. "Orhan Pamuk Kuyusu." *t24.com.tr/k24* 4 Aug. 2016. Accessed 20 June 2017 <http://t24.com.tr/k24/yazi/orhan-pamuk-kuyusu,806>.

———. "The Well of Orhan Pamuk." Trans. Yasemin Gürkan. *t24.com. tr/k24* 23 Feb. 2017. Accessed 20 June 2017 <http://t24.com.tr/ k24/yazi/the-well-of-orhan-pamuk,1094>.

Contributors

Zafer Doğan graduated from the Department of Turkish Language and Literature at Boğaziçi University in 2001. He earned a master's degree in Political Science and International Relations from Yıldız Technical University and finished his PhD there in 2011. He is a lecturer at the Atatürk Institute for Modern Turkish History at the same university. Doğan is the author of *Orhan Pamuk edebiyatında tarih ve kimlik söylemi* (İthaki 2014).

Elif Türker Gümüş graduated from the Department of Turkish Language and Literature at Gazi University and received an MA from the Department of Turkish Literature at Bilkent University. She is at present working on her doctoral thesis on Marcel Proust and Abdülhak Şinasi Hisar in the Department of Turkish Language and Literature at Kocaeli University. Since 2009, she has been an instructor teaching Turkish in the Department of Turkish Language and Revolution History at Doğuş University. She has authored a novel published by İletişim in 2015 titled *Sevgili Alef*.

Hande Gürses received her PhD in Literary Studies from University College London. She has published her work on Orhan Pamuk in *Fear and Fantasy in a Global World* (Brill/Rodopi 2015) and *Global Perspectives on Orhan Pamuk* (Palgrave 2012). She is currently co-editing a new volume titled *Animals, Plants, and Landscapes: An Ecology of Turkish Literature and Film*. Her teaching and research interests include comparative literature, animal studies and ecocriticism. She is a lecturer at the Comparative Literature Program, University of Massachusetts Amherst.

E. Khayyat is assistant professor at Rutgers University. He received his PhD from Columbia University, where he studied at the Department of English and the Institute for Comparative Literature and Society. Before Rutgers he taught in Frankfurt and Istanbul, Paris and New York, mostly philosophy of literature and religion. Among his awards and fellowships are a UNESCO award, the Marjorie Hope Nicolson doctoral fellowship and an ICLS fellowship at Columbia University, visiting fellowships at Gutenberg in Mainz, Science Po in Paris, Woolf Institute in Cambridge, and Jamia Millia Islamia of Delhi, among others. He's a member of the founding board of Harvard University's Institute for World Literature. His forthcoming book *How to Turn Turk* engages Erich Auerbach's pioneering works of contemporary literary and cultural history, some of which were produced at Istanbul University in the 1940s, against the background of his Turkish colleagues Ahmet Hamdi Tanpınar and Halide Edib's analogous works.

Beyza Lorenz earned her PhD in Comparative Literature from Penn State in 2014. Previously, she received an MA in Anatolian Civilizations and Cultural Heritage Management from Koç University and a BA in Western Languages and Literatures from Boğaziçi University. Her research interests lie in the intersection of space, modernity and empire. She is particularly interested in how authors negotiate the problematic relationship between the center and the periphery as well as the self and the Other in their thematic use of space. She is currently a lecturer in Turkish Language and Literature at UCLA and the coordinator of the Middle East and North Africa Studies Lab in the Center for Near Eastern Studies at UCLA.

Adam McConnel received his MA and PhD in History from Sabancı University in Istanbul. He successfully defended his PhD dissertation, titled "Dean Acheson and the Turkish-American Alliance, 1945-1953," in June 2014. His research interests are focused on Republican Turkish history and Turkish-American relations. Currently, McConnel teaches Turkish history (İnkılap Tarihi) at Sabancı University and regularly contributes commentary on current Turkish socio-political topics to Serbestiyet.com and the Anatolian Agency. He has lived and worked in Istanbul since 1999.

Eda Özgül is an assistant professor at Bahçeşehir University, where she has been a faculty member since 2006. She completed her PhD in 2013 at Marmara University with her dissertation titled "Modernity as a Crisis of Memory: A Possibility for a Reflexive Remembering." She holds an undergraduate degree in sociology and a master's degree in cinema and television. Her research interests include modernity, poststructuralism, history and memory, time/space and narration in art, literature and cinema. She has several academic publications and she has translated from English to Turkish *Imperialisms: Historical and Literary Investigations, 1500-1900*, edited by Balachandra Rajan and Elizabeth Sauer, and *Searching for Memory: The Brain, The Mind and The Past* by Daniel Schacter.

Contributors 251

İnci Sarız-Bilge is a doctoral student in Comparative Literature at the University of Massachusetts Amherst. She teaches world literature and works as an activist translator. Native of Turkey, she holds degrees in Translation Studies from Boğaziçi University and in Comparative Literature from Bilgi University in Istanbul. Her current project focuses on the interplay of translation and censorship, particularly as it pertains to ideological entanglements under authoritarian regimes. Her research interests also include life-writing and gender, memory studies, and cognitive approaches to literature.

Sevinç Türkkan teaches modern Turkish literature and intellectual history at the University of Rochester. Her work has appeared or is forthcoming in *Türkisch-deutsche Studien: Jahrbuch, Translation and Literature, Teaching Translation, Global Perspectives on Orhan Pamuk, Post-1960 Novelists in Turkey, Making Connections, International Journal of the Humanities* and elsewhere. Her translations from German appeared in *Best European Fiction* edited by Aleksandar Hemon (Dalkey Archive Press). Her translation of Aslı Erdoğan's book *The Stone Building and Other Places* is forthcoming from City Lights Books (2017). She is the co-editor (with David Damrosch) of *Approaches to Teaching the Works of Orhan Pamuk* (MLA, 2017) and she is at work on a book manuscript titled *Translation Criticism and the Construction of World Literature*.

Hülya Yağcıoğlu has earned her PhD degree in English Literature from Boğaziçi University, Turkey, with her dissertation entitled "The Innocence of Objects: Commodification, Collecting and Fetishism in *The Age of Innocence* and *The Museum of Innocence*." She also holds a BA degree in English literature and an MA degree in cultural studies. She currently works as an assistant professor in the English and Writing Studies Department at Zayed University, UAE. Before coming to UAE, she taught at universities in Turkey and Oman. A member of ACLA, BCLA and NCSA, she has presented papers at international conferences in Canada, Germany, Oman, Turkey, UK, and USA. She has published book chapters and articles in the field of comparative literature, especially on the interaction between material culture and literature. Her research areas include comparative literature, cultural studies, literary criticism, and modern Turkish and American fiction.

ibidem.eu